NEW ITALIAN SELF TAUGHT

Language Series titles available in
Barnes & Noble paperback editions

New French Self Taught
New German Self Taught
New Italian Self Taught
New Spanish Self Taught

THE QUICK, PRACTICAL WAY TO

READING · WRITING · SPEAKING · UNDERSTANDING

NEW ITALIAN
SELF TAUGHT

Revised by

MARIO PEI, *Columbia University*

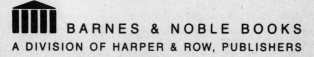
BARNES & NOBLE BOOKS
A DIVISION OF HARPER & ROW, PUBLISHERS
New York, Cambridge,
Philadelphia, San Francisco, London,
Mexico City, São Paulo, Sydney

This work was originally published by Funk & Wagnalls Company.

First BARNES & NOBLE BOOKS edition published 1982.

ISBN: 0-06-463616-X

84 85 86 10 9 8 7 6 5 4 3

CONTENTS

FOREWORD

In the present revision, corrections and changes have been made throughout, and outmoded expressions have been brought up to date. One outstanding new feature, and perhaps my principal contribution to this revision, has been a new phonetic introduction constructed in accordance with the principles of the International Phonetic Alphabet (see inside front and back covers) and the application of this transcription method to the transcribed pronunciations that appear throughout the new edition. It is my hope that this system of scientific transcription will serve to impart the authentic sounds of the Italian language as spoken by native speakers of the language.

Mario Pei

Columbia University
New York

The Method Explained

Every man and woman of intelligence realizes the imperative need of having command of a foreign language. The realization becomes more acute day by day as the fact is borne in on us that what once were known, in the old-fashioned phrase, as the "ends of the earth" are now, so to speak, practically our front lawn. Traveling by airplane we reach the remotest regions in flashes of time. By radio we know hour by hour what farthest distant peoples have on their minds and on their tongues. So it becomes increasingly necessary that we be able to tell them in their own language what we think and what we want to do.

Whether in professional, diplomatic, social, or commercial life, a sound and sure knowledge of our fellow man's language is the great essential of understanding among men and nations of the world.

The method used in this book is not new and has been successfully followed by thousands of students. By experiment and research, it was discovered many years ago that a thorough and workable command of a foreign language is not learned by long and arduous memorization of the grammatical rules of a language. Modern educational science now follows the far more efficient method that is presented in these pages. It is the most rational and simple method ever devised for learning a foreign language.

THE PRACTICAL MASTERY OF FOREIGN LANGUAGES

To think in a language not your mother tongue means that you will express yourself with sympathetic understanding of the people who speak that language. It means that you can converse easily and naturally as a good neighbor and a good friend. It is the great achievement of the method in this book that it enables its users easily and speedily to speak a foreign language just as fluently as their own. In doing this the student becomes accustomed to thinking in that language as well.

LANGUAGE AND GRAMMAR

are in no sense synonymous, although some school methods might lead us to suppose so.

Grammar is the science of language and, while necessary and desirable, is not so important as the ability to speak the language itself. Can anyone doubt this? Consider the majority of people you meet. Listen to their speech and examine it. Do they know the rules of English grammar? Do not even the very young children of educated persons express themselves correctly without ever having studied a single line of grammatical definitions? Yet,

THE STUDY OF GRAMMAR IS MADE EASY

"but it must be taught," as was said long ago by the great Erasmus, "at the proper time and kept within proper limits."

Colloquial mastery must precede it. Grammar will not then confuse, but will assist the pupil. It will cease to be a drudgery and will become a plain and simple explanation of forms and idioms already learned. It will no longer be an uncertain foundation, but will cap the edifice that has been reared by practical linguistic exercises. This is the true purpose of grammar, and in this sense it is taught throughout this book. A celebrated explorer and the master of many languages once wrote: "The only correct and scientific method by which a foreign language can be learned is to adopt

NATURE'S OWN WAY

by which all persons, whether children or adults, educated or otherwise, rapidly and correctly acquire the language which they constantly hear and which they are instinctively impelled to imitate when living in a foreign country."

It has often been observed that foreigners in the United States learn English seemingly with ease and surely with rapidity. Many of them know nothing of the principles of grammar. Some of them may be too young or may lack sufficient education to be able to read or write their native language. Despite such handicaps they master English sufficiently well within a few months to be able to make themselves understood. The quality of the English they acquire depends greatly on the kind of people they associate with. Judging by the facility with which foreigners in this country acquire English, it becomes obvious that when Americans live in a foreign country they must find some system which will enable them to obtain command of the language of that country in this same manner.

WHAT IS THE SYSTEM WHICH WE INSTINCTIVELY FOLLOW WHEN LIVING IN A FOREIGN COUNTRY?

At first the mind is confused by the multiplicity of foreign sounds heard. We try to grasp the ideas expressed in the strange tongue, and failing to do so we naturally are bewildered.

This state of mental confusion generally passes in about three or four weeks. The ear has become accustomed to some of these sounds and instinctively we begin to imitate the PHRASES we have heard most frequently pronounced by the persons surrounding us, and which, at the same time, are most necessary to our wants.

Now, what is our greatest necessity? Which of the needs of humanity is of paramount importance to young and old alike? It is nourishment—eating and drinking.

Consequently, the first sentences usually mastered are such as these: "*Please give me something to eat,*" or "*Please bring me the menu,*" or "*Please let me have a steak and some potatoes.*"

Such sentences are necessary to everyone; and it may be remarked that nature, through the mastery of these first simple sentences, points out

THE TRUE AND ONLY WAY

in which languages can be learned.

It is THROUGH SENTENCES, *and never through single, isolated words.* The verbs are the soul and backbone of all speech, and it is only by and through the proper study of verbs that mastery of a language can be attained.

To return to the sentence: "*Please bring me the menu.*" Not knowing any other expression, you cling to these words and use them again and again for your various needs.

For instance, when you want matches, or an umbrella, or some towels, instead of saying to the attendant: "*Please bring me the menu,*" you will point to the object and say to him: "*Please bring me ——— .*"

Consider here the simplicity of this mode of teaching. By mastering this first little phrase, you have been furnished with a "sentence-mold" by the use of which hundreds of correct sentences may be composed.

The attendant, understanding your abbreviated phrase and gesture, "*Please bring me* —— ," will give you the words "*matches*," "*umbrella*," or "*some towels*" in the language of the country in which you are living. You repeat these new words over and over again until they come quite naturally to you. In this way you go on from day to day, in fact from hour to hour, until after a few months you are able to express yourself readily and fluently. This is the process by which sounds become language. This is the mode in which any foreign language is learned when we live in a foreign country.

For those studying a foreign language here at home, it is necessary to use a text book containing practical idiomatic speech.

AN INDISPENSABLE VADE-MECUM

Language is divided into the Language of Literature and the Language of Every-day Life.

What part of English is used by the majority of people? The language of literature or the expressions of common life? What do our children speak when they enter school and receive their first lessons in spelling and reading? *The language of every-day life.* They understand and MUST be able to understand and follow their teachers before they can proceed to the study of English grammar. They MUST know common, every-day English before they can comprehend and appreciate the beauties of Shakespeare, Milton, and Tennyson.

Throughout this book the aim has been to give nothing but practical phrases and sentences which are used in the ordinary transactions of life. The proper selection of the vocabulary of practical life is the first distinguishing feature of the method according to which the lessons that follow have been prepared. Highly important as this part of the method is, it is a mere detail of the whole plan. The student must not overlook the fact that

DISCONNECTED, ISOLATED WORDS ARE NOT LANGUAGE

A person might learn a whole dictionary by heart and yet not be able to converse. As long as a child can use single words only, he cannot carry on a conversation. This book is based on the well tested theory that instead of beginning studies with little bits of baby sentences that no adult was ever known to use, the start should be made with connected, rational sentences, such as are employed in every-day language. Also, instead of learning phrases—the construction of which is the same as that of our native tongue—the student, from the beginning, should learn idiomatic sentences, the formation of which is utterly different from our mode of speaking. We must learn

TO THINK IN THE FOREIGN LANGUAGE ITSELF

No one can speak a foreign tongue properly who does not think in it. This is so old a maxim no one can doubt it. Yet the difficulty of learning to think in a foreign language seems at first insurmountable.

Is it possible to learn to think in a foreign language without actually living in the country of that language? Of course when we live in a foreign country and hear nothing but the foreign vernacular, it is easy to understand how we acquire the power of thinking in that foreign language.

But how can we hope to obtain the same results here in the United States where we cannot always associate with foreigners, where we speak nothing but English and think in English only, where the cares and duties of the day continually crowd in upon us, and where the little of a foreign language we learn today is almost forgotten by tomorrow? With all these drawbacks and disadvantages how can we learn to think in a foreign tongue?

No adult can learn as a child learns. In mastering its own tongue, the child reaches not only the power of expression but also the ability to think. From the perception of external facts he proceeds to mental conceptions. Each new word is a discovery to him. Each sound reveals to him a new world. Language is the basis of the child's whole mental development and underlies the acquisition of all his knowledge.

The adult, on the other hand, has passed beyond these preliminary stages. His intellect has been developed and trained. His memory is not nearly so fresh and retentive as that of an untutored child. He can already express his thoughts in one language, and in studying other tongues he aims solely at the acquirement of a new vehicle of sounds which will enable him to convey to natives of other countries the thoughts he expresses at home.

What is the meaning of the phrase, "to learn a foreign language"? It means to translate our thoughts into words and to express them in the foreign tongue. It must be accomplished by a sort of mental reconstruction. Life's scenes have to be represented anew in strange sounds which, constantly repeated, will become second nature to us. Again and again we have to *hear* and *repeat* these sounds. Again and again we must apply them until at last they are as familiar to us as the sounds of our native speech. The learner can, of course, *repeat* aloud over and over again and gain a great deal in this way. It is a valuable adjunct to this book to have also the International Phonetic Alphabet charts inside the front and back covers for ready reference.

Then there will no longer be talk of translation from one language into another. The words will have become so deeply impressed upon our memory that we shall utter them as unconsciously as we speak our mother tongue.

Language appeals, at first at least, chiefly to the *ear, tongue,* and *memory*, but though our intellect superintends the whole initiatory process, it cannot come into real action until the foreign sounds come just as unconsciously to us as the sounds of our mother tongue.

Remember also—the ear is the natural organ of language. If you desire to speak in a foreign language, listen to foreign speech and imitate what you have heard until the habit becomes second nature to you. This is The Method of Nature and this is

THE SECRET OF MASTERING A LANGUAGE

Thousands of persons have been successfully instructed by this method. Pupils as well as teachers of languages have testified to the splendid results that have been achieved by following this system. In the first place, all sentences are practical phrases based on the actual occurrences of every-day life.

After a few preliminary exercises, an advance is made with phrases that refer to speaking and understanding a language. Thereafter, as an introduction to life in a foreign land, the student continues his studies by entering a store to make some purchases. The next lesson takes him to the railway station. He buys railway tickets, checks his baggage, boards the train, arrives at his destination, takes a taxicab, drives to his hotel, engages a room, goes to the dining-room, gives his order to the waiter, eats his meal, and at the end of the day retires to his room.

Surely these are actual scenes in every-day life and occurrences with which every adult is familiar.

When such lessons have been thoroughly mastered, the next advance is to conversational exercises. English is now discarded and the foreign language alone is used. No new words are introduced and

EVERY SENTENCE IS BASED ON EXERCISES PREVIOUSLY LEARNED

By a conscientious use of this book the person who works with it will gain a mastery of foreign words, phrases, and sentences. Each phrase gradually presents conceptions and facts as clearly to the student as the English equivalents. Translation becomes unnecessary. The student's life is thus lived over again in the foreign language. His individuality is reconstructed and in this way the foreign language becomes in reality a "tongue" to the learner.

The study of it is no longer a laborious translation. The words cease to be meaningless printed signs and are immediately associated with living facts. The student no longer doubts and hesitates, but expresses his ideas as readily in the foreign language as in his own. He has acquired a new instrument of thought and action in his career. He is looking down a new vista of progress and achievement.

DIRECTIONS FOR PRIVATE STUDY

It has been made clear in the preceding pages that this book places its principal emphasis on the language of practical, every-day life. The words which the beginner is about to learn are therefore divided into the *necessary* and the *less necessary* ones. This is a simple, common-sense division. The necessary words, the expressions all men use and understand, must be mastered first.

How the necessary words were chosen can easily be illustrated. Consider, for instance, the three words, *money*, *fan*, and *chisel*. How do they compare with each other?

The word *money* is so important that no one can get on without the use of it—and, we might add, the substance of it. Everybody has to employ it and everyone must consequently know it. It is plainly a necessary word.

Fan belongs to a different class of expressions. Though no doubt necessary, the word, as well as the object itself, is by no means so imperatively necessary as *money;* it therefore belongs to another class, namely, the class of words which, though they ought to be learned, may be learned later.

Finally, there is the word *chisel.* One might live for twenty years in a foreign country without having any use for this word which to a carpenter is an absolute necessity. For the ordinary student the word belongs in the class of scarcely necessary expressions.

The user of this book must realize that what he is learning is basic. Every effort has been made to give only phrases and sentences used in the common transactions of life. The selection of the words used in this book is based on wide scientific research.

As the reader proceeds with the study of these pages and begins to acquire a vocabulary of essential terms, he should stop from time to time to test the various uses he can make of the words he has at his command. Lepsius, the famous Egyptologist, limited the number of words necessary for conversation on all general subjects to six hundred. Ogden and Richards' vocabulary for basic English is only eight hundred words. As his vocabulary grows from page to page, the student of this book will be surprised at the number of ideas it will enable him to express.

The learner may be puzzled at first by the long and sometimes complex sentences to which he is introduced, but he will soon realize that these are sentences we are in the habit of using in ordinary circumstances. This book rightly places an emphasis on idiomatic sentences constructed in a manner utterly foreign to our way of speaking.

The student must strive constantly to free himself from the habit of thinking in English. He must master each idiom to which he is introduced. These peculiar forms of expression common to every language are the lifeblood of language.

The complete mastery of a foreign tongue is best attained by training the eye, ear, tongue, and memory at one and the same time: the ear by giving the sound and intonation of every word and phrase; the eye by seeing the spelling; the tongue by pronouncing the words; and the memory by the continuous repetition of words and phrases so that the student no longer thinks *about* them but *in* them.

The person studying with this book should practice aloud as much as possible, for it is helpful to exercise the tongue and the ear at the same time. When he has read the English equivalent of a sentence and knows its meaning perfectly, he should read and pronounce the foreign sentence again and again until the words have become associated with their meaning.

After the main sentence has been mastered, the student will proceed with the variaticns given in the exercises. Study should be pursued without undue haste. One should be sure that he has thorough mastery of each section he studies before he proceeds to the next. In a few days the phrases will become second nature to the learner. He will no longer think *about* them but *in* them. He will begin to think in the foreign language itself, and will be able to form hundreds of new phrases by inserting a new noun here, a verb there, an adverb in another place, and so on.

The study of grammar is carried on with each sentence. The footnotes, which explain the grammatical peculiarities, *must* therefore be carefully studied. A full grammatical outline is found at the end of the book.

The vocabularies included in the book have been especially designed to increase the student's knowledge of *necessary* words and phrases.

The proverbs that have been included contain some of the basic folk wisdom common to so many nations. To learn the foreign equivalents of proverbs familiar to all of us is an easy and effective method of fixing words and phrases in the memory.

PART ONE

CONTENTS

THE ITALIAN ALPHABET

The Italian alphabet contains 21 letters. To these may be added k, w, x and y, employed only in foreign words, thus making 25 in all.

The forms of the letters are the same as in English:—

Characters		Names	Pronunciation
A	a	*a*	a
B	b	*bi*	bi
C	c	*ci*	tʃi
D	d	*di*	di
E	e	*e*	ɛ
F	f	*effe*	'ɛf-fe
G	g	*gi*	dʒi
H	h	*acca*	'ak-ka
I	i	*i*	i
L	l	*elle*	'ɛl-le
M	m	*emme*	'ɛm-me
N	n	*enne*	'ɛn-ne
O	o	*o*	ɔ
P	p	*pi*	pi
Q	q	*qu*	ku
R	r	*erre*	'ɛr-re
S	s	*esse*	'ɛs-se
T	t	*ti*	ti
U	u	*u*	u
V	v	*vu*	vu
Z	z	*zeta*	'dzɛ-ta

Foreign letters

K	k	*cappa*	'kap-pa
W	w	*vu doppio*	vu 'dop-pjo
X	x	*ics*	iks
Y	y	*ipsilon*	'ip-si-lon

k, w, x, y

The letters **k, w, x,** and **y** are used only in words of foreign extraction that cannot be rendered in Italian, as in whiskey, Whig, etc.

PHONETIC SYMBOLS

In this text, pronunciation is indicated by the phonetic symbols used by the International Phonetic Association (IPA).

Each phonetic symbol represents only one sound.

A single letter of the alphabet may have different pronunciations. For example, *e* in *tengo* is pronounced ɛ, whereas *e* in *vedo* is pronounced *e*.

Frequently several combined letters of the alphabet represent only one sound, but a single sound can never be represented by more than one phonetic symbol. For example, *ascia* has five letters, but only three sounds, and will therefore be represented by only three symbols: ′aʃa.

Sometimes there are several ways of spelling the same sound, but this sound is always represented by the same symbol.

Thus, in ki, k is spelled *ch* (*chi*)
in ′ka de, k is spelled *c* (*cade*)
in kwi, k is spelled *q* (*qui*)

ITALIAN PRONUNCIATION

I—VOWELS

General Instructions.

Pronounce the English word *I* very slowly. You will notice that you are really saying a series of vowel sounds, starting with *a* as in *father*, with the mouth wide open, and ending with *i* as in *machine*, with the mouth almost closed. This composite sound is called a diphthong. Four of the five so-called vowels of English (*a, i, o, u*) are diphthongs, and even *e* is a diphthong in some local pronunciations. No Italian vowel is ever pronounced as a diphthong. In pronouncing the English word *I*, the open mouth produced an a, the closed mouth produced an i. Each position of the mouth produces a different sound. Therefore, in pronouncing Italian vowels, be sure to keep tongue, lips and jaw tense and firm in exactly the same position throughout the entire sound. Otherwise you will produce a diphthong.

All Italian sounds are produced with the tongue convex (⌒), never concave (⌣). The tip of the tongue must not be permitted to turn up and back.

A. There are seven vowel sounds in Italian. They are: a, ɛ, e, i, ɔ, o, u. Note that in written Italian, ɛ and e are both represented by *e*, and ɔ and o are both represented by *o*.

Symbol	Tongue	Lips	Jaw	Examp
1. i	Very high in front of mouth, tip pressed firmly against lower teeth.	Corners drawn well back.	Almost closed.	′i vi ′vi ni fi ′ni
2. e	Still very high in front, but not quite so high as for i. Tip still against lower teeth.	Corners drawn back a little less than for i.	Slightly more open than for i.	′se te ′pe re
3. ɛ	A little lower in front than for e. Tip still against lower teeth.	Corners drawn back a little less than for e.	More open than for e.	′bɛ ne ′lɛ pre ′fɛ sta
4. a	Lowered, with tip still against lower teeth.	Relaxed.	Well open.	′fa ma ′la ma ′fa ta
5. ɔ	Slightly raised toward back of mouth. Tip no longer touches teeth.	Rounded and slightly protruding.	A little less open than for a.	′lɔ de ′kɔ sa ′tɔ ri
6. o	A little higher in back of mouth than for ɔ. Tip a little further from teeth.	Quite far forward and slightly pursed.	Very much more closed than for ɔ.	′do ne ′po ne ′mol to
7. u	Very high and pulled well back in the mouth.	As far forward as possible.	Almost closed	′fu m ′lu na ′mu le

Note well: the sounds of ɛ and ɔ can occur *only* in stressed syllables (they may, however, optionally occur in syllables bearing a secondary stress in compound words: ′fje ro; fje ra ′men te or fje ra ′men te). All other vowel sounds may be stressed or unstressed. The difference in pronunciation between ɛ and e, and between ɔ and o, can make a difference in the meaning of a word:

ɛ (*è*) = is; e (*e*) = and
′vɛn ti (*venti*) = *winds;* ′ven ti (*venti*) = twenty
ɔ (*ho*) = I have; o (*o*) = or
′lɔ ro (*l'oro*) = the gold; ′lo ro (*loro*) = to them

II—SEMI-VOWELS

When the sounds u, i are pronounced immediately before or after any vowel, a new sound is produced, which is half way between a consonant and a vowel. This is called a semi-vowel. The semi-vowel and the accompanying vowel are always in the same syllable. A semi-vowel cannot be pronounced by itself; it must be accompanied by a vowel.

Symbol	Derived from			Examples
1. j	i	ia	becomes ja	'bjan ko, 'pja no, 'kja mo
		iɛ	becomes jɛ	'fjɛ ro, 'ljɛ ve, 'vjɛ ne (stressed)
		ie	becomes je	fje ra 'men te, lje ve 'men te (unstressed)
		iɔ	becomes jɔ	'fjɔ ko, 'pjɔ ve, 'vjɔ la (stressed)
		io	becomes jo	fjo ka 'men te, pjo 'vo so (unstressed)
		iu	becomes ju	'fju me, 'kju do, 'pju ma
		ai	becomes aj	maj, daj, saj
		ɛi	becomes ɛj	sɛj, lɛj, bɛj
		ei	becomes ej	kwej, dej, pej
		ɔi	becomes ɔj	pɔj
		oi	becomes oj	noj, voj, koj
		ui	becomes uj	kuj, luj, fuj
2. w	u	ua	becomes wa	kwa, 'kwa si, 'kwan to
		uɛ	becomes wɛ	'gwɛr ra, dwɛl lo
		ue	becomes we	'kwe sto, 'ak kwe
		ui	becomes wi	kwi, 'kwin di, kon 'kwi sta
		uɔ	becomes wɔ	'kwɔ re, 'bwɔ no, 'wɔ mo
		au	becomes aw	'aw ra, 'law ro, aw 'rɔ ra
		eu	becomes ew	ew 'rɔ pa

TRIPHTHONGS

Occasionally, two semi-vowels combine with a vowel to produce a triphthong (three vocalic and semivocalic sounds in one syllable):

1.	wɔj	uɔi	uɔi becomes wɔj	twɔj, bwɔj, vwɔj
2.	jɛj	iɛi	iɛi becomes jɛj	mjɛj
3.	waj	uai	uai becomes waj	gwaj
4.	wjɛ	uiɛ	uiɛ becomes wjɛ	'kwjɛ to

III—CONSONANTS

General Instructions.

Italian consonants, like Italian vowels, are pronounced with the tongue convex, the tip pointed downward.

Try to pronounce each consonant with the tongue in the same position as the accompanying vowel. Do not permit the consonant to spoil the purity of the vowel.

A. Breath consonants: In pronouncing consonants like p, t, k, use as little breath as possible, saying the consonant and the accompanying vowel almost simultaneously, without any breath between them.

Examples: 'te ko, 'pa pa, 'tɔ po

B. Dental consonants: l, n, t, d, s, z are produced with the tongue firmly against the upper teeth, the tip of the tongue pointing downward toward the lower teeth. In English the tongue is concave, with the tip touching the upper gums.

Examples: 'ni do, 'la to, 'se te, ko 'si, do 'lɛn te

C. Special symbols: The phonetic symbol for most consonants is the same as the corresponding small printed letter. Four special symbols appear in our transcription:

1. ʃ, pronounced like *sh* in *she*. Examples: 'fa ʃa, 'ʃa me, 'ʃɔ pe ro.

2. λ: place the tip of the tongue against the lower teeth, pronounce *l* with the tongue touching the palate, as for j. The nearest English sound is lj as in *million*. The Italian sound is like lj pronounced so close together that they form one sound. Examples: 'a λo, λi, mi 'λo re.

3. ɲ: place the tip of the tongue as for λ, pronounce *n* exactly as above. The nearest English sound is nj as in *onion*. Examples: 'ba ɲo, 'skri ɲo, gwa da 'ɲa re.

4. ʒ: pronounce like *s* in *pleasure*. This sound occurs by itself only in Tuscan dialectal pronunciation ('ʒɔ ja), being replaced in all other parts of Italy by dʒ, which is pronounced like English *j* in *jet*. Examples: 'a dʒo, man 'dʒa re, dʒi 'ra re.

D. Special sounds:

1. Italian r is produced by trilling the tip of the tongue, which begins its movement from a position against the back of the lower teeth. The tongue is convex, not concave, and points downward. Closest English sound is the British *r* of *very*. Examples: 'ru pe, 'ɛ ra, a 'mo re.

2. Italian s between vowels is pronounced by some speakers as z, by others as s. The pronunciation is optional, and both forms are acceptable. Examples: 'kɔ za (or 'kɔ sa); ko 'zi (or ko 'si); 'pre ze (or 'pre se).

3. In addition to the sound of ʃ, Italian also has the combination sound tʃ. This sound, unless initial or doubled, is less explosive and energetic than English *ch* of *church*, and many Italian speakers pronounce it midway between the sounds represented in English by *sh* and *ch*. Examples: 'pa tʃe, 'tʃe na, tʃa 'sku no.

4. Two other composite sounds are ts and dz (or tts and ddz between vowels), both of which are represented in writing by *z* or *zz* (note, however, that in the common ending *-zione*, the sound is invariably ts). Examples: 'mat tso, 'pot tso, na 'tsjo ne; 'mɛd dzo, 'rad dzo, 'dzin ga ro.

SINGLE AND DOUBLE CONSONANT SOUNDS

These must be carefully distinguished, as they very frequently make a difference in the meaning of a word. In the written language, the double consonant is normally written twice. In speech, if the consonant sound is one that can be prolonged (f, v, s, l, m, n, r), it is continued beyond the normal period that would be devoted to a single consonant. If the sound is one that cannot be prolonged by reason of complete closure of the vocal passage followed by a sudden, explosive release (p, t, k, b, d, g), then the period of closure that precedes the release is prolonged. Examples: 'ɛ ko, 'ɛk ko; 'fa to, 'fat to; 'ru pe, 'rup pe; 'fu ga, 'fug ga; 'ka de, 'kad de; 'ɛ be, 'ɛb be; 'tu fo, 'tuf fo; 'be ve, 'bev ve; 'ka tʃo, 'kat tʃo; 'a dʒo, 'mad dʒo; 'ka sa, 'kas sa; 'a la, 'al la; 'fu mo, 'fum mo; 'se no, 'sen no; 'ɛ ra, 'ɛr ra.

SYLLABIFICATION

The division of words into syllables is not merely a written-language convention that shows you how to divide a word at the end of a line of writing. It is a basic element of pronunciation. With correct syllabification, you stand a good chance of sounding like a native speaker. Without it, you will always sound like a foreigner, no matter how correct your pronunciation may be otherwise.

A syllable consists of one full vowel, which may or may not be preceded or followed by one or more consonants or semi-vowels. In English, the most frequent syllabic arrangement consists of consonant-plus-vowel-plus-consonant, though vowel-plus-consonant and consonant-plus-vowel are not uncommon. In Italian, the typical arrangement is consonant-plus-vowel, though other arrangements are possible. This means that most Italian syllables end in vowel sounds, which are fully and clearly pronounced; it is the vowels rather than the consonants that have prominence. In the English syllabic arrangement, the fact that the vowel of the syllable is most often followed by a consonant tends to shorten and slur the vowel sound if the syllable is unstressed. This never happens in Italian. Compare English gen/er/al with Italian ge/ne/ra/le. The only clear vowel sound of the English word is the *e* of the first syllable, which is stressed. The *e* of the second syllable and the *a* of the third, being unstressed, are reduced to the sound of *e* in *the man*. In phonetic representation, the English word appears as 'dʒɛn ər əl, the Italian word as dʒe ne 'ra le. If you pronounce the Italian word syllable by syllable, pausing between each syllable, then gradually speed up your pronunciation as you repeat, you will have a reasonable facsimile of a native Italian speaker.

RULES OF SYLLABIFICATION

I. The basic and all-important rule of Italian syllabification is that a single consonant sound between two vowels goes with the following, not with the preceding vowel:

Examples:
generale — dʒe ne 'ra le
ripetere — ri 'pɛ te re
felicità — fe li tʃi 'ta

II. Two consonants are generally separated, one going with the preceding, the other with the following vowel:

Examples:

partire	— par ′ti re
alzandosi	— al ′tsan do si
indarno	— in ′dar no

A. A double consonant (mm, nn, ff, tt, etc.) is divided as above. Note, however, that the sound is not *repeated*, but merely *prolonged*. In the case of consonant sounds produced by a complete closure of the vocal passage followed by a sudden release (tt, kk, pp, dd, gg, bb), the first written consonant merely marks a lengthening of the period of closure before the release. Examples: ′fum mo, ′fat to, sek ′ka re.

B. *R* and *l* are combined with a preceding consonant to form a new syllable.

Examples:

segreto	— se ′gre to
aprire	— a ′pri re
applicare	— ap pli ′ka re

Exceptions — *r, l* are separated from a preceding *r, l, m, n.*

Examples:

parlare	— par ′la re
alloro	— al ′lɔ ro
Enrico	— en ′ri ko
correre	— ′kor re re

C. The written groups *gl, gn, ch, gh, sc* (before *e* or *i*) represent single consonant sounds, and must not be separated:

Examples:

aglio	— ′a λo
agnello	— a ′ɲɛl lo
antichi	— an ′ti ki
laghi	— ′la gi
fascia	— ′fa ʃa

D. Groups of st, sp, sk, etc., are not separated, and go with the following vowel:

Examples:

questo	— ′kwe sto
aspetto	— a ′spɛt to
ascoltare	— a skol ′ta re

III.   When there are three consonants, separate the first consonant from the rest:

Examples:
 sorprendere — sor 'prɛn de re
 sembrare   — sem 'bra re
 altro   — 'al tro
 dentro   — 'den tro

Exceptions — groups of spr, str, skr, etc., are not separated, but go with the following vowel:

Examples:
 aspro   — 'a spro
 lastra   — 'la stra
 distruzione — di stru 'tsjo ne
 iscriversi — i 'skri ver si

SPELLING AND PRONUNCIATION

Italian employs a certain number of conventional spellings to indicate certain sounds:

1.   The written letter *h* is always silent. It is used initially only in four forms of the verb *avere*, "to have" (*ho, hai, ha, hanno*, pronounced ɔ, aj, a, 'an no).

2.   The written group *ch* is used before the written vowels *e* and *i* to represent the sound of k (*chi*, "who," pronounced ki; *che*, "what," pronounced ke).

3.   The written group *gh* is used before the written vowels *e* and *i* to represent the sound of g (*laghi*, "lakes," pronounced 'la gi).

4.   The written group *sch* is used before the written vowels *e* and *i* to represent the sound of sk (*schifo*, "nausea," pronounced 'ski fo).

5.   Between the written letters *c, g, sc* and a following *a, o* or *u*, a written *i*, normally silent, is used to indicate that *c* is to have the sound of tʃ, *g* the sound of dʒ, *sc* the sound of ʃ (*ciò*, "that," pronounced tʃɔ; *Giovanni*, "John," pronounced dʒo 'van ni; *sciopero*, "strike," pronounced 'ʃɔ pe ro).

The following syllabic chart will indicate the written representation for each of six sounds (tʃ, k, dʒ, g, ʃ, sk) before each vowel:

Sound		Written Representation				English Equivalent
tʃ	cia	ce	ci	cio	ciu	ch
k	ca	che	chi	co	cu	k
dʒ	gia	ge	gi	gio	giu	j
g	ga	ghe	ghi	go	gu	g (hard)
ʃ	scia	sce	sci	scio	sciu	sh
sk	sca	sche	schi	sco	scu	sk

To put it still another way: a silent *i* serves to indicate a palatal pronunciation of a written *c*, *g* or *sc* before *a*, *o* or *u*; a silent *h* serves to indicate a velarized (guttural) pronunciation of a written *c*, *g* or *sc* before *e* or *i*.

LINKING AND KINDRED PHENOMENA

1.   Italian words seldom end in consonants. The consonants that occasionally appear at the end of a word are *r*, *l*, *n* and *d*. When a word ends in one of these consonants, and the next word begins with a vowel, the syllabic structure of Italian calls for the carrying of the final consonant over to the following initial vowel, so that they form a syllable together:

Examples:	non è vero? — nɔ nɛ 'vero
	per avere — pe ra 've re
	ed egli — e 'de ʎi

2.   When two words are in the same thought group and are closely related grammatically, and the first ends in a vowel while the second begins with a consonant, there is a perceptible doubling (lengthening) of the initial consonant of the second word. This doubling occasionally appears in writing (*ebbene*, from *e bene; fammi* from *fa mi*), but for the most part goes unwritten:

Examples:	a casa — ak 'ka sa
	è nero — ɛn 'ne ro

3.   When two words are in the same thought group and are closely related grammatically, and the first ends in a vowel while the second begins with a vowel, there is a tendency for the final vowel of the

first word to drop out or merge with the initial vowel of the second. This phenomenon is often indicated in writing by an apostrophe (*quell'uomo* from *quello uomo; vent'anni* from *venti anni*). Regardless of the spelling, three pronunciations are often heard for such groups: ven 'tan ni; ven 'tjan nï; 'ven ti 'an ni.

STRESS

In Italian, most words are stressed on the next to the last syllable:

ma 'ri to   a 'man te   in tel li 'dʒɛ́n te

There are also, however, numerous words stressed on the final syllable, or on the third from the end:

tʃit 'ta   vir 'tu   ko 'si
'prɛn de re   'ra pi do   'wɔ mi ni

Occasionally, for the most part because of pronoun forms that are added to verb forms, but also because of recessive accent in the third person plural of verbs, the stress falls on the fourth syllable from the end:

par 'lan do λe ne   'dan do me lo   'in di ka no

The written language normally does not indicate where the stress falls, save in words that end in a final stressed vowel, like *città* or *virtù*.

In our transcription, we indicate by a *preceding* accent mark (') the stressed syllable for all words of more than one syllable, including doubtful cases involving a written *i* or *u* that might be interpreted as indicating either the vowel sound (i, u), or the semi-vowel sound (j, w):

bat te 'ri a   de mo kra 'tsi a   'tu e   'pru a

INTONATION

This refers to the musical lilt of the voice as it speaks connected sentences. Each language has its own distinctive intonation or lilt for various types of statements, commands, questions, etc. The intonation of a language can be taught by the use of musical notation or of a xylophone. It can also be acquired by listening carefully to your records and imitating not only the sounds, but also the intonation of the speaker. Listen for the melody and rhythm of the individual syllables, of each thought group taken as a unit, and, finally, for the music of the entire sentence.

REFERENCE LIST OF SPELLINGS WITH THEIR REGULAR PRONUNCIATIONS

Spelling		Pronunciation	Examples	
a	a	(fata, arma)	'fa ta	'ar ma
b	b	(basso, labaro)	'bas so	'la ba ro
bb	bb	(abbasso, labbro)	ab 'bas so	'lab bro
c (before a, o, u, consonant)	k	(eco, comando)	'ɛ ko	ko 'man do
c (before e, i)	tʃ	(cena, baci)	'tʃe na	'ba tʃi
cc (before a, o, u, consonant)	kk	(ecco, tacco)	'ɛk ko	'tak ko
cch (before e, i)	kk	(facchino, bacche)	fak 'ki no	'bak ke
cci (before a, o, u)	ttʃ	(faccia, acciaio)	'fat tʃa	at 'tʃa jo
ch (before e, i)	k	(chiedere, chiudo)	'kje de re	'kju do
ci (before a, o, u)	tʃ	(ciò, cacio)	tʃɔ	'ka tʃo
cq (only before u)	kk	(acqua, tacquero)	'ak kwa	'tak kwe ro
d	d	(dado, dico)	'da do	'di ko
dd	dd	(Adda, cadde)	'ad da	'kad de
e (stressed or unstressed)	e	(freddo, sete)	'fred do	'se te
e (stressed only)	ɛ	(lepre, bene)	'lɛ pre	'bɛ ne
f	f	(figlio, tufo)	'fi λo	'tu fo
ff	ff	(tuffo, affare)	'tuf fo	af 'fa re
g (before a, o, u, consonant)	g	(gola, magro)	'go la	'ma gro
g (before e, i)	dʒ	(giro, agi)	'dʒi ro	'a dʒi
gg (before a, o, u, consonant)	gg	(legga, fuggo)	'leg ga	'fug go
gg (before e, i)	ddʒ	(legge, raggi)	'led dʒe	'rad dʒi

Spelling		Pronunciation		Examples	
ggh	(before *e, i*)	gg	(tegghia)	'teg gja	
ggi	(before *a, o, u*)	ddʒ	(maggio, leggiamo)	'mad dʒo	led 'dʒa mo
gh	(before *e, i*)	g	(leghe, ghiro)	'le ge	'gi ro
gi	(before *a, o, u*)	dʒ	(giugno, agio)	'dʒu ɲo	'a dʒo
gl	(before *i*)	ʎ	(gli, maglia)	ʎi	'ma ʎa
gn		ɲ	(bagno, agnello)	'ba ɲo	a 'ɲel lo
h		silent	(ho, hanno)	ɔ	'an no
i		i	(vini, si)	'vi ni	si
i	(before or after vowels)	j	(bianco, mai)	'bjan ko	maj
l		l	(lino, parla)	'li no	'par la
ll		ll	(falla, anello)	'fal la	a 'nel lo
m		m	(fame, mira)	'fa me	'mi ra
mm		mm	(andammo, fummo)	an 'dam mo	'fum mo
n		n	(nero, vieni)	'ne ro	'vje ni
o	(stressed or unstressed)	o	(sole, volo)	'so le	'vo lo
o	(stressed only)	ɔ	(cosa, toro)	'kɔ sa	'tɔ ro
p		p	(padre, capo)	'pa dre	'ka po
pp		pp	(mappa, apporre)	'map pa	ap 'por re
q	(only before *u*)	k	(qui, eloquio)	kwi	e 'lɔ kwjo
r		r	(rido, faro)	'ri do	'fa ro

Spelling	Phonetic	Position	Examples	Transcription
rr	rr		(corre, errore)	'kor re er 'ro re
s	s *or* z	(between vowels)	(cosa, così)	'kɔ sa ko 'si *or* 'kɔ za ko 'zi
s	s	(in other positions)	(sole, stella)	'so le 'stel la
sc	sk	(before *a, o, u*)	(scorrere, esca)	'skor re re 'ɛ ska
sc	ʃ	(before *e, i*)	(sciogliere, fasci)	'ʃɔ ʎe re 'fa ʃi
sch	sk	(before *e, i*)	(scheletro, maschi)	'ske le tro 'ma ski
sci	ʃ	(before *a, o, u*)	(lascio, fasciare)	'la ʃo fa 'ʃa re
ss	ss		(sassi, asso)	'sas si 'as so
t	t		(torre, fato)	'tor re 'fa to
tt	tt		(fatto, attore)	'fat to at 'to re
u	u		(uno, fumare)	'u no fu 'ma re
u	w	(before or after vowels)	(quasi, fauno)	'kwa si 'faw no
v	v		(vino, bevo)	'vi no 'be vo
vv	vv		(avviare, bevve)	av 'vja re 'bev ve
z	ts *or*		(zio, zucchero)	'tsi o 'tsuk ke ro
	dz		(zeta, zanzara)	'dze ta dzan 'dza ra
zi	ts	(in endings -*zia*, -*zio*)	(giustizia, comizio)	dʒu 'sti tsja ko 'mi tsjo
zz	tts *or*		(pezzo, mozzare)	'pɛt tso mot 'tsa re
	ddz		(razzo, azzardo)	'rad dzo ad 'dzar do

NOTES

1. The following letters of the alphabet do not occur in native Italian words: *k, w, x, y*. Where they occur in foreign words, pronounce as in the language from which the word is derived.

2. The letter *j* occasionally appears in older writings, either to indicate the phonetic sound of j, today represented by *i* (*majale*, today spelled *maiale*), or to indicate a final contraction of a phonetic j with a final -*i* ending (*mugnaio*, plural *mugnaj*, today spelled *mugnai*).

3. In words borrowed from Greek, *k* and *ch* are rendered by Italian *c* (before *a, o, u*, consonant), by Italian *ch* (before *e, i*); Greek *y* is rendered by Italian *i*; thus, the word appearing in English as *psychosis* will appear in Italian as *psicosi*.

4. Greek-derived *ph* and *th* are rendered in Italian spelling by *f* and *t*, respectively; thus, the words appearing in English as *Philadelphia, telegraph, arithmetic, theme*, will appear in Italian as *Filadelfia, telegrafo, aritmetica, tema*.

IDIOMATIC WEALTH OF ITALIAN

"La lingua italiana è una delle più ricche del mondo. Fra gli idiomi moderni il francese e l'italiano sono i più ricchi e perciò stesso contano naturalmente moltissimi idiotismi."

"The Italian language is one of the richest tongues in the world. Among modern tongues French and Italian rank highest in expressions, and as a matter of course contain many idioms."

ITALIAN AND AMERICAN CHARACTERISTICS

"Gli Italiani sono naturalmente cortesi. La cortesia italiana è innata e si trova nella classe povera non meno che nella ricca. ... Forse gli Americani sono meno espansivi di noi Italiani. Comunque ciascun paese ha le sue proprie caratteristiche e maniere. E se anche fosse come lei dice, d'altra parte vi sono molte cose ben più importanti della cortesia che noi dovremmo imparare da loro."

"Italian people are polite by nature. Italian politeness is inborn and is found among the poorest as well as the richest. ... Perhaps Americans are less expansive than we Italians. However, each country has its own characteristics and ways. And even if it were as you say, we on the other hand might learn many things from you which are much more important than politeness."

FRASE PRINCIPALE

Che vuol fare questa mattina? Vorrei partire col primo aeroplano per
Roma; ma, disgraziatamente, ciò mi è impossibile, perchè aspetto un
mio amico da Boston e devo restare a New York finchè egli arrivi in
piroscafo o in treno o in autobus.

PRONUNCIATION

Ke vwɔl 'fa-re 'kwe-sta mat-'ti-na? vor-'rɛj par-'ti-re kol 'pri-mo
a-e-ro-'pla-no per 'ro-ma, ma, di-sgra-tsja-ta-'men-te, tʃɔ mi ɛ
im-pos-'si-bi-le, per-'ke a-'spɛt-to un 'mi-o a-'mi-ko da 'bɔs-ton e
'de-vo re-'sta-re a nju jɔrk fin-'ke 'e-ʎi ar-'ri-vi in pi-'rɔ-ska-fo o in
'trɛ-no o in 'aw-to-bus.

Che (ke)

vuol¹(ella)² ? (vwɔl 'el-la)

fare ('fa-re)

questa mattina ('kwe-sta mat-'ti-na)

---

¹ The final vowel of any word, when preceded by either *l*, *m*, *n*, or *r*, is very
frequently dropped for euphony's sake, but not necessarily so, except in a few
cases, which will be pointed out further on.

² *Lei* or *Ella* (frequently omitted in speech) is the polite form of addressing a
person in Italian. This mode of address is quite peculiar to the Italian language.
Formerly the term *Vossignoria* was used (not unlike the English *"your Lordship"*
or the Spanish *"Vuestra Merced = Usted"*) which being *feminine* requires the
third person singular feminine, as: *Vossignoria ha,* your Lordship has. This word
"Vossignoria" is now obsolete; the construction, however, remains, and is always
employed, when a person is politely spoken to, as: Have you? ha (Lei)? (has *she*,
i. e. Vossignoria); *comanda?* (*ella* left out), what do you want? (literally: does she
command?). In mercantile style and in conversation with inferiors, etc., the
second person plural is used, as in French and in English, as: *Avete voi?* Have you?
(*avez-vous?*) The *second person singular*, as in French, is used in addressing relations
and intimate friends, as: *Hai?* (hast thou) have you? *Vuoi?* (wilt thou) will you?
Avevi? (hadst thou) had you?

MAIN SENTENCE

What do you want to do this morning? I should like to leave by (Lit. with)[3] the first airplane for Rome, but, unfortunately, that is (Lit. to me) impossible; for I expect a friend from Boston, and I must stay in New York till he arrives either by steamer, train or bus.

---

[3] Throughout the Language Phone Text-books the abbreviation—Lit.:—indicates the literal translation of the Italian text.

1. Che vuole[1]? ('vwɔ-le)
2. Che vuol fare?
3. Che cosa vuol fare stamane[2]? ('kɔ-sa) (sta-'ma-ne)
4. Che cosa vuol fare domani? (do-'ma-ni)
5. Vuol farlo[3]? ('far-lo)
6. Vuol farlo domani?
7. Vuol farlo oggi? ('ɔd-dʒi)

>   (io) voglio ('i-o vɔ-λo)
>   (tu) vuoi (tu vwɔj)
>   (egli) vuole ('e-λi'vwɔ-le)
>   (noi) vogliamo (noj vo-'λja-mo)
>   (voi) volete (voj vo-'le-te)
>   (essi) vogliono ('es-si 'vɔ-λo-no)

8. Io non[4] voglio farlo stamattina. (non)
9. Perchè[5] non vuol farlo oggi? (per-'ke)

>   (io) non voglio
>   (tu) non vuoi
>   (egli) non vuole
>   (noi) non vogliamo
>   (voi) non volete
>   (essi) non vogliono

10. Quando vuol farlo?
11. Lo[6] può fare stamattina? (pwɔ). Può farlo stamattina?

---

[1] The Italian verb seldom requires the personal pronouns *io, tu, egli, ella, noi, voi, essi*, the persons being sufficiently marked by the terminations of the verb.

[2] *Stamane, stamattina* are contractions of *questa mane, questa mattina*. In like manner *stasera* and *stanotte* are used instead of *questa sera*, this evening, and *questa notte*, this night.

[3] The so-called *conjunctive personal pronouns*, me, thee, him, her, it, us, you, them, *follow* the verb in the *infinitive*, which, in this case, drops its final vowel, and are contracted into one word. The pupil should commit these pronouns to memory:

mi	me
ti	thee
lo	him
la	her
gli	to him
le	her (to her)
ci	us (to us)
vi	you (to you)
li	them

1. What do you want?
2. What do you want to do?
3. What (Lit. thing) do you want to do this morning?
4. What do you want to do to-morrow?
5. Will you do it?
6. Do you want to do it to-morrow?
7. Do you want to do it to-day?

> I want
> you want (familiar singular, f.s.)
> he wants
> we want
> you want
> they want

8. I do not want to do it this morning.
9. Why do you not want to do it to-day?

> I do not want
> you do not want (f.s.)
> he does not want
> we do not want
> you do not want
> they do not want

10. When do you want to do it?
11. Can you do it (Lit.: It can [you] do) this morning?

---

le	them
loro	them (to them); this pronoun, exceptionally, always follows the verb, and is detached from it (do loro il libro, I give them the book).
si	one's self

[4] The negation in Italian must be placed *before* the verb—*io non voglio*—I will not.

[5] The *accento grave* (`) (from left to right) is used to show that the stress is on the final vowel of the word. The acute accent (´) (from right to left) is used only in dictionaries and grammars to mark the syllable on which the stress is laid.

[6] The conjunctive personal pronouns in Italian precede the verb in all cases, except in the imperative affirmative, in the infinitive, or in the gerund, in which cases they follow the verb, and form only one word with the same, *Io lo voglio*, I want it; *Non la vogliamo*, we do not want her; *farlo*, to do it. We say in English: Will you do it? In Italian: *It* will you do? *Lo vuol fare?* Or: Will you do *it? Vuol farlo?* (In the latter case *lo* is added directly to *far* with which it forms only one word.)

12. No, non posso farlo stamane. No, non lo posso fare stamane. (nɔ) ('pɔs-so)

> (io)posso ('pɔs-so)
> (tu)puoi (pwɔj)
> (egli)può (pwɔ)
> (noi)possiamo (noj pos-'sja-mo)
> (voi)potete (voj po-'te-te)
> (essi)possono ('pɔs-so-no)

13. Può farlo domani? Sì, posso farlo domani mattina. Lo può fare domani? Sì, lo posso fare domani mattina.

PARLARE
(par-'la-re)

14. Parla italiano[1]? ('par-la i-ta-'lja-no)

15. Lo parlo un poco. (lo 'par-lo un 'pɔ-ko)

16. Lo parla bene? ('par-la) ('bɛ-ne)

17. No, signore, non lo parlo molto bene. (si-'ɲo-re) ('mol-to)

> (io)parlo ('par-lo)
> (tu)parli ('par-li)
> (egli)parla ('par-la)
> (noi)parliamo (par-'lja-mo)
> (voi)parlate (par-'la-te)
> (essi)parlano ('par-la-no)

18. Può esprimersi in italiano? (e-'spri-mer-si)
Può farsi capire in italiano?[2] ('far-si) (ka-'pi-re)

19. Lo parlo abbastanza per farmi intendere (ab-ba-'stan-tsa) ('far-mi) (in-'tɛn-de-re)

20. Non posso esprimermi molto bene in italiano, però lo parlo abbastanza per farmi intendere *or* per farmi comprendere.

21. Parla italiano questo[3] signore? ('kwe-sto)

22. Sì, lo parla correntemente. (kor-ren-te-'men-te)

---

[1] Words indicating *nationality* are used with a capital initial only when used as nouns, as: Gli Italiani, the Italians.

[2] This phrase might be translated: Can you make yourself understood in Italian? The two Italian phrases given above mean the same thing exactly. Synonymous

12. No, I can not do it (Lit.: [I] not can do it. Or: [I] not it can do) this morning.

> I can
> you can (f.s.)
> he can
> we can
> you can
> they can

13. Can you do it to-morrow? Yes, I can do it to-morrow morning

TO SPEAK

14. Do you speak Italian? (Lit.: Speak [you] Italian?)
15. I speak it slightly. (Lit.: [I] it speak a little.)
16. Do you speak it well? (Lit.: It speak you well?)
17. No, sir, I do not speak it very well.

> I speak
> you speak (f.s.)
> he speaks
> we speak
> you speak
> they speak

18. Can you express yourself in Italian?

19. I speak it sufficiently to make myself understood. (Lit.: understand.)
20. I cannot express myself (Lit.: [I] not can express me) very well in Italian, but I speak it sufficiently to make myself understood.
21. Does this gentleman speak Italian? (Lit.: Speaks Italian this gentleman?)
22. Yes, he speaks it fluently.

---

expressions are frequently introduced to accustom the student to variety of expression.

[5] *Questo* and for the feminine *questa*, before vowels: *quest'*.

24

23. È italiano[1]?

24. Sì, signore, è italiano.

> (io)sono ('i-o 'so-no)
> (tu)sei (tu sɛj)
> (egli)è ('e-ʎi ɛ)
> (ella)è ('el-la ɛ)
> (noi)siamo (noj 'sja-mo)
> (voi)siete (voj 'sje-te)
> (essi)sono ('es-si 'so-no)
> (esse)sono ('es-se 'so-no)

25. E Lei, signore, è americano od[2] italiano? (e) (si-'ɲo-re) (a-me-ri-'ka-no) (od)

26. Perchè me lo[3] domanda? (per-'ke me lo do-'man-da)

27. Glielo domando perchè parla inglese benissimo. ('ʎe-lo do-'man-do) (in-'gle-se be-'nis-si-mo)

28. Sono italiano, ma mia madre era americana ed io parlo italiano ed inglese correntemente. ('mi-a 'ma-dre 'ɛ-ra a-me-ri-'ka-na)

29. È difficile la lingua italiana? (dif-'fi-tʃi-le la 'lin-gwa)

30. Sono nato a Firenze e l' italiano è la mia lingua materna. ('so-no 'na-to a fi-'rɛn-tse) ('mi-a 'lin-gwa ma-'tɛr-na)

31. È molto difficile la pronuncia italiana? (pro-'nun-tʃa)

32. La pronuncia italiana[4] non è molto difficile, anzi è facilissima. ('mol-to) ('an-tsi ɛ fa-tʃi-'lis-si-ma)

33. Mi riesce assai difficile pronunciare correttamente frasi italiane. (mi ri-'ɛ-ʃe) (pro-nun-'tʃa-re kor-rɛt-ta-'men-te)

34. Credo che la pronuncia italiana sia molto difficile. ('kre-do) ('si-a)

35. Al contrario la pronuncia inglese è assai più difficile della[5] nostra. (al kon-'tra-rjo) (in-'gle-se) (as-'saj) (pju) ('del-la 'nɔ-stra)

---

[1] We say in English: Are you an Italian? In Italian this is expressed by: Are you Italian? *Lei è italiano?*

[2] The words: *e* (and), *a* (to, at), *o* (or) often take a *d* before a vowel and become *ed, ad, od,* for the sake of euphony.

[3] We have seen that the conjunctive pronouns are placed *before* the verbs. When a verb governs two conjunctive pronouns, the dative must *precede* the

23. Is he an Italian?

24. Yes, sir, he is an Italian.

> I am
> you are (f.s.)
> he is
> she is
> we are
> you are
> they are (masc.)
> they are (fem.)

25. And you, sir, are you an American or an Italian?

26. Why do you ask me that? (Lit.: Why me it you-ask?)

27. I ask this question, (Lit.: You it I ask) because you speak English so well.

28. I am an Italian, but my mother was an American, and I speak both Italian and English fluently.

29. Is Italian a difficult language? (Lit.: Is difficult the language Italian?)

30. I was born in Florence, and Italian is my mother-tongue.

31. Is Italian pronunciation very difficult?

32. Italian pronunciation is not very difficult, on the contrary it is very easy.

33. It is (Lit. succeeds) very difficult for me to pronounce Italian sentences correctly.

34. I think Italian pronunciation is very difficult.

35. On the contrary, English pronunciation is much more difficult than ours.

---

accusative. See Grammar, Part X., for more extensive rules on this subject. In this case, the dative pronouns *mi, ti, ci, vi, si* change to *me, te, ce, ve, se.*

[4] Adjectives denoting *nationality, color,* and *shape,* are usually placed after the *noun.* See Part X.

[5] See Part X. for the declension of the article.

36. L' inglese è la mia[1] propria lingua. ('mi-a 'prɔ-prja 'lin-gwa)

37. Lei è nato a Nuova York? No, signore; sono nato a Chicago. (ɛ 'na-to) (a 'nwɔ-va)

38. La pronuncia italiana è molto più facile della loro. Abbiamo regole fisse per la pronuncia. (ab-'bja-mo 're-go-le 'fis-se)

Avere—Indicativo Presente

AFFERMATIVAMENTE	INTERROGATIVAMENTE
(Io) ho	ho (io)?
(tu) hai	hai (tu)?
(egli) ha	ha (egli)?
(ella) ha	ha (ella)?
(noi) abbiamo	abbiamo (noi)?
(voi) avete	avete (voi)?
(essi) hanno	hanno (essi)?
(esse) hanno	hanno (esse)?

NEGATIVAMENTE	INTERROGATIVAMENTE E NEGATIVAMENTE
(io) non ho	non ho (io)?
(tu) non hai	non hai (tu)?
(egli) non ha	non ha (egli)?
(ella) non ha	non ha (ella)?
(noi) non abbiamo	non abbiamo (noi)?
(voi) non avete	non avete (voi)?
(essi) non hanno	non hanno (essi)?
(esse) non hanno	non hanno (esse)?

---

[1] Possessive adjectives in Italian are generally preceded by the definite article, thus:

il mio	il tuo	il suo	my, thy (your), his, her, its
la mia	la tua	la sua	

36. English is my own tongue.

37. Were you born in New York? No, sir; I was born in Chicago.

38. Italian pronunciation is much easier than yours. We have definite rules for pronunciation.

"To Have"—Present Indicative

AFFIRMATIVE	INTERROGATIVE
I have	have I?
you have (f.s.)	have you? (f.s.)
he has	has he?
she has	has she?
we have	have we?
you have	have you?
they have	have they?
they have	have they?

NEGATIVE	INTERROGATIVE AND NEGATIVE
I have not	have I not?
you have not (f.s.)	have you not? (f.s.)
he has not	has he not?
she has not	has she not?
we have not	have we not?
you have not	have you not?
they have not	have they not?
they have not	have they not?

---

il nostro	il vostro	il loro	
la nostra	la vostra	la loro	our, your, their

See Part X.

CONIUGAZIONE DEI VERBI REGOLARI[1]
Modo Indicativo
PRESENTE
Affermativamente

1.ᵃ Parlare	2.ᵃ Ricevere	3.ᵃ Sentire
(Io) parlo	ricevo	sento
(tu) parli	ricevi	senti
(egli) parla	riceve	sente
(noi) parliamo	riceviamo	sentiamo
(voi) parlate	ricevete	sentite
(essi) parlano	ricevono	sentono

Negativamente

(Io) non parlo	non ricevo	non sento
(tu) non parli	non ricevi	non senti
(egli) non parla	non riceve	non sente
(noi) non parliamo	non riceviamo	non sentiamo
(voi) non parlate	non ricevete	non sentite
(essi) non parlano	non ricevono	non sentono

1. Favorisca[2] pronunciarmi questa parola. (fa-vo-'ris-ka pro-nun-'tʃar-mi 'kwe-sta pa-'rɔ-la)
2. Mi fa la gentilezza di pronunciarla un' altra volta? (fa) (dʒen-ti-'let-tsa) (u-'nal-tra 'vɔl-ta)

favorisco
favorisci
favorisce
favoriamo
favorite
favoriscono

[1] There are three regular conjugations in Italian ending respectively in *are*, *ere*, and *ire*. By dropping these endings we get the root or stem of the verb, thus *parl*, *ricev*, and *sent*. This stem remains unaltered throughout the entire conjugation in all regular verbs. To the stem various terminations are added, by which persons, tenses, and moods are distinguished, and which are common to all verbs of the same conjugation. For the present tense of the first, second and third conjugations, the following terminations are added:

CONJUGATION OF THE REGULAR VERBS
Indicative Mood
PRESENT TENSE
Affirmative

1st To speak	2d To receive	3d To feel, to hear
I speak	I receive	I feel
you speak (f.s.)	you receive (f.s.)	you feel (f.s.)
he speaks	he receives	he feels
we speak	we receive	we feel
you speak	you receive	you feel
they speak	they receive	they feel

Negative

I do not speak	receive	feel
you do not speak (f.s.)	receive	feel
he does not speak	receive	feel
we do not speak	receive	feel
you do not speak	receive	feel
they do not speak	receive	feel

1. Will you please pronounce this word for me? (Lit.: Favor to pronounce [to] me this word.)
2. Will you please pronounce it once more? (Lit.: Do me the kindness to pronounce it another time.)

I do a favor
you do a favor (f.s.)
he does a favor
we do a favor
you do a favor
they do a favor

1st	2nd	3rd
-o	-o	-o
-i	-i	-i
-a	-e	-e
-iamo	-iamo	-iamo
-ate	-ete	-ite
-ano	-ono	-ono

For a complete table of terminations and further rules, see Part X.

² Verbs of the third conjugation in *ire*, as a rule, are irregular in the present tense like *favorire;* and the same irregularity is repeated in the subjunctive and in the imperative moods.

> faccio **or** fo
> fai
> fa
> facciamo
> fate
> fanno

3. Come si[1] pronuncia questa parola? ('ko-me si)

4. Non posso pronunciare questa parola. Vuol favorire pronunciarmela un' altra volta? ('pɔs-so pro-nun-'tʃa-re) (pro-nun-'tʃar-me-la)

5. Sa come si pronuncia questa parola? (sa)

> so (sɔ)
> sai (saj)
> sa (sa)
> sappiamo (sap-'pja-mo)
> sapete (sa-'pe-te)
> sanno ('san-no)

6. Sì, ora so come si pronuncia ('o-ra)
7. Comprende[2] l' italiano? (kom-'prɛn-de)
8. Lo capisco pochissimo. (lo ka-'pi-sko po-'kis-si-mo)
9. Mi intende quando parlo in italiano? (in-'tɛn-de 'kwan-do 'par-lo i-ta-'lja-no)
10. La intendo quando parla adagio e distintamente.[3] (a-'da-dʒo) (di-stin-ta-'men-te)
11. Non mi capisce quando parlo in fretta? (ka-'pi-ʃe) ('fret-ta)

12. No, signore, non la comprendo quando parla così in fretta. (si-'ɲo-re) (ko-'si)
13. Mi faccia il favore di parlare adagio e distintamente. Sono americano e non la capisco quando parla così in fretta. ('fat-tʃa) (fa-'vo-re di)
14. Mi faccia il favore di ripetere questa frase. Non la comprendo quando parla così in fretta. (ri-'pɛ-te-re) ('fra-se)
15. Mi comprende ora?

---

[1] The reflexive form in Italian is very frequently used instead of the passive form, as: *Si dice*, it is said; *Si pronuncia*, it is pronounced.

[2] The English auxiliary verb *to do* as it is used in interrogative and negative sentences, is never made use of in Italian.

I make
you make (f.s.)
he makes
we make
you make
they make

3. How is this word pronounced? (Lit.: How itself pronounces this word?)
4. I cannot pronounce this word. Will you be kind enough to pronounce it once more for me?

5. Do you know how this word is pronounced?

I know
you know (f.s.)
he knows
we know
you know
they know

6. Yes, now I know how it is pronounced.
7. Do you understand Italian?
8. I understand it very little.
9. Do you understand me when I speak Italian?

10. I understand you when you speak slowly and distinctly.

11. Do you not understand me when I speak rapidly (Lit.: in a hurry)?
12. No, sir, I do not understand you when you speak so fast.

13. Will you please speak (Lit.: do me the favor of speaking) slowly and distinctly. I am an American, and I do not understand you when you speak so fast.
14. Please repeat this sentence. I do not understand you when you speak so fast.
15. Do you understand me now?

---

[3] Adverbs of manner are usually formed by adding *mente* to the feminine form of the adjectives, thus: *Distinto* (distinct), *distinta*, *distintamente; perfetto* (perfect), *perfetta*, *perfettamente*. In Part X. will be found further adverbs.

16. Sì, ora la capisco[1] perfettamente. (per-fet-ta-'men-te)

17. Che dice? ('di-tʃe)

> (io) dico ('di-ko)
> (tu) dici ('di-tʃi)
> (egli) dice (di-tʃe)
> (essa) dice ('es-sa)
> (noi) diciamo (di-'tʃa-mo)
> (voi) dite ('di-te)
> (essi) dicono ('es-si 'di-ko-no)
> (esse) dicono ('es-se)

18. Che dice?

19. Che dice quest'[2] uomo? ('kwe-'stwɔ-mo)

20. Intende quel che dice quest' uomo? No, non lo intendo.

> (io) intendo
> (tu) intendi
> (egli) intende
> (ella) intende
> (noi) intendiamo
> (voi) intendete
> (essi) intendono
> (esse) intendono

21. Comprende tutto quel che dico? ('tut-to kwel)

22. Sì, comprendo tutto quel che dice, se parla adagio e distinta- mente.

23. Non capisco questa parola; favorisca ripeterla.

24. La capisce adesso? Sì, ora la capisco. (a-'dɛs-so)

25. Che significa questa parola? (si-'ɲi-fi-ka) (pa-'rɔ-la)

26. Che significa questa parola in inglese?

27. Che significa?

28. Mi faccia la gentilezza di ripeterlo. Non comprendo quel che signifîchi[3]. (si-'ɲi-fi-ki)

---

[1] *Capisco* (I understand), from *capire*, as a verb of the third conjugation, is conjugated like *favorire*, as are most verbs ending in *ire*:

capisco	capiamo
capisci	capite
capisce	capiscono

16. Yes, now I understand you perfectly.

17. What do you say?

> I say
> you say (f.s.)
> he says
> she says
> we say
> you say
> (m.) they say
> (f.) they say

18. What does he say?

19. What does this man say?

20. Do you understand what (Lit.: that which) this man says? No, I do not understand him.

> I understand
> you understand (f.s.)
> he understands
> she understands
> we understand
> you understand
> they understand
> they understand

21. Do you understand everything (Lit.: all that which) I say?

22. Yes, I can understand everything you say, if you speak slowly and distinctly.

23. I do not understand this word; please repeat it.

24. Do you understand it now? Yes, now I understand it.

25. What does this word mean?

26. What does this word mean in English?

27. What does it mean?

28. Please repeat it. I do not understand what it means.

---

[2] *Questo* and *questa* (this), before a vowel drop *o* and *a* and take an apostrophe instead.

[3] The subjunctive is very frequently used in Italian, even more so than in French.

29. Abbia la bontà di spiegare questa parola. ('ab-bja) (bon-'ta) (spje-'ga-re)

30. Favorisca spiegarmi un' altra volta questa parola.

31. Sa quel che significhi in inglese questa parola?

32. Sì, ora so quel che significa questa parola.

33. Mi fa la gentilezza[1] di spiegarmi questa frase italiana? Non so quel che significhi in inglese. (spje-'gar-mi)

34. Comprende ora quel che significhi questa frase?

35. Sì, ora so quel che significa questa frase, e posso dirla in italiano ed in inglese.

36. Mi riesce difficile pronunciare[2] tutte[3] queste[3] frasi. Credo che la pronuncia italiana sia molto difficile.

37. Invece la pronuncia italiana è facilissima. Le parole italiane si pronunciano secondo regole precise. (in-'ve-tʃe) (pre-'tʃi-se)

38. Sa quel che significhi "dire di nuovo"? No, non lo so. ('di-re di 'nwɔ-vo)

39. "Dire di nuovo" significa ripetere. Posso dire: "Favorisca ripeter questo" o "Favorisca dirlo di nuovo." Queste due frasi significano la stessa cosa.

IN UN NEGOZIO; IN UNA BOTTEGA
(ne-'gɔ-tsjo)

1. Che cosa[4] vuol fare in questa bottega? Voglio comprare qualche cosa. (bot-'te-ga) (kom-'pra-re 'kwal-ke 'kɔsa)

2. Che cosa vuol comprare? Voglio comprare un cappello. (kap-'pɛl-lo)

3. Favorisca accompagnarmi. Voglio comprare un cappello e non parlo abbastanza l' italiano. (ak-kom-pa-'ɲar-mi) (ab-ba-'stan-tsa)

4. Buon giorno.[5] Il mio amico vorrebbe comprare un cappello. (bwɔn 'dʒor-no) (a-'mi-ko)

---

[1] This is only one of the many ways to express the same idea in Italian.

[2] The infinitive form of Italian verbs is often employed as a noun.

[3] Adjectives, pronouns and nouns ending in o become *feminine*, as a rule, by changing this termination into a: *Questo, questa* (this), *tutto, tutta* (all), *italiano, italiana,* (Italian), etc. And while the masculine form becomes plural by changing

29. Have the kindness to explain this word.

30. Please explain this word once more to me.

31. Do you know what this word means in English?

32. Yes, now I know what this word means.

33. Do me the kindness to explain this Italian sentence to me. I do not know what it means in English.

34. Do you understand now what this sentence means?

35. Yes, now I know what this sentence means, and can say it in Italian and in English.

36. It is hard for me to pronounce all these sentences. I think (that) Italian pronunciation is very difficult.

37. On the contrary the Italian pronunciation is very easy. Italian words are pronounced according to definite rules.

38. Do you know what "dire di nuovo" means? No, I don't know.

39. "Dire di nuovo" means to repeat. I can say: "Please repeat that." or "Please say it again." These two sentences mean the same thing.

IN A STORE—IN A SHOP

1. What do you want to do in this store? I want to buy something.

2. What do you want to buy? I want to buy a hat.

3. Please come with me. I want to buy a hat, and I do not speak Italian (well) enough.

4. Good day. My friend would like to buy a hat.

---

o into *i*, the feminine *a* is changed into *e. Tutto, tutti; tutta, tutte;* etc.

⁴ *Che, che cosa,* and *cosa* are used for "what," thus: *che vuoi? che cosa vuoi?* and *cosa vuoi?*

⁵ *Buon giorno,* good day, good morning; *buona serà,* good evening; *buona notte,* good night.

5. Che qualità di cappello vuole? (kwa-li-'ta)

6. Ne voglio uno di feltro ('fel-tro)

7. Che numero ha? ('nu-me-ro)

8. Il numero sette. ('sɛt-te)

9. Provi questo. ('prɔ-vi)

10. M'[1] è troppo stretto. ('trɔp-po 'stret-to)

11. Vorrei pure un paio di guanti. (vor-'rɛ-i 'pu-re) ('pa-jo) ('gwan-ti)

12. Di che qualità li desidera? Di pelle. (li de-'si-de-ra) ('pɛl-le)

13. Di che numero? Del numero sei.

> duemila (du-e-'mi-la)
> un milione (mi-'ljo-ne)
> due milioni (mi-'ljo-ni)
> un miliardo (mi-'ljar-do)
> due miliardi (mi-'ljar-di)

14. Le vanno bene questi guanti? Sì, mi vanno benissimo (le 'van-no 'bene) ('gwan-ti) (be-'nis-si-mo)

15. E come le va questo cappello? Bene, benissimo! (va)

> vado or vo ('va-do) (vɔ)
> vai (vaj)
> va (va)
> andiamo (an-'dja-mo)
> andate (an-'da-te)
> vanno ('van-no)

16. Favorisca farmi vedere altri[2] guanti; questi non mi vanno bene. ('far-mi ve-'de-re 'al-tri)

17. Quanto costa questo cappello? Questo costa dieci dollari. ('kɔs-ta)

18. E quanto costano questi guanti[3]? Tre dollari. ('kɔs-ta-no) ('dɔl-la-ri)

---

[1] The i of mi (me), ti (thee), gli (himself), si (oneself), ci (us), vi (you), and di (of), may or may not be dropped before a vowel.

[2] *Altro, altra, altri, altre.*

5. What kind of a hat do you want?

6. I want a felt hat. (Lit.: Of them [I] want one of felt.)

7. What size do you wear? (Lit.: What number have [you]?)

8. Size seven.

9. Try on this one.

10. It is too small for (Lit.: tight to) me.

11. I would also like a pair of gloves.

12. What kind of gloves do you want? Kid gloves. (Lit.: of skin.)

13. What size? Size six.

> 2,000
> 1,000,000
> 2,000,000
> 1,000,000,000
> 2,000,000,000

14. Do these gloves fit you? Yes, they fit me very well.

15. And how does this hat fit you? Very, very well.

> I go
> you go (f.s.)
> he goes
> we go
> you go
> they go

16. Please show me some other gloves; these do not fit me well.

17. How much is this hat? This one costs ten dollars.

18. And how much are these gloves? Three dollars.

---

[3] In Italian, adjectives must agree in gender and number with the noun they modify. *Guanti* is pl. and masc., hence *questi* must be pl. and masc. too. *Cappello* is sing. and masc., hence *questo* must also be sing. and masc.

NUMERI CARDINALI—CARDINAL NUMBERS

uno,[1] due ('u-no, 'du-e)	1, 2
tre, quattro (tre, kwat-tro)	3, 4
cinque, sei ('tʃin-kwe, sɛj)	5, 6
sette, otto ('sɛt-te, 'ɔt-to)	7, 8
nove, dieci ('nɔ-ve, 'djɛ-tʃi)	9, 10
undici ('un-di-tʃi)	11
dodici ('do-di-tʃi)	12
tredici ('tre-di-tʃi)	13
quattordici (kwat-'tɔr-di-tʃi)	14
quindici ('kwin-di-tʃi)	15
sedici ('se-di-tʃi)	16
diciassette (di-tʃas-'sɛt-te)	17
diciotto (di-'tʃɔt-to)	18
diciannove (di-tʃan-'nɔ-ve)	19
venti ('ven-ti)	20
ventuno (ven-'tu-no)	21
ventidue (ven-ti-'du-e), ecc.	22, etc.
trenta ('trɛn-ta)	30
trentuno (tren-'tu-no), ecc.	31, etc.
quaranta (kwa-'ran-ta)	40
cinquanta (tʃin-'kwan-ta)	50
sessanta (ses-'san-ta)	60
settanta (set-'tan-ta)	70
ottanta (ot-'tan-ta)	80
novanta (no-'van-ta)	90
cento ('tʃen-to)	100
duecento (du-e-'tʃɛn-to), ecc.	200, etc.
mille ('mil-le)	1,000
mille (e) cento	1,100
mille duecento	1,200
mille trecento	1,300

---

[1] Cardinal numbers, with the exception of *uno* (one), *mille* (one thousand) and *milione* (one million), are invariable.

VOCABOLARIO

La Lingua; Le Lingue

VOCABULARY

The Language; The Languages

Lei ha una buona pronuncia.	You have a good pronunciation.
La sua pronuncia è pessima.	His pronunciation is very bad.
L' accento	The accent
Gli accenti	The accents
Ella non accentua bene questa sillaba.	You do not stress this syllable properly.
Accentui bene questa sillaba.	Put the right accent on this syllable.
Pronunciare	To pronounce
Lei pronuncia bene.	You pronounce well.
Lei pronuncia male.	You pronounce badly.
Lei non pronuncia correttamente questa parola.	You do not pronounce this word correctly.
Lei non pronuncia bene questa parola.	You do not pronounce this word correctly (well).
Lei pronuncia male questa parola.	You pronounce this word incorrectly (badly).
Correggere	To correct
Lo sbaglio, l' errore	The mistake, the error
Lo sproposito, lo strafalcione	The blunder
Mi faccia il favore di correggermi quando faccio uno sbaglio nel pronunciare.	Please correct me when I make a mistake in pronunciation.

PROVERBI

A cavallo donato non si guarda in bocca.

A chi fa male, mai mancano scuse.

A chi vuole, non mancano modi.

Ad ognuno par più grave la croce sua.

Al buon vino non bisogna frasca.

Al male estremo, rimedio violento.

Bisogna battere il ferro mentre è caldo.

Cattivo è quel vento che a nessuno è prospero.

Chi ascolta alla porta, ode il suo danno.

Chiave d'oro apre la porta di ferro.

Chi ben congettura, bene indovina.

Chi bestia va a Roma bestia ritorna.

Chi si marita in fretta stenta adagio.

Cosa ben fatta è fatta due volte.

Dove l'oro parla, ogni lingua tace.

PROVERBS

Don't look a gift horse in the mouth.

Who does evil is never short of excuses.

Where there's a will there's a way.

To every man his own cross appears the heaviest.

Good wine needs no bush.

Desperate ills need desperate remedies.

Strike while the iron is hot.

It is an ill wind that blows nobody any good.

An eavesdropper always hears himself damned.

A golden key opens the iron door.

The best prophet is the best guesser.

He that goes to Rome a fool returns a fool.

Marry in haste and repent at leisure.

A thing well done is doubly done.

Where gold speaks every tongue is silent.

PART TWO

CONTENTS

IN UNA BOTTEGA
(*Continuazione*)

19. È troppo. Sono carissimi (′trɔp-po) (′so-no ka-′ris-si-mi)

> sono
> sei (sɛj)
> è
> siamo (′sja-mo)
> siete (′sje-te)
> sono

20. Oh! no signore; sono a buon mercato, **or** a buon prezzo. (bwɔn mer-′ka-to) (′prɛt-tso)
21. Desidera pagare questi guanti adesso?
22. Sì, **voglio** pagarli adesso. Ecco il denaro. Grazie infinite. Mille grazie. (′ɛk-ko) (de-′na-ro) (′gra-tsje in-fi-′ni-te)
23. Vuol pagare ora questo cappello? (pa-′ga-re)
24. No, favorisca mandarlo all' albergo col conto: lo pagherò là. (man-′dar-lo kol ′kon-to al-lal-′bɛr-go) (pa-ge-′ro)
25. Non **ho abbastanza** denaro con me. (ab-ba-′stan-tsa)
26. Ha **denaro in tasca?** (′tas-ka)
27. Quanto **denaro ha in dosso?** (′dɔs-so)
28. Ha molto denaro in dosso?

29. Ne ho molto poco. (′pɔ-ko)
30. Non ho molto denaro in tasca. Mandi questo cappello all'albergo. Lo pagherò là. (′man-di)

CONIUGAZIONE DEL TEMPO FUTURO
Prima Coniugazione

parlerò	pagherò	mangerò
parlerai	pagherai	mangerai
parlerà	pagherà	mangerà
parleremo	pagheremo	mangeremo
parlerete	pagherete	mangerete
parleranno	pagheranno	mangeranno

IN A STORE
(*Continuation*)

19. Too much. They are very expensive.

> I am
> you are (f.s.)
> he or she is
> we are
> you are
> they are

20. Oh, no, sir; they are cheap. (Lit.: at good **market, or** at **good** price.)

21. Do you want to pay for these gloves now?

22. Yes, I want to pay for them now. Here is the **money.** Many thanks. (Lit.: A thousand thanks.)

23. Do you wish to pay for this hat now?

24. No, please send it with your bill to the hotel; I will pay for it there.

25. I have not money enough with me.

26. Have you money with you? (Lit.: in pocket?)

27. How much money have you with you? (Lit.: on you.)

28. Have you much money with you? (Lit.: Have [you] much money in back?)

29. I have very little.

30. I have not much money with me. Send this hat to the hotel; I will pay for it there.

CONJUGATION OF THE FUTURE TENSE
First Conjugation

I shall speak	I shall pay	I shall eat
you will speak	you will pay	you will eat (f.s.)
he will speak	he will pay	he will eat
we shall speak	we shall pay	we shall eat
you will speak	you will pay	you will eat
they will speak	they will pay	they will eat

Seconda Coniugazione

venderò	riceverò	vivrò
venderai	riceverai	vivrai
venderà	riceverà	vivrà
venderemo	riceveremo	vivremo
venderete	riceverete	vivrete
venderanno	riceveranno	vivranno

Terza Coniugazione

partirò	sentirò	favorirò
partirai	sentirai	favorirai
partirà	sentirà	favorirà
partiremo	sentiremo	favoriremo
partirete	sentirete	favoritete
partiranno	sentiranno	favoriranno

L'ARRIVO—L'ALBERGO—LE STANZE

(ar-'ri-vo al-'bɛr-go 'stan-tsa)

1. Che vuol fare al nostro arrivo? ('nɔs-tro)

2. Sono molto stanco. Vorrei andare immediatamente ad un buon[1] albergo. ('stan-ko) (vor-'rɛj) (im-me-dja-ta-'men-te ad)

> vorrei (vor-'rɛj)
> vorresti (vor-'res-ti)
> vorrebbe (vor-'reb-be)
> vorremmo (vor-'rem-mo)
> vorreste (vor-'res-te)
> vorrebbero (vor-'reb-be-ro)

3. A che albergo vuol andare[2]? All' albergo Excelsior.

4. Vuol andarci a piedi? No, prenderò un tassì. (an-'dar-tʃi) ('pjɛ-di) (pren-de-'rɔ un tas-'si)

5. Sono molto stanco. Non posso andar a piedi fino all' albergo. Piglierò un tassì. ('fi-no) (pi-ʎe-'rɔ)

---

[1] *Buono* (good), follows the same rule as *uno*, hence: *Buon amico, buon libro, buono scolare, buona casa, buon'amica.* See Part X.

Second Conjugation

I shall sell	I shall receive	I shall live
you will sell	you will receive	you will live (f.s.)
he will sell	he will receive	he will live
we shall sell	we shall receive	we shall live
you will sell	you will receive	you will live
they will sell	they will receive	they will live

Third Conjugation

I shall leave	I shall feel	I shall favor
you will leave	you will feel	you will favor (f.s.)
he will leave	he will feel	he will favor
we shall leave	we shall feel	we shall favor
you will leave	you will feel	you will favor
they will leave	they will feel	they will favor

THE ARRIVAL—THE HOTEL—THE ROOMS

1. What do you want to do when we get there? (Lit.: on our arrival?)
2. I am very tired. I should like to go at once to a good hotel.

> I should like
> you would like (f.s.)
> he or she would like
> we should like
> you would like
> they would like

3. To which hotel do you want to go? To the Hotel Excelsior.
4. Do you want to walk there? (Lit.: go there on foot.) No, I am going to take a taxi.
5. I am very tired. I cannot walk to the hotel. I am going to take a taxi.

---

[2] See Grammar, Part X., for a list of verbs governing other verbs without a preposition.

6. Va a piedi fino all' albergo o desidera pigliare un tassì? (de-'si-de-ra pi-'ʎa-re)

7. Non sono stanco; andrò a piedi. (an-'drɔ)

8. Ha bagaglio? (ba-'ga-ʎo)

9. Ha molto bagaglio?

10. Quanto bagaglio ha?

11. Ho pochissimo[1] bagaglio. Prenderò il tranvia (tramvia, tramvai) (pren-de-'rɔ) (tran-'vi-a, tram-vaj)

12. Ho molto bagaglio. Non posso andare a piedi sino all' albergo. Prenderò un tassì. ('si-no)

13. Autista, all' albergo Excelsior.

14. Buon giorno; può darmi una buona stanza? ('stan-tsa)

15. Può darmi una buona stanza al primo piano? ('pri-mo 'pja-no)

16. Sono stanchissimo[1] e desidero coricarmi subito. (stan-'kis-si-mo) (ko-ri-'kar-mi 'su-bi-to)

17. Favorisca darmi una buona stanza al primo piano.

18. Favorisca darmi una buona stanza al secondo piano. (se-'kon-do)

19. Quanto domandate per questa camera? (do-man-'da-te) ('ka-me-ra)

20. Quanto costa al giorno questa stanza? (al-'dʒor-no)

21. Quanto fate pagare al giorno per questa stanza? ('fa-te pa-'ga-re)

22. Questa stanza costa sei dollari al giorno. ('dɔl-la-ri)

23. Le posso dare questa stanza a buon mercato.

24. Questa stanza è troppo cara. Non voglio prenderla. Favorisca farmene vedere un' altra.

25. Non ho più nessun' altra stanza a questo piano, ma gliene[2] posso dar una grandissima ed a buon prezzo al terzo. (pju nes-'su 'nal-tra) (ma 'ʎe-ne) ('u-na gran-'dis-si-ma ed a bwɔn 'prɛt-tso al 'tɛr-tso)

---

[1] The absolute superlative of adjectives (meaning *very*) is formed by changing either *o* or *a* into *issimo* or *issima* respectively. Words ending in *co* or *go*, *ca* or *ga* change these terminations in *chissimo*, *ghissimo*, *chissima* or *ghissima* respectively. For more rules and exceptions see Part X.

6. Are you going to walk to the hotel, or do you want to take a taxi?

7. I am not tired; I am going to walk.

8. Have you (any) baggage?

9. Have you much baggage?

10. How much baggage have you?

11. I have very little baggage. I am going to take the street-car.

12. I have a great deal of baggage. I cannot walk to the hotel. I am going to take a taxi.

13. Driver, to the Hotel Excelsior!

14. Good day; can you give me a good room?

15. Can you give me a good room on the first floor?

16. I am very tired, and I wish to go to bed at once.

17. Please give me a good room on the first floor.

18. Please give me a good room on the second floor.

19. How much do you ask for this room?

20. How much is this room per day?

21. How much do you charge (Lit.: make pay) for this room per day?

22. This room is six dollars per day.

23. I can give you this room cheap.

24. This room is too dear. I will not take it. Please let me see another.

25. I have no other room on this floor; but I can give you a very large and inexpensive room on the third floor.

---

² See rules on personal pronouns in Part X.

26. Non mi piace dimorar su in alto. Potrei avere una stanza a pian
    terreno? (pja-tʃe di-mo-ʹrar su) (ʹal-to) (po-ʹtrɛj a-ʹve-re)
    (pjan ter-ʹre-no)

<blockquote>
potrei (po-ʹtrɛj)
potresti (po-ʹtres-ti)
potrebbe (po-ʹtreb-be)
potremmo (po-ʹtrem-mo)
potreste (po-ʹtre-ste)
potrebbero (po-ʹtreb-be-ro)
</blockquote>

27. Questa camera è grande[1] e bella. Per quanto me la dà? (ʹgran-de)
    (ʹbɛl-la) (da)
28. Questa stanza è molto a buon mercato. Costa solo tre dollari al
    giorno.
29. Benissimo, la piglio. Abbia la bontà di farmi portar su il bagaglio
    e di pagare l' austista. (ʹpi-ʎo)
30. Portiere, a che piano potreste darci alloggio? Portiere, a che
    piano potreste alloggiarci? (por-ʹtjɛ-re) (ʹdar-tʃi al-ʹlɔd-dʒo)
    (al-lod-ʹdʒar-tʃi)
31. Non lo so; devo chiamare l' albergatore, il proprietario, il diret-
    tore. (ʹde-vo kja-ʹma-re lal-ber-ga-ʹto-re, il pro-prje-ʹta-rjo, il
    di-ret-ʹto-re)
32. Buon giorno, signore. Ella vorrebbe delle stanze?
33. Quante stanze vorrebbe?
34. Potrebbe darci un salotto e due camere da letto contigue[2]?
    (ʹsa-la) (ʹlɛt-to) (kon-ʹti-gwe)
35. A che piano ci potrebbe dare queste stanze?
36. Al secondo. Non ci potrebbe dare delle stanze a pian terreno?

37. Sì, signore. Eccone tre che fanno per loro. (ʹɛk-ko-ne tre) (ʹlo-ro)
38. Quanto fate pagare al giorno?
39. Quattro dollari. (ʹkwat-tro ʹdɔl-la-ri)
40. Son troppo care. (ʹka-re)
41. Posso darle stanze del[3] mezzanino a miglior prezzo. (med-dza-
    ʹni-no)

---

[1] See Part X. on adjectives ending in e.
[2] Adjectives must agree with the nouns they qualify.
[3] See Declensions of the Article in Part X.

26. I do not like to be up high. Could I have a room on the ground floor?

> I could
> you could (f.s.)
> he or she could
> we could
> you could
> they could

27. This room is large and beautiful. At what price can you give it to me?

28. This room is very cheap. It is only three dollars a day.

29. Very well, I will take it. Please send (Lit.: have carried) my baggage up and pay the taxidriver.

30. Doorman,[4] on what floor could you put us? (Lit.: give us lodging?)

31. I don't know. I will have to call the innkeeper, the proprietor, the manager.

32. Good-day, sir. You would like [to have] some rooms?

33. How many rooms would you like?

34. Could you give us a parlor and two adjoining bedrooms?

35. On what floor could you give us these rooms?

36. On the second floor. Could you not give us some rooms on the ground floor?

37. Yes, sir. Here are three that will suit you.

38. How much do you charge per day?

39. Four dollars.

40. They are too expensive.

41. I can give you some cheaper rooms on the mezzanine floor.

---

[4] The student will of course remember that hotel rooms in the United States are allotted by a room clerk and guests are shown to their rooms by a bell-boy.

42. Ditemi il prezzo più basso. Ditemi l' ultimo prezzo.

43. Tre dollari al giorno?

44. Ebbene! Prenderò le stanze del mezzanino.

45. Desidera pranzare adesso, signore? (pran-'dza-re)

46. No, grazie. Sono stanchissimo e desidero coricarmi subito. (ko-ri-'kar-mi)

47. Desidera altro? No, grazie. Ho quanto mi occorre. ('al-tro) ('gra-tsje) (ok-'kor-re)

48. Non vedo zolfanelli nella¹ stanza. Cameriere, portatemi una scatola di fiammiferi. ('ve-do) (dzol-fa-'nɛl-li) (ka-me-'rjɛ-re) (por-'ta-te-mi) ('ska-to-la) (fjam-'mi-fe-ri)

49. Ecco² i fiammiferi. Desidera altro?

50. No. grazie; null'altro. Voglio coricarmi subito. (nul-'lal-tro) (ko-ri-'kar-mi)

51. Buona notte, signore. Buon riposo. ('bwɔ-na 'nɔt-te) (ri-'pɔ-so)

> mi occorre
> ti occorre
> gli occorre
> le occorre
> ci occorre
> vi occorre
> occorre loro ('lo-ro)

Vorrei partire col primo aeroplano per Roma; ma disgraziatamente, ciò mi è impossibile.

vorrei (vor-rɛj)
partire (par-'ti-re)
col (kol)
primo aeroplano ('pri-mo a-e-ro-'pla-no)
per (per)
Roma ('ro-ma)
ma (ma)
disgraziatamente (di-sgra-tsja-ta-'men-te)
ciò (tʃɔ)
mi (mi)
è (ɛ)
impossibile (im-pos-'si-bi-le)

---

¹ See Part X. about the prepositions that form only one word with the article.
² *Ecco*, here is, here are.

42. Tell me your lowest (final) price.
43. Three dollars a day.
44. All right! I will take the rooms on the mezzanine floor.
45. Do you wish to dine now, sir?
46. No, thank you; I am very tired and want to go to bed at once.

47. Do you wish anything else? No, thank you; I have everything I need.
48. I do not see (any) matches in the room. Boy, bring me a box of matches.

49. Here are the matches. Do you wish anything else?
50. No, thanks; nothing else. I wish to retire at once.

51. Good-night, sir. Sleep well. (Lit.: Good rest.)

> I need
> you need (f.s.)
> he needs
> she needs
> we need
> you need
> they need

I should like to leave by the first airplane for Rome, but unfortunately, that is impossible.

I should like (I would like)
to leave (to start, to set out)
by the
first airplane
for
Rome
but,
unfortunately,
that
to me
is
impossible.

UN VIAGGIO

1. Che vuol fare domani mattina[1]? Vorrei partire per Firenze col primo[2] treno. (do-'ma-ni mat-'ti-na) ('trɛ-no)

2. Perdoni, signore; vorrei partire per Firenze. Mi fa la gentilezza di dirmi dove è la stazione della ferrovia? (per-'do-ni) ('dir-mi) (sta-'tsjo-ne) (fer-ro-'vi-a)

3. Scusi; dov' è la Stazione Centrale[3]? ('sku-si) (do-'vɛ) (tʃen-'tra-le)

4. Perdoni; per dove si va alla Stazione Centrale?

5. Scusi; qual' è la sala d' aspetto? (a-'spɛt-to)

6. Perdoni; dov' è l'ufficio dei biglietti? (uf-'fi-tʃo dej bi-'ʎet-ti)

7. Scusi, voglio andare a Firenze. Dov' è l'ufficio-biglietti?

8. Perdoni, voglio partire col treno espresso per Firenze. Potrebbe dirmi dove sia l' ufficio-biglietti? (e-'sprɛs-so)

9. Vada diritto avanti. ('va-da di-'rit-to a-'van-ti)

10. L' ufficio-biglietti si trova a destra. ('trɔ-va) ('dɛ-stra)

11. Perdoni, mi potrebbe dire da che lato si trovi l'ufficio-biglietti? ('la-to)

12. Da che lato si trova l'ufficio-biglietti? A destra. A sinistra. (si-'ni-stra)

13. Favorisca darmi un biglietto per Firenze. (bi-'ʎet-to) (fi-'rɛn-tse)

14. Di che classe? Di seconda. ('klas-se) (se-'kon-da)

15. Favorisca darmi un biglietto di seconda per Venezia. (ve-'nɛ-tsja)

16. Lo vuole solo di andata, o di andata e ritorno? (lo) ('so-lo) (an-'da-ta) (ri-'tor-no)

17. Favorisca darmi un biglietto di andata e ritorno.

18. Quanto costa il biglietto per Venezia?

19. Quanto costa un biglietto di seconda classe per Napoli? ('na-po-li)

20. Quanto costa un biglietto di ritorno di terza classe? ('tɛr-tsa)

21. Dieci dollari, signore. Eccoli.[4] Ed ecco il Suo biglietto col resto. ('rɛs-to)

22. Voglio consegnare il baule. Dov' è l' ufficio dei bagagli? (kon-se-'ɲa-re) (uf-'fi-tʃo)

---

[1] *Domani mattina*, to-morrow morning. *La mattina*, the morning.

[2] The student should commit to memory by frequent repetition both the Cardinal and the Ordinal numbers.

[3] Adjectives ending in *e* have the same termination for both genders.

A JOURNEY

1. What do you want to do to-morrow morning? I should like to leave by the first train for Florence.
2. Excuse me, sir; I should like to leave for Florence. Will you please tell me where the railroad station is?

3. Excuse me, where is the Central Station?
4. Pardon me, which is the way to the Central Station?
5. Excuse me, which is the waiting-room?
6. I beg your pardon, where is the ticket office?
7. Excuse me; I want to go to Florence. Where is the ticket office?
8. Pardon me; I want to leave by the express train for Florence. Could you tell me where the ticket office is?
9. Go straight ahead.
10. The ticket office is (Lit.: finds itself) on the right side.
11. I beg your pardon; could you please tell me on which side the ticket office is?
12. On which side is the ticket office? On the right. On the left.

13. Please give me a ticket to Florence.
14. Which class? Second.
15. Please give me a second class ticket to Venice.
16. Do you want it only one way or round trip? (Lit.: only of going, or of going and return)
17. Please give me a return-ticket.
18. How much is the ticket to Venice?
19. How much is a second-class ticket to Naples?
20. How much is a third-class return ticket?
21. Ten dollars, sir. Here you are. And here is your ticket with the change.
22. I want to check the trunk. Where is the baggage room?

---

4 Expressions like: Here I am, here you are (f.s.), here he is, here she is, here we are, here you are, here they (masc. and fem.) are, are rendered by *ecco* joined with the pronouns *mi, ti, lo, la, ci, vi*, etc., as: *eccomi, eccoti, eccolo, eccola, eccoci, eccovi, eccoli, eccole.* Here is my father, *ecco mio padre;* Here he is, *eccolo.*

23. Potrebbe dirmi dove sia l' ufficio dei bagagli? Vorrei consegnare questo baule.

24. Chiamerò il facchino: egli consegnerà il Suo baule. (kja-me-'ro) (fak-'ki-no)

25. Facchino, questo signore vuol consegnare il suo baule.

26. Benissimo. Dove va, signore?

27. Vado a Napoli.

28. Ha il biglietto? Sì, l' ho. Eccolo.

29. Favorisca darmelo.[1] Vada ora nella sala d' aspetto. Io consegnerò il suo baule e le[1] porterò lo scontrino. (skon-'tri-no)

30. Ecco lo scontrino. Lei ha *soprappeso*[2] da pagare. (so-prap-'pe-so)

31. Mille grazie. Ecco il denaro per il soprappeso. E quanto devo a lei? ('mil-le)

32. Non abbiamo tariffa. Dia quel che crede. (ta-'rif-fa) ('di-a) ('kre-de)

33. Capisco. È una mancia, non è vero? (ka-'pi-sko) ('man-tʃa)

34. Sì, signore, così è. Grazie infinite, signore. Gli Americani sono generosi; danno sempre buone mance. (ko-'si) (in-fi-'ni-te) ('dan-no 'sɛm-pre 'bwɔ-ne 'man-tʃe)

35. A che ora[3] parte questo treno? ('par-te)

do (dɔ)
dai (daj)
dà (da)
diamo ('dja-mo)
date ('da-te)
danno ('dan-no)

dia ('di-a)
dia
dia
diamo ('dja-mo)
diate ('dja-te)
diano ('di-a-no)

---

[1] The student should very frequently consult the table representing the Personal Pronouns in Part X.

[2] *Soprappeso*, instead of *sopra peso*. In compound words the initial consonant of the second part is generally doubled if the first part ends with a vowel. Thus *da vero* becomes *davvero*, really; and *e bene* is contracted into *ebbene*, and well.

23. Could you please tell me where the baggage room is? I would like to check this trunk?

24. I will call the porter; he will check your trunk (for you).

25. Porter, this gentleman wants to have his trunk checked.

26. All right, Where are you going, sir?

27. I am going to Naples.

28. Have you your ticket? Yes, I have it; here it is.

29. Please give it to me. Now go into the waiting-room. I will check your baggage, and bring you the check.

30. Here is your check. You have some excess weight to pay.

31. Many thanks. Here is the money for the excess weight. And how much do I owe you?

32. We have no rate. Give what you like.

33. I understand. That's a tip, is it not?

34. Yes, sir, that's what it is. Ever so much obliged to you! Americans are always generous; they always give good tips.

35. At what time does this train leave?

> I give
> you give (f.s.)
> he or she gives
> we give
> you give
> they give
>
> that I may give
> that you may give (f.s.)
> that he or she may give
> that we may give
> that you may give
> that they may give

---

[3] The student should familiarize himself with the way of giving or asking the *time*, which he will find fully explained in Part X.

parto ('par-to)
parti ('par-ti)
parte ('par-te)
partiamo (par-'tja-mo)
partite (par-'ti-te)
partono ('par-to-no)

36. Questo treno partirà fra cinque minuti. (par-ti-'ra fra 'tʃin-kwe mi-'nu-ti)

partirò
partirai
partirà
partiremo
partirete
partiranno

37. C' è un vagone per fumatori? (tʃɛ) (va-'go-ne) (fu-ma-'to-ri)

38. Eccolo, e c' è molto posto. ('pɔs-to)

39. Sa quando arriverà a Napoli questo treno? Alle otto di sera. Ecco un orario. (ar-ri-ve-'ra) (o-'ra-rjo)

> I leave
> you leave (f.s.)
> he or she leaves
> we leave
> you leave
> they leave

36. This train leaves (Lit.: will leave) in five minutes.

> I shall leave
> you will leave (f.s.)
> he will leave
> we shall leave
> you will leave
> they will leave

37. Is there a smoking-car?

38. Here it is, and there is plenty of room.

39. Do you know when this train will arrive in Naples? At eight P. M. Here is a time-table.

CONVERSATIONAL EXERCISES

What they are and how they should be studied

Having thoroughly mastered the foregoing sentences, the student must now familiarize himself with the Conversational Exercises.

They consist of purely practical phrases, such as we are in the habit of using in common, every-day life. But as every person employs of necessity his own peculiar mode of diction,

Diversity of Expression

must be acquired from the very start by the student of foreign tongues.

The most commonplace thought can be expressed in numerous ways, and throughout the Language Phone text-books, and especially in the Conversational Parts, appear many sentences which, though worded differently, are identical in their meaning.

The Advantages of this Plan

are self-evident. The student is no longer confined to a single phrase, but becomes familiar with a variety of expressions. He does not learn only *one* sentence by which he may state his wants, but controls *the whole colloquial vocabulary on any one subject*, and is thus enabled to carry on a conversation with almost anyone.

At the same time

The Conversations are Graded

in such a manner that only such constructions, idioms, moods and tenses are given as have been previously mastered by the student.

Mere questions and answers of the guide-book style have—as far as possible—been avoided. Later all conversations are carried on in Italian.

All phrases used are, so to speak,

Sentence-Molds

They are intended to teach the pupil to *think* in Italian, and with this end in view they should always be studied *aloud* and rendered frequently in Italian until the student can utter them just as smoothly and rapidly in the foreign language as in his own.

Let it always be remembered that

Repetitio est mater studiorum.

(Repetition is the mother of studies.)

Nothing is so essential in mastering a foreign tongue as constant repetition.

Gutta cavat lapidem, non vi, sed saepe cadendo.

(The drop [of water] hollows the stone, not by force, but by often falling.)

VOCABOLARIO	VOCABULARY
Continuazione	*Continuation*
Lei ha fatto uno sbaglio.	You have made a mistake.
Che significa questo?	What does this mean?
Il senso, il significato	The sense, the meaning
Usare, impiegare	To use, to employ
Questa parola non si usa in questo senso.	This word is not used in this sense.
Come si impiega questa parola?	How is this word used?
La frase	The sentence
Vorrei fare delle compre; delle spese.	I would like to do some shopping; [make] some purchases.
Quanto costa?	How much does it cost?
Quanto vale questo?	How much is this worth?
È questo il prezzo più basso?	Is this the cheapest price?
È questo l' ultimo prezzo?	Is this the last [lowest] price?
Il conto	The bill
La ricevuta	The receipt
Favorisca mandare all' albergo questi oggetti col conto saldato.	Please send these goods with a receipted bill to the hotel.

PART THREE

CONTENTS

62

NUMERI ORDINALI
('nu-me-ri or-di-'na-li)

il primo, la prima ('pri-mo, 'pri-ma)
il secondo, la seconda, ecc. (se-'kon-do, se-'kon-da)
il terzo ('tɛr-tso)
il quarto ('kwar-to)
il quinto ('kwin-to)
il sesto ('sɛs-to)
il settimo ('sɛt-ti-mo)
l' ottavo, l' ottava (ot-'ta-vo)
il nono ('nɔ-no)
il decimo ('dɛ-tʃi-mo)
l' undicesimo **or** l' undecimo, **or** il decimo primo (un-di-'tʃe-si-mo, un-'dɛ-tʃi-mo)
il dodicesimo, **or** il decimo secondo (do-di-'tʃe-si-mo)
il tredicesimo, **or** il decimo terzo (tre-di-'tʃe-si-mo)
il quattordicesimo, **or** il decimo quarto (kwat-tor-di-'tʃe-si-mo)
il quindicesimo, **or** il decimo quinto (kwin-di-'tʃe-si-mo)
il sedicesimo, **or** il decimo sesto (se-di-'tʃe-si-mo)
il diciasettesimo, **or** il decimo settimo (di-tʃa-sɛt-'te-si-mo)
il diciottesimo, **or** il decimo ottavo (di-tʃot-'te-si-mo)
il diciannovesimo, **or** il decimo nono (di-tʃan-no-'ve-si-mo)
il ventesimo (ven-'te-si-mo)
il ventesimo primo, ecc., **or** il ventunesimo (ven-tu-'ne-si-mo)
il trentesimo (tren-'te-si-mo)
il quarantesimo (kwa-ran-'te-si-mo)
il cinquantesimo (tʃin-kwan-'te-si-mo)
il sessantesimo (ses-san-'te-si-mo)
il settantesimo (set-tan-'te-si-mo)
l' ottantesimo (ot-tan-'te-si-mo)
il novantesimo (no-van-'te-si-mo)
il centesimo (tʃen-'te-si-mo)
il millesimo (mil-'le-si-mo)
il milionesimo (mi-ljo-'ne-si-mo)
l' ultimo ('ul-ti-mo)
il penultimo (pe-'nul-ti-mo)

THE ORDINAL NUMBERS

the 1st
the 2d
the 3d
the 4th
the 5th
the 6th
the 7th
the 8th
the 9th
the 10th
the 11th
the 12th
the 13th
the 14th
the 15th
the 16th
the 17th
the 18th
the 19th
the 20th
the 21st, etc.
the 30th
the 40th
the 50th
the 60th
the 70th
the 80th
the 90th
the 100th
the 1,000th
the 1,000,000th
the last
the last but one

DOMANDE PER CHIEDERE LA STRADA
(do-'man-de) ('kjɛ-de-re) ('stra-da)

1. Perdoni,[1] signore; potrebbe indicarmi[2] la Via Alessandro Manzoni? (in-di-'kar-mi) ('vi-a a-les-'san-dro man-'dzo-ni)
2. Mi fa la gentilezza d' indicarmi il cammino che[3] mena alla Via Michelangelo Buonarroti? (kam-'mi-no) ('mɛ-na 'al-la) (mi-ke-'lan-dʒe-lo bwɔ-nar-'rɔ-ti)
3. Per favore, per dove si passa per andare in via Torino? (per fa-'vo-re) ('pas-sa) (to-'ri-no)
4. Scusi, è quì vicino l' Albergo degli Angioli? (vi-'tʃi-no) (de-'ʎan-dʒo-li)
5. Per piacere, per dove si va al Teatro della Scala? (pja-'tʃe-re) (te-'a-tro 'del-la 'ska-la)
6. Scusi, è questa la via che[3] conduce al Teatro Alessandro Manzoni? (kon-'du-tʃe)
7. Abbia la gentilezza d' insegnarmi per dove si va alla stazione della ferrovia.
8. Favorisca dirmi se è questa la strada che conduce al teatro.
9. Sì, signore, vada diritto sino[4] a Porta Orientale. ('pɔr-ta o-rjen-'ta-le)
10. Prenda la seconda strada a destra, poi vada avanti diritto sino ad una piazza. ('pjat-tsa)
11. Varchi il ponte ed attraversi la piazza. Non può sbagliare. ('var-ki) ('pon-te) (at-tra-'vɛr-si)
12. È distante di quì? No, non è distante. (di-'stan-te)
13. Desidera che l' accompagni? Mi farà un gran favore. (ak-kom-'pa-ɲi) (fa-'ra) (gran)

PER FARE COMPRE—SPESE
('kom-pre) ('spe-se)

1. Che vuol fare stamane (**or** stamattina)?
2. Vorrei[5] uscire per fare alcune spese (u-'ʃi-re) (al-'ku-ne)
3. E dove vuol far le compre?

---

[1] See Part X. about the Imperative Mood.
[2] Part X. gives a list of verbs governing other verbs without an intervening preposition.
[3] *Che* in this case is a relative pronoun; while *chi?* who? is an interrogative pronoun.

QUESTIONS TO INQUIRE ONE'S WAY

1. Excuse me, sir; could you please tell me where Alessandro Manzoni Street is?
2. Will you kindly show me the way (that leads) to Michelangelo Buonarroti Street?

3. If you please, which is the way to Turin Street?

4. I beg your pardon, is the Hotel of the Angels near by? (Lit.: Excuse, is here near the Hotel of the Angels?)
5. Pardon me, how do I go (Lit.: through where does one go) to the Scala Theatre?
6. Excuse me, is this the way to Alessandro Manzoni Theatre?

7. Will you be kind enough to tell me the way to the railroad station?
8. Please tell me whether this is the street that leads to the theatre.
9. Yes, sir, go straight ahead as far as the Porta Orientale.

10. Take the second street on the right, then go straight ahead till you come to a square.
11. Go across the bridge, then across the square. You cannot miss your way.
12. Is it far from here? No, it is not far.
13. Do you wish me to accompany you? You will be doing me a great favor.

PURCHASES—SHOPPING
(Lit.: To make purchases—to do expenses)

1. What do you want to do this morning?
2. I should like to go out to do some shopping.
3. And where do you want to make your purchases?

---

4 *Sino a*, or *fino a*, as far as, up to, etc.
5 For the formation of the future and the conditional tenses see Part X.

66

4. Per dir la verità non lo so nemmen·io. Lei ha visitato Milano già varie volte. Mi saprebbe dire dove potrei comprare buoni guanti? (dir) (ve-ri-'ta) (non) (nem-'men) (vi-si-'ta-to) (dʒa 'va-rje 'vɔl-te)

5. Non desidera altro?

6. No, devo pure comperare alcune coserelle per mia moglie. ('pu-re) (ko-se-rɛl-le)

> devo **or** debbo ('de-vo) ('deb-bo)
> devi ('de-vi)
> deve ('de-ve)
> dobbiamo (dob-'bja-mo)
> dovete (do've-te)
> devono **or** debbono ('de-vo-no) ('deb-bo-no)

7. Ha bisogno di forcine, di una spazzola per i capelli, di uno spaz-zolino da denti, d' un pettine e d' altre bagatelle. (bi-'sɔ-ɲo) (for-'tʃi-ne) ('spat-tso-la) (spat-tso-'li-no) ('dɛn-ti) ('pɛt-ti-ne) (ba-ga-'tɛl-le)

8. Favorisca venir con me, perchè non so dove si possano ottenere tutte queste cose. (ve-'nir) ('pɔs-sa-no ot-te-'ne-re 'tut-te 'kwes-te 'kɔ-se)

9. Lei troverà tutto quì vicino. Desidera uscir subito? (tro-ve-'ra)

10. Sì, subito. Mia moglie desidera uscire ed ha bisogno di tutti questi oggetti. (bi-'sɔ-ɲo)

11. Benissimo! In un buon negozio quì dirimpetto Lei potrà ottenere tutto l'occorrente. (ne-'go-tsjo) (di-rim-'pɛt-to) (po-'tra) (ok-kor-'rɛn-te)

12. Si compra a buon mercato in quel negozio? (mer-'ka-to)

13. Vi¹ si vende tutto a buon mercato. Lei sa benissimo che questi articoli di toeletta sono a miglior mercato qui che in America. (ar-'ti-ko-li) (to-e-'let-ta) ('so-no) (mi-'ʎor) (a-'mɛ-ri-ka)

14. Ecco il negozio. È molto grande, non è vero?—Sì, è grande e bello. ('gran-de)

15. Che desidera comperare in primo² luogo?—Dei guanti. ('lwɔ-go) (dej 'gwan-ti)

¹ *Vi* and *ci*, besides being personal pronouns, are also adverbs and mean both of them: *there*.

4. To tell you the truth, I don't know myself. You have been several times in Milan; could you tell me where I could buy some good gloves?

5. Is that all you want?

6. No, I also have to buy some small things for my wife.

> I must
> you must (f.s.)
> he must
> we must
> you must
> they must

7. She needs hairpins, a hair-brush, a tooth-brush, a comb, and some other trifles.

8. Please come with me, as I do not know where to get all these things.

9. You will find everything near by. Do you want to go out at once?

10. Yes, at once. My wife wishes to go out, and needs all these articles.

11. All right; in a very good store directly opposite you can get everything you need.

12. Do you buy cheap in that store?

13. Everything is inexpensive there. You know perfectly well that toilet articles are cheaper here than in America.

14. Here is the store. It's very large, isn't it? Yes, it is large and handsome.

15. What do you want to buy first? Gloves.

---

[2] Cardinal and ordinal numbers are very important and rather difficult. The student ought to practice them often till he masters them fully.

16. Voglio due paia[1] di guanti. Un paio nero ed un paio marrone.
    Favorisca farmi vedere buoni guanti di pelle. ('pa-ja) ('pa-jo
    'ne-ro) (mar-'ro-ne) (ve-'de-re) ('pɛl-le)
17. Li desidera chiari? ('kja-ri)
18. Non troppo chiari. Me li dia d' un colore che non sia troppo chiaro.
19. Quanto vuol pagare?—Un prezzo moderato. (mo-de-'ra-to)
20. Per tremila lire posso darle buonissimi guanti. (tre-'mi-la)
    ('dar-le)
21. Quanto fa in moneta americana? (mo-'ne-ta)
22. Seicento venti lire fanno un dollaro. (sɛj-'tʃɛn-to 'ven-ti)
23. Seicento venti lire fanno un dollaro in moneta americana. Non
    le sembrano a buon prezzo? ('sem-bra-no)
24. Sì, ciò mi sembra molto a buon mercato. Per tre dollari non si
    comprano guanti come questi negli Stati Uniti. ('sem-bra)
    ('mol-to) ('kom-pra-no) ('ne-λi 'sta-ti u-'ni-ti)
25. Desidera provarseli? (pro-'var-se-li)
26. Questi guanti[2] non mi vanno. Sono troppo stretti — sono troppo
    larghi.[3] ('stret-ti) ('lar-gi)
27. Quanto fa in tutto?
28. In tutto sono diecimila lire. (djɛ-tʃi-'mi-la 'li-re)

DA UNA MODISTA
(mo-'di-sta)

1. Buon giorno, signora. Posso servirla?
2. Vorrei un cappello. (kap-'pɛl-lo)
3. Come lo vuole, signora?
4. Lo vorrei piccolo e guarnito di fiori. (gwar-'ni-to) ('fjo-ri)
5. Eccone uno grazioso assai, signora. È l' ultima moda. ('ɛk-ko-ne)
   (gra-'tsjo-so as-'saj) ('ul-ti-ma 'mɔ-da)
6. Favorisca provarselo. (pro-'var-se-lo)
7. Come mi va? (va)
8. Non le potrebbe star meglio. (po-'treb-be star 'mɛ-λo)
9. Il cappello le sta a meraviglia. (me-ra-'vi-λa)

---

[1] Very frequently masculine Italian nouns have an irregular feminine plural,
as: *il paio*, the pair; *le paia*, the pairs.

[2] Adjectives must agree in gender and number with their substantives.

16. I want two pairs of gloves, a pair of black ones and a pair of brown ones. Please show me some good kid gloves.

17. Do you want them light brown?
18. Not too light; give me a shade that is not too light.
19. How much do you want to pay? A moderate price.
20. For 3000 lire I can give you very good gloves.

21. How much is that in American money?
22. Six hundred twenty lire make one dollar.
23. Six hundred twenty lire are equal to a dollar in American money. Don't they seem cheap to you?
24. Yes, that seems very cheap to me. For four and a half dollars we cannot get gloves like these in the United States.

25. Do you want to try them on?
26. These gloves do not fit me; they are too tight — too big (Lit.: wide.)
27. How much does that amount to altogether?
28. That amounts to ten thousand lire all told.

AT A MILLINER'S

1. Good-morning, madam; what can I do for you?
2. I should like a hat.
3. How do you want it, madam?
4. I want a little one, trimmed with flowers.
5. Here is a very pretty one, madam. It is the very latest style.

6. Please try it on.
7. How does it look on me? (Lit.: go to me.)
8. It couldn't fit you any better.
9. The hat is wonderfully becoming to you.

---

[3] Adjectives ending in *go* and *co* generally form their plural by changing these terminations into *ghi* and *chi*, thus: *largo, larghi; bianco, bianchi,* white.

10. Quanto costa questo cappello?—Seimila lire.

11. Lei me lo darà a miglior mercato, ne son sicura. (ne son si-'ku-ra)

12. Volontieri se lo potessi fare. Ma noi vendiamo solo a prezzi fissi. (vo-lon-'tjɛ-ri) ('prɛt-tsi 'fis-si)

13. È questo l' ultimo prezzo?—Sì, signora, è proprio il prezzo più basso. ('prɔ-prjo)

14. Non voglio mercanteggiare, ma questo prezzo mi sembra esorbitante. (mer-kan-ted-'dʒa-re) ('sem-bra e-sor-bi-'tan-te)

15. Non potrebbe accordarmi un piccolo ribasso sul prezzo? (akkor-'dar-mi) (un 'pik-ko-lo ri-'bas-so sul)

16. Ebbene, trattandosi di una nuova cliente, farò un' eccezione per una **volta tanto**[1], e glielo lascerò per cinquemila cinquecento. (trat-'tan-do-si) (kli-'ɛn-te) (et-tʃet-'tsjo-ne) ('vɔl-ta 'tan-to) ('ʎelo la-ʃe-'rɔ) ('tʃin-kwe-'mi-la tʃin-kwe-'tʃɛn-to)

17. In questo caso me lo mandi. Ecco il mio indirizzo. ('ka-so) ('man-di) ('ɛk-ko) (in-di-'rit-tso)

SALUTI

1. Buon giorno, come sta?

2. Benissimo, grazie. ('gra-tsje)

3. E come sta Sua moglie?

4. Mia moglie sta molto bene, grazie.

5. E Lei, come sta?—Benissimo, grazie.

6. E come sta Suo fratello? (fra-'tɛl-lo)

7. Spero che ora stia bene. ('spɛ-ro) ('sti-a)

8. Io sto benissimo, grazie; ma il mio povero fratello, mi rincresce (mi dispiace) dirlo, non può ancora uscire. È ancora debolissimo. ('pɔ-ve-ro) (rin-'kre-ʃe) (di-'spja-tʃe) ('dir-lo) (pwɔ an-'ko-ra) (u-'ʃi-re) (de-bo-'lis-si-mo)

9. Mi dispiace moltissimo. Ha un buon medico? (di-'spja-tʃe) (mol-'tis-si-mo) ('mɛ-di-ko)

10. Sì, il nostro medico è molto buono; ma mio fratello è stato aggravatissimo e, come Le ho detto, è ancora debolissimo. ('sta-to) (ag-gra-va-'tis-si-mo) (le ɔ 'det-to) (de-bo-'lis-si-mo)

---

[1] *Tanto* is sometimes used instead of *solo, solamente*, only. *Una volta tanto, una volta solamente*, only once.

10. How much is this hat? Six thousand lire.
11. You will let me have it cheaper, I'm sure.
12. Gladly, if I could. But we sell only at fixed prices.

13. Is that the lowest price? Yes, madam, the very lowest.

14. I don't want to bargain, but that price seems excessive.

15. Couldn't you give me a small reduction on the price?

16. Well, as you are a new customer, I will, for once, make an exception. I'll give it to you for five thousand five hundred lire.

17. Well, then, send it to me. Here is my address.

GREETINGS

1. Good-morning, how are you?
2. Very well, thank you.
3. And how is your wife?
4. My wife is quite well, thank you.
5. And how are you, yourself? Quite well, thanks.
6. And how is your brother?
7. I hope he is well now.
8. I am very well, thanks, but my poor brother, I am sorry to say, cannot go out yet. He is still very weak.

9. I am very sorry to hear that. Have you a good physician?

10. Yes, our physician is very good, but my brother was very ill, and is still very weak, as I told you.

11. Però si rimetterà presto (si rimetterà presto in salute). È molto giovane ancora, la sua costituzione è buona, ed alla sua età si ricupera facilmente la salute. (ri-met-te-'ra) ('prɛ-sto) (sa-'lu-te) ('dʒo-va-ne) (ko-sti-tu-'tsjo-ne) (e-'ta) (ri-'ku-pe-ra) (fa-tʃil-'men-te)

12. Dio lo volesse[1]! Piacesse a Dio[1]! (pja-'tʃes-se) ('di-o) (vo-'les-se)

13. Domani ritornerò, perchè mi preme di tenermi informato sullo stato di Suo fratello. Frattanto gli faccia i miei saluti. (ri-tor-ne-'rɔ) (te-'ner-mi) (in-for-'ma-to) ('sul-lo 'sta-to) (di 'su-o) (frat-'tan-to) (ʎi 'fat-tʃa) (i miɛj sa-'lu-ti)

14. Arrivederci. (ar-ri-ve-'der-tʃi)

FRASI IMPIEGATE NEL FARE UNA VISTA
(im-pje-'ga-te) ('vi-si-ta)

1. È in casa il signor[2] Serpi? No, signore, non c' è. ('ka-sa) ('sɛr-pi)
2. Peccato! (pek-'ka-to)
3. Ma il signor Serpi ritornerà presto. Favorisca entrare e si accomodi. (ri-tor-ne-'ra) (en-'tra-re) (ak-'kɔ-mo-di)
4. No, grazie, non posso aspettare. Favorisca rimettergli la mia carta, e gli dica che mi rincresce molto non aver potuto vederlo. (as-pet-'ta-re) (ri-'met-ter-ʎi) ('kar-ta) (ʎi 'di-ka) (rin-'kre-ʃe) (non a-'ver po-'tu-to ve-'der-lo)
5. È venuto qualcuno[3]? (ve-'nu-to kwal-'ku-no)
6. No, signora, nessuno[4] è venuto. (nes-'su-no)
7. C' è qualcuno che suona il campanello. Andate a vedere chi è. (swɔ-na) (kam-pa-'nɛl-lo) (an-'da-te)
8. Il signor Pedrazzini desidera salutarla. (pe-drat-'tsi-ni) (sa-lu-'tar-la)
9. Fatelo entrare nel salotto e ditegli che sarò subito da lui. ('fa-te-lo) (sa-'lɔt-to) ('di-te-ʎi) (sa-'rɔ)
10. È in casa la signora Marchesa? (si-'ɲo-ra mar-'ke-sa)
11. Sì, signora; favorisca entrare.
12. Ah! buon giorno, mia cara; quanto mi rallegro di rivederla. (bwɔn 'dʒor-no) (ral-'lɛ-gro) (ri-ve-'der-la)

---

[1] Idiomatic expressions very frequently used in Italian.

[2] *Signore* and *Signora*, except when used in addressing the person directly, must be preceded by the definite article.

11. But he will soon get well. He is still quite young, his constitution
is good, and, at his age, people recover rapidly.

12. Let us hope so! (Lit.: [May] God will it! May it please God!)
13. To-morrow I will call on you again, because I want to know how
your brother is getting along. Meanwhile give him my regards.

14. Good-bye.

PHRASES USED IN MAKING A CALL

1. Is Mr. Serpi at home? No, sir, he is not in.
2. What a pity!
3. But Mr. Serpi will be back soon. Please come in and sit down.
(Lit.: make yourself comfortable.)
4. No, thanks! I can't wait. Please give him my card, and tell him
I am sorry to have missed him.

5. Did anyone call?
6. No, madam; no one called.
7. There is somebody ringing the bell. Go and see who it is.

8. Mr. Pedrazzini wishes to greet you.

9. Show him into the parlor, and tell him I shall be with him in a
moment.
10. Is the Marchioness at home?
11. Yes, madam, please come in.
12. Ah, good morning, my dear. I am so happy to see you again.

---

[3] *Qualcuno;* fem. *qualcuna,* somebody, someone.
[4] *Nessuno; nessuna,* no one, nobody.

13. La disturbo forse? (di-'stur-bo 'for-se)

14. In nessun modo; anzi sono felicissima di rivederla. La prego, s' accomodi. (nes-'sun 'mɔ-do) (fe-li-'tʃis-si-ma) ('prɛ-go)

15. Non preferisce sedersi sul divano? (pre-fe-'ri-ʃe se-'der-si sul di-'va-no)

16. Grazie, sto benissimo quì. (stɔ)

17. Grazie, ho poco tempo; non posso mettermi a sedere. ('pɔ-ko 'tɛm-po) ('pɔs-so 'met-ter-mi) (se-'de-re)

18. È un secolo che non La vedo. ('sɛ-ko-lo) ('ve-do)

19. Non si fa mai vedere, **or** non si fa più viva. (maj) (fa pju 'vi-va)

20. Sono stata in campagna. ('sta-ta) (kam-'pa-ɲa)

21. Come sta Lei, e come sta tutta la famiglia?

22. Grazie mille, stiamo tutti molto bene. ('stja-mo)

23. Me ne rallegro moltissimo. (ral-'lɛ-gro)

24. E come stanno tutti in casa? Godono tutti ottima salute, grazie. ('stan-no) ('gɔ-do-no) ('ɔt-ti-ma)

25. Quanto son contenta di rivederla! (kon-'tɛn-ta)

26. Quando ha ricevuto[1] nuove di Suo fratello? (ri-tʃe-'vu-to) ('nwɔ-ve)

27. Ha avuto sue nuove?

28. È un gran pezzo che non abbiamo più sue nuove. (gran 'pɛt-tso) (ab-'bja-mo)

29. Aspettiamo sue notizie di giorno in giorno. (as-spet-'tja-mo) (no-'ti-tsje)

30. Che fa? Ci lascia già? ('la-ʃa)

31. Par che abbia molta fretta.

---

[1] The corresponding past participles of the three regular conjugations end respectively in *ato*, *uto* and *ito*, as: *parlato*, spoken; *ricevuto*, received, and *sentito*, felt or heard.

13. Perhaps I am disturbing you?

14. Oh, not at all; on the contrary, I am delighted to see you again. Please sit down.

15. Wouldn't you rather sit on the sofa?

16. Thanks, I am very comfortable here.

17. Thank you, I have very little time; I cannot sit down.

18. I haven't seen you for a long time. (Lit.: a century.)

19. You are quite a stranger. (Lit.: You never let yourself be seen, you no longer come alive.)

20. I have been in the country.

21. And how are you and your family?

22. Thank you, we all enjoy good health.

23. I am very glad to hear that.

24. And how is everybody at your home? They all enjoy excellent health, thank you.

25. I am so glad to see you again!

26. When did you hear from (Lit.: receive news from) your brother?

27. Have you heard from him?

28. We have not had any news from him for a long time.

29. We expect news from him from day to day.

30. What are you doing? Are you leaving us already?

31. You seem to be in a great hurry.

32. Devo andarmene[1]; mio marito m'aspetta. (an-'dar-me-ne) ('mi-o ma-'ri-to ma-'spɛt-ta)

33. Mi rincresce[2] (mi dispiace) di lasciarla, ma devo andarmene. (la-'ʃar-la) (an-'dar-me-ne)

34. Devo ritornare a casa.

35. Spero che tornerà presto a farmi visita.

36. Ebbene, quando avremo il piacere di rivederla? (a-'vre-mo il pja-'tʃe-re)

37. Ritornerò presto, glielo prometto. (ri-tor-ne-'rɔ) (pro-'met-to)

38. Non manchi. ('man-ki)

39. Non si disturbi, La[3] prego. L'accompagnerò sino alla porta. (di-'stur-bi) (ak-kom-pa-ɲe-'rɔ) ('pɔr-ta)

40. I miei saluti a Suo marito.

41. Con chi ho l' onore di parlare? Con Pietro Antonelli. ('piɛ-tro an-to-'nɛl-li)

42. Ho il piacere di parlare col signor D'Azeglio? Per l' appunto. (pja-'tʃe-re) (par-'la-re) (da-'dze-ʎo)

43. Arrivederla, signore.

Buon giorno.

Buona sera ('bwɔ-na 'se-ra)

44. Mi faccia presto l' onore d' un' altra visita. ('vi-si-ta)

45. L' onore è tutto mio.

46. Mi sento molto onorato. ('sɛn-to 'mol-to o-no-'ra-to)

47. Ebbene, arrivederla presto.

48. Arrivederci. Addio.

---

[1] *Andarsene*, to go away.

Present Tense of the Indicative

me ne vado	I am going away
te ne vai	you are going away (f.s.)
se ne va	he is going away
ce ne andiamo	we are going away
ve ne andate	you are going away
se ne vanno	they are going away

32. I must go; my husband is waiting for me.

33. I am sorry to leave you, but I must go.

34. I have to go home.
35. I hope you will soon call again.
36. Well, when shall we have the pleasure of seeing you again?

37. I'll come back again soon, I promise you.
38. Don't fail (to do so).
39. Please do not trouble yourself. I shall see you to the door.

40. (Give) my regards to your husband.
41. With whom have I the honor of speaking? With Peter Antonelli.

42. Is this Mr. D' Azeglio? That's right, sir.

43. Good-bye, sir. Good morning. Good evening.

44. Please call again soon. (Lit.: Do me soon the honor of another visit.)
45. You are very kind. (Lit.: The honor is all mine.)
46. I feel greatly honored.
47. Well, see you again soon.
48. Good-bye. Farewell (Lit.: To God).

---

[2] IMPERSONAL VERB

mi rincresce	I am sorry
ti rincresce	you are sorry (f.s.)
gli rincresce	he is sorry
le rincresce	she is sorry
ci rincresce	we are sorry
vi rincresce	you are sorry
rincresce loro	they are sorry

[3] The student already knows that in polite conversation *Lei* (lit. she) is used as a polite "you." In the same way other pronouns referring to this "she" for "you" must be in the feminine.

VOCABOLARIO
Continuazione

VOCABULARY
Continuation

L' ufficio	The office
Il cassiere	The cashier
La cassa	The cashier's desk
Pagare	To pay
A quanto ascende questo?	
A quanto monta questo?	How much does that amount to?
Quanto importa questo?	
Il denaro, il danaro	The money
Moneta spicciola = spiccioli	The change
Moneta spezzata = spezzati	
Non ho spiccioli (moneta spicciola).	
Non ho spezzati (moneta spezzata).	I have no change with me.
Ha moneta spicciola?	Have you any change with you?
Non mi torna il conto.	You did not give me the correct change.

Cambiare

To Change

Può cambiarmi un biglietto di cento dollari?	Can you change a hundred dollar bill for me?
Il biglietto	The bill
La carta monetata	The paper-money
Vuol (desidera) oro o carta?	Do you want gold or paper?
Vendere	To sell
Il venditore	The salesman
A che prezzo lo vende? (lo dà)?	At what price do you sell this?
Quanto vuole per questo articolo?	How much do you charge for this article?
Quanto domanda?	How much do you ask for it?
È troppo caro; non lo voglio a questo prezzo.	That is too dear; I don't want it at this price.
La qualità	The quality
Non mi piace questa qualità.	I don't like this quality.
Le piace questa?	Do you like this one?

Mi piace di più.	I like it better.
Il panno	The cloth
La seta	The silk
La lana	The wool
Il cotone	The cotton
Il vestito, l'abito	The dress, the suit
I vestiti, gli abiti	The dresses, the suits
Un vestito di seta	A silk dress
Un vestito di lana	A woolen dress
Un vestito di cotone	A cotton dress

PROVERBI

La parola è d'argento, il silenzio
è d'oro.

Troppi cuochi rovinano il brodo.

Quando la miseria entra dalla
porta, l'amore se ne va dalla
finestra.

Non v'è rosa senza spina.

Il buon sangue non mente.

Non è tutt'oro ciò che riluce.

Quando il gatto non c'è, i topi
ballano.

Aiutati, che Dio t'aiuta.

Meglio tardi che mai.

Dimmi con chi vai e ti dirò chi sei.

Meglio un uccello in gabbia che
due in frasca.

Ogni nube ha una fodera d'argento.

Pietra mossa non fa muschio.

La necessità è il migliore dei
maestri.

Albero che cresce storto non può
raddrizzare i suoi rami.

Al bisogno si conosce l'amico.

PROVERBS

Speech is silver, silence is golden.

Too many cooks spoil the broth.

When poverty comes in at the
door, love flies out of the
window.

No rose without thorns.

Blood will tell.

All is not gold that glitters.

When the cat is away the mice
will play.

Help yourself and God will help
you.

Better late than never.

You are known by the company
you keep.

A bird in the hand is worth two
in the bush.

Every cloud has a silver lining.

A rolling stone gathers no moss.

Necessity is the mother of
invention.

As the twig is bent the tree is
inclined.

A friend in need is a friend
indeed.

PART FOUR

CONTENTS

CONVERSAZIONE
(kon-ver-tsa-'tsjo-ne)

1. Comprende l' italiano? (kom-'prɛn-de li-ta-'lja-no)
2. Lo capisco un poco, però non tanto. (ka-'pi-sko) (pe-'rɔ)
3. Mi comprende quando parlo in fretta?
4. La intendo quando parla adagio e distintamente; ma quando comincia a parlare rapidamente, o, piuttosto, quando parla naturalmente, a stento capisco qualche parola. (in-'tɛn-do) (a-'da-dʒo) (di-stin-ta-'men-te) (ko-'min-tʃa) (ra-pi-da-'men-te) (pjut-'tɔ-sto) (na-tu-ral-'men-te) ('sten-to) (ka-'pi-sko) ('kwal-ke) (pa-'rɔ-la)
5. Che peccato!
6. Al Suo udito manca la pratica. ('su-o u-'di-to 'man-ka la 'pra-ti-ka)
7. Deve ascoltare di più gli Italiani quando parlano fra loro. (a-skol-'ta-re) (pju) (ʎi-ta-'lja-ni) ('par-la-no) (fra 'lo-ro)
8. Ho procurato di farlo, però mi pare che gli Italiani parlino molto più in fretta di noi. (pro-ku-'ra-to)
9. Le sembra così. Col tempo e colla pratica l' udito si abituerà[1] ed allora vedrà quanto sarà facile intendere qualsiasi conversazione. ('sem-bra ko-'si) ('tɛm-po) ('pra-ti-ka) (u-'di-to) (a-bi-twe-'ra) (al-'lo-ra) (ve-'dra) (sa-'ra) ('fa-tʃi-le) (kwal-'si-a-si)
10. Piacesse a Dio! Ma Lei s' è servita[2] or ora d' un' espressione che m'è nuova. Che significa letteralmente: "Allora vedrà"? (sɛ ser-'vi-ta or 'o-ra du-ne-spres-'sjo-ne ke mɛ nwɔ-va) (si-'ɲi-fi-ka let-te-ral-'men-te)
11. "Allora ella vedrà" vuol dire letteralmente: "Then you will see." Comprende ora quel che vuol dire "Allora vedrà"? (vwɔl 'di-re)
12. Sì, ora lo capisco e desidero che mi dia sempre la traduzione letterale. (tra-du-'tsjo-ne let-te-'ra-le)

---

[1] *The future* and *the conditional* are always formed in the same way as far as the endings are concerned.

[2] Reflexive or pronominal verbs are conjugated with two pronouns, one, the subject, in the nominative, which is frequently not expressed; the other usually in the accusative and which cannot be dispensed with:

CONVERSATION

1. Do you understand Italian?

2. I understand it a little, but not very well.

3. Do you understand me when I speak rapidly?

4. I understand you when you talk slowly and distinctly, but when you begin to speak rapidly, or, rather, when you talk naturally, I can scarcely understand a few words.

5. What a pity!

6. Your ear lacks training.

7. You ought to listen more to Italians when they converse with one another.

8. I have tried to do that, but it seems to me that the Italian people talk a great deal faster than we do.

9. That (only) seems so to you. With time and practice your ear will get accustomed (to it) and then you will see how easy it will be to understand any conversation.

10. I hope so. (Lit.: may it please God!) But you have just used an expression which is new to me. What is the literal meaning of "Allora vedrà"?

11. "Allora vedrà" means, literally, "Then you will see." Do you understand now what "Allora vedrà" means?

12. Yes, now I understand it, and I wish that you would always give me the literal translation.

---

mi servo	I use, etc.	mi son servito
ti servi		ti sei servito
si serve		(egli) s' è servito
ci serviamo		(ella) s' è servita
vi servite		ci siamo serviti
si servono		vi siete serviti
		(essi) si sono serviti
		(esse) si sono servite

13. La traduzione letterale, amico mio, è impossibile in molti casi. (a-'mi-ko)

14. E perchè?

15. Perchè ogni lingua ha le sue particolarità, i suoi idiotismi, i suoi modi di dire che non si possono mai tradurre letteralmente. ('o-ɲi 'lin-gwa) ('su-e par-ti-ko-la-ri-'ta) (i-djo-'ti-smi) ('mɔ-di di 'di-re) ('pɔs-so-no) (maj tra-'dur-re)

16. Ci sono in italiano molti[1] idiotismi?

17. La lingua italiana, amico mio, è una delle più ricche[2] del mondo. Fra gli idiomi moderni il francese e l' italiano sono i più ricchi e perciò hanno naturalmente moltissimi idiotismi. ('rik-ke) ('mon-do) (i-'djɔ-mi) ('rik-ki) (per-'tʃɔ) ('an-no)

18. Vuol avere la bontà di citare alcuni degli idiotismi più usati? Intendo parlare di quelli che si impiegano nella conversazione ordinaria. (tʃi-'ta-re) (al-'ku-ni) ('de-ʎi) (u-'sa-ti) (im-'pjɛ-ga-no) (or-di-'na-rja)

19. Certamente! Per ora formeremo alcuni idiotismi con "fare." Cominci. (tʃer-ta-'men-te) (for-me-'re-mo)

20. Oh! ciò è assai facile! Ieri faceva cattivo tempo. (tʃɔ) (as-'saj) (fa-'tʃe-va) (kat-'ti-vo)

21. A meraviglia! Mi dica qualche cosa sul tempo d' oggi. (me-ra-'vi-ʎa) ('kwal-ke) ('ɔd-dʒi)

22. Ieri faceva cattivo tempo, ma oggi fa bellissimo tempo. (bel-'lis-si-mo)

23. Fa molto vento? Tira un gran[3] vento? ('ti-ra) ('vɛn-to)

24. Stanotte spirava un vento fortissimo, soffiava un vento gagliardo, ma oggi s' è calmato. (sta-'nɔt-te) (spi-'ra-va) (sof-'fja-va) (ga-'ʎar-do) (kal-'ma-to)

25. Ha letto i giornali? Quali sono le previsioni del tempo per domani? (dʒor-'na-li) ('kwa-li) (pre-vi-'sjo-ni)

26. Ecco il giornale. Vediamo; eccolo quì. Le probabilità[4] per domani sono che avremo venti di ponente fortissimi con acquazzoni. (ve-'dja-mo) (po-'nɛn-te) (for-'tis-si-mi) (ak-kwat-'tso-ni)

---

[1] When *molto* modifies an adjective or an adverb, it is used adverbially and is invariable; when it modifies a noun, it must agree with the same in gender and number, because it is then an adjective.

[2] See Part X. about the degrees of comparison. *Ricco*, rich; *più ricco*, richer; *il più ricco*, the richest; *ricchissimo*, very rich.

13. Literal translations, my friend, are in many cases impossible.

14. Why?

15. Because every language has its own peculiarities, its own idioms and modes of expression which can never be translated literally.

16. Are there many idiomatic expressions in Italian?

17. The Italian language, my friend, is one of the richest tongues in the world. Among modern tongues French and Italian are among the richest, and therefore have many idioms.

18. Would you have the kindness to mention some of the most widely used idioms? I mean (to speak of) those which come up in everyday conversation.

19. Certainly! For the time being, we shall form some idioms with "fare." Begin.

20. Oh, that's very easy! Yesterday the weather was bad (Lit.: it made bad weather).

21. Wonderful! Tell me something about to-day's weather.

22. Yesterday the weather was bad, but to-day we have lovely weather.

23. Is it very windy? (Lit.: does it make much wind? Does a great wind draw?)

24. A very strong wind was blowing last night, but to-day it has calmed down.

25. Have you read the papers? What are the weather forecasts for to-morrow?

26. Here is the paper. Let us see; here it is. The probabilities for to-morrow are that we shall have strong westerly winds, with showers.

---

[3] *Grande,* large, grand, great, drops usually the last syllable before a consonant, except before *s impura.* Before a vowel it drops *e* and takes an apostrophe instead: *Grand' uomo,* great man.

[4] *Nouns* ending with an accented vowel do not change in the plural: *La probabilità, le probabilità; la virtù, le virtù.*

27. Lei traduce benissimo. D' ora in poi Le darò delle frasi sul tempo col verbo "fare." (tra-'du-tʃe) (pɔj) (da-'rɔ)

28. Che tempo fa[1] oggi? Fa un tempo magnifico, incantevole! (ma-'ɲi-fi-ko) (in-kan-'te-vo-le)

29. Apriamo la finestra e vediamo come è il tempo. (a-'prja-mo) (fi-'nɛ-stra)

30. Risplende il sole, ma fa freddo. (ri-'splɛn-de) ('so-le)

31. Credo che avremo cattivo tempo; il barometro indica pioggia. (ba-'rɔ-me-tro) ('in-di-ka) ('pjɔd-dʒa)

32. Ha ragione[2]; il barometro si è abbassato; temo che pioverà. (a ra-'dʒo-ne) (ab-bas-'sa-to) ('te-mo) (pjo-ve-'ra)

33. Benissimo! Vedo che capisce a meraviglia questi idiotismi. (ka-'pi-ʃe)

34. Son quì tutte le espressioni idiomatiche in cui si impiega il verbo "fare"? (i-djo-'ma-ti-ke) (kuj) ('vɛr-bo)

35. Oh! no; noi impieghiamo "fare" unitamente ad altri verbi; come, per esempio, col verbo "scrivere," "far scrivere." (im-pje-'gja-mo) (u-ni-ta-'men-te) (e-'sem-pjo) ('skri-ve-re)

36. Ah! mi ricordo[3]; Lei ha già spiegato questi idiotismi. (ri-'kɔr-do) (spje-'ga-to)

37. È vero; ma ora mi faccia[4] vedere se li sa impiegare a proposito. Formi una frase. ('ve-ro) ('fat-tʃa) (pro-'pɔ-si-to)

38. Su che, signore?—Oh! su quel che più Le aggrada. (ag-'gra-da)

39. Benissimo. Farò del mio meglio.—Dove va?—Vado dal[5] sarto. (fa-'rɔ del 'mi-o 'mɛ-ʎo) ('sar-to)

40. Che va a fare dal sarto?—Vado a farmi fare un vestito nuovo. (ves-'ti-to)

41. Molto bene! Che fa sua sorella? (so-'rɛl-la)

42. Mia sorella si fa fare una veste dalla signora Luigia. ('dal-la si-'ɲo-ra lu-'i-dʒa)

43. Benissimo! Ora mi traduca. (tra-'du-ka)

44. Come vuole che sia guarnito il Suo cappello?—Come vuole far guarnire il suo cappello? (gwar-'ni-to) (gwar-'ni-re)

---

[1] On the idiomatic use of *fare* see Part X.

[2] On the omission of the article and the idiomatic use of *avere* see Part X.

[3] See the conjugation of a pronominal or reflexive verb in Part X.

[4] Irregular verbs will be found in Part X.

27. You translate very well. From now on I will give you some phrases about the weather with the verb "fare."

28. What kind of weather is it (Lit.: does it make) to-day? The weather is splendid, delightful!

29. Let us open the window and see how the weather is.

30. The sun is shining, but it is (Lit.: it makes) cold.

31. I think we are going to have bad weather; the barometer points to rain.

32. You are right; the barometer has fallen; I am afraid it is going to rain.

33. Excellent! I see you understand these idioms perfectly.

34. Are these all the idiomatic expressions in which "fare" is used?

35. Oh, no; we use "fare" in connection with other verbs, as, for instance, with "scrivere," to write, "far scrivere," to have something written.

36. Ah, I remember; you explained these idioms already.

37. Quite so, but show me now if you can employ them correctly. Form a sentence.

38. About what, sir? Oh, about anything you like best.

39. Very well; I shall do my best. Where are you going? I am going to the tailor's.

40. What are you going to do at the tailor's? I am going to have a new suit made.

41. Excellent! What is your sister doing?

42. My sister is having a dress made at Mme. Louise's.

43. Very good. Now translate for me.

44. How do you wish to have your hat trimmed?

---

[5] *Da*, from and at. In this second acceptation it is like the French *chez*. *Dal dottore*, At the doctor's—*chez le docteur*.

45. Favorisca guarnirlo di fiori e d' un nodo di nastro azzurro. Scelga un bell' azzurro scuro; ciò mi starà bene e s' accompagnerà col mio vestito. (gwar-'nir-lo) ('fjo-ri) ('nɔ-do) ('na-stro) (ad-'dzur-ro) ('tʃel-ga) ('sku-ro) (tʃɔ) (sta-'ra) (ak-kom-pa-ɲe-'ra)

AVERE

1. Lei si rammenta (si ricorda) il verbo "avere" che abbiamo studiato nel primo libro? (ram-'men-ta) (ri-'kɔr-da) ('vɛr-bo a-'ve-re) (stu-'dja-to)

2. Sì, me lo ricordo (me lo rammento) benissimo; ma noi abbiamo studiato solamente il presente dell' indicativo. (ri-'kɔr-do) (ram-'men-to)

3. Benissimo; ma ella deve studiare il verbo per intero, perchè è usato frequentissimamente ed offre molte difficoltà agli Inglesi ed agli Americani. (stu-'dja-re) (in-'tɛ-ro) (u-'sa-to) (fre-kwen-tis-si-ma-'men-te) ('ɔf-fre) (dif-fi-kol-'ta) ('a-ʎi in-'gle-si) (a-me-ri-'ka-ni)

4. Ebbene, lo studi. Lo troverà nel decimo libro che contiene la grammatica della lingua italiana. ('stu-di) (kon-'tjɛ-ne) (gram-'ma-ti-ka)

5. Lo studi bene e nella prossima lezione le insegnerò gli idiotismi del verbo avere. A rivederla. ('prɔs-si-ma) (le-'tsjo-ne) (in-se-ɲe-'rɔ)

6. Arrivederla, signore.

FARE

1. Ah! buon giorno, caro signore! Sono contento di vederla. Come sta? Come va colla salute? (kon-'tɛn-to)

2. Benone, grazie. E Lei, come sta di salute oggi? (be-'no-ne)

3. Assai bene, grazie mille. Questo tempo di primavera mi piace assai. (pri-ma-'vɛ-ra) ('pja-tʃe)

4. "Tempo di primavera?" Mi scusi se ripeto queste parole, ma l' espressione m' è affato nuova e non so quel che voglia dire. (ri-'pɛ-to) (pa-'rɔ-la) (af-'fat-to) ('vɔ-ʎa)

45. Please trim it with flowers and a blue ribbon bow. Choose a pretty navy blue. That will be becoming to me, and will match my suit.

AVERE (To Have)

1. You remember the verb "avere," which we studied in the first book?

2. Yes, I remember it perfectly, but we studied only the Present Indicative.

3. Very well, but you ought to study the whole verb, as it is very commonly used, and presents many difficulties to Englishmen and Americans.

4. Well, study it. You will find it in the Tenth Book, which contains the grammar of the Italian language.

5. Study it well, and in our next lesson I will teach you the idioms of the verb "avere." Good-bye!

6. Good-bye, sir.

TO MAKE, TO DO

1. Ah! good-morning, my dear sir! I am delighted to see you. How are you? How is your health?

2. Very well, thank you. And how are you to-day?

3. I am very well, thank you. This spring weather just suits me.

4. "Spring weather?" Pardon me if I repeat these words, but the expression is quite new to me, and I don't know what it means.

5. Lei sa senza dubbio, che abbiamo quattro stagioni, cioè: la primavera, l' estate, l' autunno, e l' inverno, ma probabilmente i nostri nomi italiani Le sono nuovi. (sono nuovi per lei) (ʹsɛn-tsa ʹdub-bjo) (ab-ʹbja-mo ʹkwat-tro sta-ʹdʒo-ni) (tʃo-ʹɛ) (e-ʹsta-te) (aw-ʹtun-no) (in-ʹvɛr-no) (pro-ba-bil-ʹmen-te) (ʹnɔ-stri ʹnɔ-mi)

6. Lo sono infatti. Mi permetta di ripeterli dopo di Lei: la primavera, l' estate, l' autunno, e l' inverno. (per-ʹmet-ta) (ri-ʹpɛ-ter-li) (ʹdɔ-po)

7. Ben detto! La sua pronuncia è eccellente. (bɛn ʹdet-to) (et-tʃel-ʹlɛn-te)

8. Lei mi sta adulando,[1] signor professore. Loro Italiani sono complimentosi assai (sono pieni di complimenti, fanno molti complimenti). (kom-pli-men-ʹto-si) (as-ʹsaj) (ʹpjɛ-ni) (kom-pli-ʹmen-ti)

9. Complimentosi no, ma gentili (cortesi). Gli Italiani sono naturalmente cortesi (gentili di natura, per natura). La cortesia italiana è innata e si trova nella classe povera non meno che[2] nella ricca. (dʒen-ʹti-li) (kor-ʹte-si) (na-tu-ral-ʹmen-te) (na-ʹtu-ra) (kor-te-ʹsi-a) (ʹme-no) (ʹrik-ka)

10. Vorrei poter dire lo stesso dei miei compatriotti. Temo che le nostre maniere Le abbiano a parere alquanto (piuttosto) rozze. (po-ʹter) (ʹstes-so) (miɛj) (kom-pa-tri-ɔt-ti) (ʹnɔ-stra) (ma-ʹnjɛ-ra) (ʹab-bja-no) (pá-ʹre-re) (al-ʹkwan-to) (pjut-ʹtɔ-sto) (ʹrod-dze)

11. Se Le devo dire apertamente la verità, mi pare che sotto questo aspetto Lei esageri. Forse gli Americani sono meno espansivi di noi Italiani. Comunque ciascun paese ha le sue proprie caratteristiche e maniere. E se anche fosse come Lei dice, d'altra parte vi sono molte cose ben più importanti della cortesia che noi dovremmo imparare da Loro. Ma ritorniamo alla nostra conversazione. (e-ʹsa-dʒe-ri) (ʹfor-se) (e-span-ʹsi-vi) (ko-ʹmun-kwe) (tʃa-ʹskun pa-ʹe-se) (ka-rat-te-ʹri-sti-ke) (ma-ʹnjɛ-rɛ)

12. Ho dimenticato interamente di che parlavamo. (di-men-ti-ʹka-to) (in-te-ra-ʹmen-te) (par-la-ʹva-mo)

---

[1] *Lei mi sta adulando,* You are flattering me; *io sto scrivendo,* I am writing; *sto mangiando,* I am eating, are examples of the progressive conjugation **very** frequently and elegantly employed among educated people.

5. You know, of course, that we have four seasons, that is, spring, summer, autumn and winter, but I suppose our Italian names are new to you.

6. Quite so; let me repeat them after you: spring, summer, autumn, winter.

7. That was very good! Your pronunciation is excellent!

8. You flatter me, professor. You Italians are always so complimentary.

9. Not complimentary, but polite. Italian people are polite by nature. Italian politeness is inborn and is found among the poor as well as the rich. (Lit.: in the poor class no less than in the rich).

10. I wish I could say the same thing about my countrymen. I am afraid our manners must appear rather rude to you.

11. Well, frankly speaking (Lit.: if I must openly tell you the truth), I think that you exaggerate in that respect. Perhaps Americans are less expansive than we Italians. However, each country has its own characteristics and ways. And even if it were as you say, there are on the other hand many things far more important than politeness which we ought to learn from you. But let us return to our subject.

12. I have quite forgotten what we were talking about.

---

[2] The two terms of the comparative degree of equality are joined together by the expressions: *tanto—quanto,* as much—as; *così—come,* so—as; *altrettanto—quanto,* just as much—as; *tale—quale,* such—as; *non meno—che,* not less—than; *del pari—che,* etc.

13. Noi parlavamo delle stagioni e gliene avevo appena detto i nomi. Se li rammenta[1] ancora? (ap-'pe-na) (ram-'men-ta) (an-'ko-ra)

14. Perfettamente: la primavera, l' estate, l' autunno e l' inverno. (per-fet-ta-'men-te)

15. Benissimo! Che tempo fa oggi?

16. Mi perdoni se l' interrompo; ma perchè dice "fa"? (in-ter-'rom-po)

17. Perchè "fare" vien impiegato parlando del tempo.

18. Strano! Eppur non mi dovrebbe parere talmente strano, perchè i Francesi e gli Spagnuoli si servono del medesimo verbo. ('stra-no) (ep-'pur) (do-'vreb-be) (tal-'men-te) (fran-'tʃe-si) (spa-'ɲwɔ-li) ('sɛr-vo-no) (me-'de-si-mo)

19. È vero. Ora per renderle famigliare quest' idiotismo, faremo un certo numero di frasi con questo verbo. ('rɛn-der-le) (fa-mi-'ʎa-re) (fa-'re-mo) ('tʃɛr-to) ('nu-me-ro)

20. Le posso fare una domanda, signor professore? ('pɔs-so) (do-'man-da) (pro-fes-'so-re)

21. Quante ne vuole! ('vwɔ-le)

22. Da qual lingua deriva il verbo "fare"? È preso forse dal latino? (de-'ri-va) ('for-se) (la-'ti-no)

23. Senza dubbio! È derivato dalla parola latina "facere." ('fa-ke-re)

24. Ah! ora vedo la sua origine latina. D' ora in poi non l' interromperò più. Desidero formare alcune frasi sul tempo per imparare ad usarle correttamente (a farne un uso corretto). ('ve-do) (o-'ri-dʒi-ne) (in-ter-rom-pe-'rɔ) ('far-ne) ('u-so kor-'rɛt-to)

---

[1] Pronominal or reflexive verbs with two pronouns:

me lo rammento	I remember it
te lo rammenti	you remember it (f.s.)
se lo rammenta	he remembers it

13. We were talking about the seasons, and I had just mentioned their names to you. Do you still remember them?

14. Perfectly: spring, summer, autumn, and winter.

15. Very good! Now, how is the weather to-day?

16. Pardon me if I interrupt you, but why do you say "fa" (makes)?

17. Because "fare" is used when speaking of the weather.

18. How peculiar! And yet it ought not to appear so strange to me, as both Frenchmen and Spaniards use the same verb.

19. That's true. Now, in order that you may become familiar with this idiom, (Lit.: to make this idiom familiar to you) we will form a certain number of sentences with this verb.

20. May I ask you a question, professor?

21. As many as you like.

22. From what language is the verb "fare" derived? It is taken perhaps from the Latin?

23. Certainly, it comes from the Latin word "facere."

24. Ah, now I see its Latin origin. Henceforth I shall not interrupt you any more. I wish to form some sentences about the weather, so that I may learn to use them correctly.

---

ce lo rammentiamo	we remember it
ve lo rammentate	you remember it
se lo rammentano	they remember it

See Part X. for further explanation.

FARE ED AVERE

(*Continuazione*)

1. Buon giorno, amico carissimo. Sono oltremodo[1] felice di vederla! Come è stata dacchè ebbi il piacere di vederla? L' ultima volta che è stata quì, Lei aveva mal di capo (mal di testa). Voglio sperare che stia meglio oggi. (ol-tre-'mɔ-do) (fe-'li-tʃe) (ve-'der-la) ('ko-me) (dak-'ke) ('eb-bi) ('ka-po) ('tɛs-ta) ('vɔ-λo) ('sti-a)

2. Grazie, sto molto meglio, anzi sto affatto bene e son pronto a continuare la nostra lezione. ('mɛ-λo) ('pron-to) (kon-ti-nu-'a-re)

3. Ne sono contentissimo, ma favorisca levarsi il soprabito e si ponga a sedere. (le-'var-si) (so-'pra-bi-to) ('pon-ga) (se-'de-re)

4. Dove mi metterò a sedere, signor professore? (met-te-'rɔ)

5. Quì su questa sedia. Ed ora incominciamo. Di che stavam parlando l' ultima volta? ('sɛ-dja) (in-ko-min-'tʃa-mo) (sta-'vam)

6. Lei ha spiegato l'uso di "fare" col parlar del tempo. (spje-'ga-to) (par-'lar)

7. Sì, sì; me lo ricordo. Ha imparato a mente (a memoria) la coniugazione del verbo "fare"? ('men-te) (me-'mɔ-rja)

8. Sì, signore. "Fare" è molto irregolare, ma con tutto ciò credo saperne[2] tutta la coniugazione. (ir-re-go-'la-re) (kon 'tut-to tʃɔ)

9. Bene, bene; vediamo! Coniughi il presente dell' indicativo. (ve-'dja-mo) ('kɔ-nju-gi)

> faccio, **or** fo ('fat-tʃo)
> fai (faj)
> fa (fa)
> facciamo (fat-'tʃa-mo)
> fate ('fa-te)
> fanno ('fan-no)

---

[1] The superlative, without direct comparison, is expressed in many ways, besides the usual termination of the adjective in *issimo*. For inst.: By repetition of the adjective, as: *nero nero*, very black; by affixes, like *arci, oltre, stra*, as in *arcibello*, very beautiful; *oltrenumero*, without number; *stragrande*, very large;

TO DO AND TO HAVE

(*Continuation*)

1. Ah, good-morning, my very dear friend! Delighted to see you! How have you been since I had the pleasure of seeing you? The last time you were here you were suffering from a headache. I trust you feel better to-day.

2. Thank you, I am a great deal better; in fact, I am quite well, and ready to go on with our lesson.

3. I am very glad, but please take off your overcoat and sit down.

4. Where shall I sit, professor?

5. Here, on this chair. And now let us start. Of what were we talking the last time?

6. You explained the use of "fare" in speaking of the weather.

7. Ah, yes, I remember. Have you learned the conjugation of the verb "fare" by heart?

8. Yes, sir. "Fare" is very irregular, but in spite of that I think I know the whole conjugation.

9. Well, let us see. Conjugate the Indicative Present.

I do, or	I am doing
you do, or	you are doing (f.s.)
he does, or	he is doing
we do, or	we are doing
you do, or	you are doing
they do, or	they are doing

---

or by expressions like these: *sopra ogni altro, oltremisura, sopra ogni dire, oltremodo,* etc.

[2] The little word *ne* has the same meaning as the French *en*, of it, of them, etc.

10. Benissimo! Ora il presente del soggiuntivo. (sod-dʒun-'ti-vo)

> che io faccia[1] ('fat-tʃa)
> che tu faccia
> che egli faccia
> che noi facciamo (fat-'tʃa-mo)
> he voi facciate (fat-'tʃa-te)
> che essi facciano ('fat-tʃa-no)

10. Very well! Now the Present Subjunctive.

> I may make
> you may make (f.s.)
> he may make
> we may make
> you may make
> they may make

VOCABOLARIO	VOCABULARY
Portare	**To Wear**
Queste mercanzie durano molto (sono di buona durata).	These goods wear very well.
L'affare, il negozio, la faccenda	The business
Il magazzino, il negozio, la bottega	The store, the shop
Il magazzino del merciaio; la merceria	The dry goods store
Il cappello	The hat
Il cappellaio	The hatter
La modista	The milliner
Il magazzino di modista	The millinery shop
La libreria	The bookstore
Il libraio	The bookseller
La carta; le carte	The paper; the papers
La cartoleria	The stationery store
La scarpa	The shoe
Il calzolaio	The shoemaker
La calzoleria	The shoestore
L'orologio	The watch
L'orologiaio	The watchmaker
Il negoziante, il mercante	The merchant
Il pane	The bread
Il panettiere, il fornaio	The baker
Il forno; la bottega di fornaio	The bakery
Il panino; la pagnottina	The roll
La focaccia	The cake
Il beccaio; il macellaio	The butcher
La carne	The meat
La beccheria; la macelleria	The butcher-shop
Il metro	The metre (a few inches more than a yard)
Il chilo (il chilogramma)	The kilo (a little more than two American pounds)
La libbra	The pound

VOCABOLARIO	VOCABULARY
Mangiare e Bere (Bevere)	**Eating and Drinking**

Mangiare	To eat
Bere	To drink
Far colazione	To breakfast or lunch
Pranzare	To dine
Cenare	To take supper
L' appetito	The appetite
Aver fame	To be hungry (= to have hunger)
Ha fame?	Are you hungry?
Sì, ho fame.	Yes, I am hungry.
Aver sete	To be thirsty (= to have thirst)
Ha sete?	Are you thirsty?
No, non ho sete.	No, I am not thirsty.

PROVERBI

Cane ch'abbaia, non morde.
Ride bene chi ride l'ultimo.
Paese che vai, usanza che trovi.

Lungo è il cammino che non ha giravolte.
Chi è cagion del suo mal, pianga se stesso.
Nessun peggior sordo di chi non vuol sentire.
Di buona volontà sta pieno l'inferno.
Giovine ozioso, vecchio bisognoso.

I frutti proibiti sono i più dolci.
I gran dolori sono muti.
Il buono è buono, ma il meglio vince.
Il danaro è fratello del danaro.
Il male per libra viene, va via per once.
Il meglio è l'inimico del bene.
In un giorno non si fe' Roma.
La comodità fa l'uomo ladro.

PROVERBS

A barking dog never bites.
He laughs best who laughs last.
When in Rome do as the Romans do.
It is a long lane that has no turning.
He who makes his bed has to lie in it.
There are none so deaf as those who will not hear.
Hell is paved with good intentions.
A young man idle, an old man needy.
Forbidden fruit is the sweetest.
Great sorrows are dumb.
Good is good, but better is better.
Money is the brother of money.
Sorrows come in pounds and go in ounces.
Better is the enemy of good.
Rome was not built in a day.
Opportunity makes the thief.

PART FIVE

CONTENTS

CONVERSAZIONE

Fare

(Continuazione)

11. Benissimo! L' imperfetto! (im-per-'fɛt-to)

> facevo
> facevi
> faceva
> facevamo
> facevate
> facevano

12. Benissimo! Ora il passato remoto. (re-'mɔ-to)

> feci
> facesti
> fece
> facemmo
> faceste
> fecero

13. Sempre meglio! Il futuro!

> farò
> farai
> farà
> faremo
> farete
> faranno

14. Bene, benissimo! Il condizionale. (kon-di-tsjo-'na-le)

> farei
> faresti
> farebbe
> faremmo
> fareste
> farebbero

CONVERSATION

Fare

(Continuation)

11. Excellent! The Imperfect.

> I was making, or   doing
> you were making, or   doing (f.s.)
> he was making, or   doing
> we were making, or   doing
> you were making, or   doing
> they were making, or   doing

12. Very good! Now the Historical Tense.

> I did, or   I made
> you did, or   you made (f.s.)
> he did, or   he made
> we did, or   we made
> you did, or   you made
> they did, or   they made

13. Still better! And the Future.

> I shall do, or   make
> you will do, or   make (f.s.)
> he will do, or   make
> we shall do, or   make
> you will do, or   make
> they will do, or   make

14. That's very good! The Conditional!

> I should do, or   make
> you would do, or   make (f.s.)
> he would do, or   make
> we should do, or   make
> you would do, or   make
> they would do, or   make

15. In verità Lei è un eccellente scolaro! Coniughi ora l'imperfetto del soggiuntivo. (sko-'la-ro) ('kɔ-nju-gi)

> che io facessi
> tu facessi
> egli facesse
> noi facessimo
> voi faceste
> essi facessero

16. Bravo, bravissimo! Senza nessun dubbio Lei avrà presto superato tutte le difficoltà della lingua italiana. ('bra-vo) (bra-'vis-si-mo) (su-pe-'ra-to)

17. Lei non sa quanto mi stia a cuore l' impararla. Nessuna lingua è importante per un maestro di musica quanto[1] la bella lingua di Dante. (ma-'e-stro) ('mu-si-ka) ('dan-te)

"AVERE" ED IL SUO USO IDIOMATICO

1. Vediamo ora il verbo "avere." Suppongo che avrà imparato a memoria la coniugazione di questo verbo. (sup-'pon-go) (a-'vra im-pa-'ra-to) (ko-nju-ga-'tsjo-ne)

2. L' ho studiato e credo di saperne tutti i modi e tempi. ('kre-do) ('mɔ-di)

3. Benissimo! Vediamo! Mi dia il presente dell' indicativo.

> ho (ɔ)
> hai (aj)
> ha (a)
> abbiamo (ab-'bja-mo)
> avete (a-'ve-te)
> hanno ('an-no)

4. Benissimo! Adesso il presente del soggiuntivo.

> che io abbia ('ab-bja)
> tu abbi **or** abbia
> egli abbia
> noi abbiamo
> voi abbiate (ab-'bja-te)
> essi abbiano ('ab-bja-no)

---

[1] In comparative sentences of equality one of the words in the following expressions: *Così—come, tanto—quanto,* etc., may be omitted.

15. You are indeed a diligent student! Now conjugate the Imperfect Subjunctive.

> I might make
> you might make (f.s.)
> he might make
> we might make
> you might make
> they might make

16. Bravo! I have no doubt that you will soon master all the intricacies of the Italian language.

17. You cannot imagine how anxious I am (Lit.: how it is to heart to me) to master it. No other tongue is so important for a music teacher as the beautiful language of Dante.

"AVERE" AND ITS IDIOMATIC USE

1. Now let us see the verb "avere." I suppose you have learned the conjugation of this verb by heart?

2. I have studied it, and I think I know all its moods and tenses.

3. Well, let us see! Give me the Present Indicative.

> I have
> you have (f.s.)
> he has
> we have
> you have
> they have

4. Very good! Now the Present Subjunctive.

> that I may have
> that you may have (f.s.)
> that he may have
> that we may have
> that you may have
> that they may have

5. **Molto bene!** Per favore, l' imperfetto.

> avevo (a-'ve-vo)
> avevi
> aveva
> avevamo (a-ve-'va-mo)
> avevate (a-ve-'va-te)
> avevano (a-'ve-va-no)

6. **A meraviglia!** Il passato remoto.

> ebbi ('eb-bi)
> avesti (a-'ve-sti)
> ebbe ('eb-be)
> avemmo (a-'vem-mo)
> aveste (a-'ve-ste)
> ebbero ('eb-be-ro)

7. **Sempre bene!** Mi coniughi ora l' imperfetto del soggiuntivo.

> che avessi (a-'ves-si)
> avessi
> avesse
> avessimo (a-'ves-si-mo)
> aveste (a-'ve-ste)
> **avessero** (a-'ves-se-ro)

8. **Non potrebbe far meglio.** Coniughi ora il futuro.

> avrò (a-'vrɔ)
> avrai (a-'vraj)
> avrà (a-'vra)
> avremo (a-'vre-mo)
> avrete (a-'vre-te)
> avranno (a-'vran-no)

9. **Andiam sempre di bene in meglio!** Favorisca darmi il condizionale.

> avrei (a-'vrej)
> avresti (a-'vre-sti)
> avrebbe (a-'vreb-be)
> avremmo (a-'vrem-mo)
> avreste (a-'vre-ste)
> avrebbero (a-'vreb-be-ro)

5. Excellent! Now the Imperfect, if you please.

> I had, or   used to have
> you had (f.s.)
> he had, or   used to have
> we had, or   used to have
> you had, or   used to have
> they had, or   used to have

6. Wonderful! Now the Historical Tense.

> I had
> you had (f.s.)
> he had
> we had
> you had
> they had

7. Still good! Now conjugate the Imperfect Subjunctive for me.

> that I might have
> that you might have (f.s.)
> that he might have
> that we might have
> that you might have
> that they might have

8. You could not do better. Now conjugate the Future.

> I shall have
> you will have (f.s.)
> he will have
> we shall have
> you will have
> they will have

9. Always better and better! Please give me the Conditional.

> I should have
> you would have (f.s.)
> he would have
> we should have
> you would have
> they would have

10. Benissimo! Ora può dirmi come si impieghi "avere" in connessione con altri verbi? (kon-nes-'sjo-ne)

11. Noi l' impieghiamo come verbo ausiliare, esattamente come in inglese, nella formazione dei tempi composti, per esempio: "Ho scritto. L' avrei fatto. Che avrebbe fatto al mio posto?" (aw-si-'lja-re) (e-sat-ta-'men-te) (for-ma-'tsjo-ne) (kom-'pɔ-sti) (e-'sem-pjo) ('pɔs-to)

12. Benissimo! Ma io devo richiamare la Sua attenzione su un punto importante in cui le due lingue non vanno sempre d' accordo. (ri-kja-'ma-re) (at-ten-'tsjo-ne) ('pun-to) (kuj) ('sɛm-pre) (dak-'kɔr-do)

13. In inglese si fa uso del passato remoto[1] parlando di fatti od eventi passati. Per esempio: "I saw him yesterday morning." In italiano, in simil caso, si usa più frequentemente il passato prossimo, quantunque il passato remoto sia pure assolutamente corretto. Così si dirà: "L' ho visto ieri mattina, o lo vidi ieri mattina." (par-'lan-do) ('fat-ti) (e-'vɛn-ti) ('si-mil) ('ka-so) (fre-kwen-te-'men-te) (kwan-'tun-kwe) (as-so-lu-ta-'men-te) (kor-'rɛt-to) (di-'ra) ('vis-to) ('vi-di)

14. È sempre così?

15. Generalmente, sì. (dʒe-ne-ral-'men-te)

16. Senza dubbio, vi sono regole sull' uso del' imperfetto e del passato remoto. Quest' ultimo si impiega specialmente in racconti, ma queste regole le vedremo più tardi. (im-per-'fɛt-to) (im-'pjɛ-ga) (spe-tʃal-'men-te) (rak-'kon-ti) (ve-'dre-mo) ('tar-di)

17. Per ora voglio solo ricordarle che generalmente impieghiamo il passato prossimo in italiano per parlare di fatti passati. È una regola di grande importanza e deve rammentarsela specialmente nel tradurre domande. (im-pje-'gja-mo) ('prɔs-si-mo) ('rɛ-go-la) (im-por-'tan-tsa) (ram-men-'tar-se-la) (tra-'dur-re)

18. E perchè domande?

---

[1] Further rules on the difference between these two tenses will be found in Part X.

10. Very, very good! Now can you tell me how we use "avere" in connection with other verbs?

11. We use it as an auxiliary verb, exactly as in English, for the formation of compound tenses, for instance: "I have written. I would have done it. What would you have done in my place?"

12. Very good! But I must call your attention to an important point where the two languages don't always agree.

13. In English, we use the past tense when talking about past actions or events. We say for instance: "I saw him yesterday morning." In such a case Italian more frequently uses the Past Indefinite Tense, although the Historical Tense may also be absolutely correct. Thus we will say: "[I] him have seen yesterday morning, or him saw yesterday morning."

14. And is it always so?

15. Generally speaking, yes.

16. Of course, there are rules for the use of the Imperfect and the Historical Tense. The latter is used in narratives especially; but these rules we shall see later.

17. Just now I only want to remind you that we generally use the Past Indefinite Tense in Italian in speaking of past actions. This is a very important rule, and you ought to remember it, especially in translating questions.

18. Why questions?

19. Perchè in italiano non c'è verbo ausiliare che risponda al nostro verbo inglese "did."

20. Per esempio, quando diciamo in inglese: "Did you do this?—Did he tell you so?—Why didn't you pay him the money which I handed you this morning?—Did you send him a telegram or did you write to him?" In italiano diciamo: "Ha fatto questo?—Glielo ha detto?—Perchè non gli ha rimesso il denaro che le ho dato stamane?—Gli ha mandato un telegramma o gli ha scritto? (e-'sem-pjo) (di-'tʃa-mo) ('ʎe-lo) (sta-'ma-ne) (man-'da-to) (te-le-'gram-ma) ('skrit-to)

21. Comprendo questo perfettamente e mi sforzerò di ricordarmi sempre questa regola. (sfor-tse-'rɔ)

22. Benissimo, ma Lei deve porla in pratica applicandola. Le regole sono buone teoricamente, ma la pratica è la cosa principale per ben possedere una lingua straniera. ('por-la) ('pra-ti-ka) (ap-pli-'kan-do-la) (te-o-ri-ka-'men-te) (prin-tʃi-'pa-le) (pos-se-'de-re) (stra-'njɛ-ra)

AVERE

(Continuazione)

23. Scriva[1] in casa un certo numero di frasi in tutte le persone ed a tutti i tempi, me le porti ed io gliele correggerò. ('skri-va) ('tʃer-to) (per-'so-ne) (kor-red-dʒe-'rɔ)

24. Lo farò. Ma mi parli del participio passato accompagnato dall'ausiliare "avere" nei tempi composti. (fa-'rɔ) (par-ti-'tʃi-pjo pas-'sa-to) (ak-kom-pa-'ɲa-to)

25. Ah! son contento che mi rivolga (che mi faccia) questa domanda. Noi abbiamo in italiano tre coniugazioni per i verbi regolari. (kon-'tɛn-to) (ri-'vɔl-ga) (ko-nju-ga-'tsjo-ni) (re-go-'la-ri)

26. Mi par di sapere tutto questo. Non finiscono forse i verbi della prima coniugazione in **are**? (fi-'ni-sko-no) ('for-se)

---

[1] The imperative mood has only two forms of its own, the second person singular and plural; all the others are taken from the subjunctive mood.

19. Because in Italian there is no auxiliary verb which corresponds to our English "did."

20. For instance, when we say in English: "Did you do this? Did he tell you so? Why didn't you pay him the money which I handed you this morning? Did you send him a telegram or did you write to him?" In Italian we say: "Have you done this? Has he told you so? Why have you not paid him the money which I have handed you this morning? Have you sent him a telegram or have you written to him?"

21. I understand this perfectly, and shall try always to remember this rule.

22. Very well, but you must practice it by applying it. Rules are good in theory, but practice is the main thing in mastering a foreign tongue.

TO HAVE

(Continuation)

23. Write a number of sentences in the various persons and tenses at home, bring them to me, and I'll correct them.

24. I will do so. But tell me about the formation of the past participle accompanied by "avere" in the compound tenses.

25. Ah, I am glad you asked me this question. We have three conjugations for regular verbs in Italian.

26. I think I know all that. The verbs of the First Conjugation end in **are**, do they not?

27. Sì, i verbi regolari della prima coniugazione terminano in **are**;
quelli della seconda in **ere**; e quelli della terza in **ire**. (ˈtɛr-mi-na-no)

28. Togliendo queste desinenze abbiamo la radice che nei verbi
regolari è invariabile. A queste radici aggiungiamo le desinenze
delle varie coniugazioni. Lei troverà nel decimo libro un quadro
completo di queste desinenze che Lei dovrebbe mandare a
memoria. (to-ˈʎɛn-do) (de-si-ˈnɛn-tse) (ra-ˈdi-tʃe) (in-va-ˈrja-bi-le) (ad-dʒun-ˈdʒa-mo) (ˈva-rje) (tro-ve-ˈra) (ˈdɛ-tʃi-mo) (ˈli-bro) (ˈkwa-dro) (kom-ˈplɛ-to) (man-ˈda-re) (me-ˈmɔ-rja)

29. Lo farò. Ma vorrei sapere come si forma il participio passato di
queste tre coniugazioni regolari. (par-ti-ˈtʃi-pjo)

30. In un modo semplicissimo. Il participio passato della prima
coniugazione finisce in **ato**, come: amare, amato; pagare, **pagato**;
dare, dato; parlare, parlato, ecc. (sem-pli-ˈtʃis-si-mo)

31. Qual' è la desinenza del participio passato dei verbi della seconda
coniugazione?

32. Essi finiscono in **uto**, come: temere, temuto; credere, creduto;
sapere, saputo. (te-ˈme-re) (te-ˈmu-to) (ˈkre-de-re) (kre-ˈdu-to)
(sa-ˈpe-re) (sa-ˈpu-to)

33. Ah! è semplicissimo. Qual' è la desinenza dei participi passati
dei verbi della terza coniugazione?

34. Finiscono in **ito**: sentire, sentito; udire, udito; capire, capito;
finire, finito. (sen-ˈti-to) (u-ˈdi-to) (ka-ˈpi-to) (fi-ˈni-to)

35. Ma queste regole s' applicano solo ai verbi regolari, non è vero?
(ˈsap-pli-ka-no)

36. Certamente. Noi abbiamo un gran numero di verbi irregolari.
Lei ne troverà una lista completa nel decimo volume. (tʃer-ta-ˈmen-te) (ˈli-sta) (vo-ˈlu-me)

37. E tutti i verbi si coniugano con "avere"? (ˈkɔ-nju-ga-no)

27. Yes, the regular verbs of the First Conjugation end in **are**; those of the Second in **ere**; and those of the Third in **ire**.

28. By dropping these endings we get the stem of the verb, which in regular verbs is invariable. To these stems we add the endings of the respective conjugations. You will find in Book X. a complete table of these endings, which you ought to memorize.

29. I will do so. But I would like to know how the Past Participle of these three regular conjugations is formed.

30. In a very simple way. The Past Participle of the First Conjugation ends in **ato**, as: amare, amato; pagare, pagato; dare, dato; parlare, parlato, etc.

31. What is the ending of the Past Participle of verbs of the Second Conjugation?

32. They end in **uto**, as: temere, temuto; credere, creduto; sapere, saputo.

33. Ah! that is very simple. What is the ending of the Past Participle of the verbs of the Third Conjugation?

34. They end in **ito**: sentire, sentito; udire, udito; capire, capito; finire, finito.

35. But these rules refer solely to the regular verbs, do they not?

36. Certainly. We have a great number of irregular verbs. You will find a complete table of them in Part X.

37. And are all verbs conjugated with "avere"?

114

38. Tutti i verbi attivi e molti verbi neutri si coniugano con "avere."
Però i seguenti si coniugano coll' ausiliare "essere." (at-'ti-vi)
('nɛw-tri) (se-'gwɛn-ti)

> andare
> stare
> entrare
> cadere
> partire
> venire
> ritornare
> uscire
> arrivare
> discendere (di-'ʃen-de-re)
> rimanere, restare

39. Noi coniughiamo pure con "essere" i verbi "divenire," "per-
venire," ecc., derivati dal verbo "venire," come pure "nascere"
e "morire." Noi diciamo: "Dove è nata? Son nato a Parigi."
"Egli è morto." "Ella è morta."

40. Credo di intendere questa regola; noi abbiamo avuto nelle nostre
lezioni precedenti un certo numero d' esempi. Ma si compiaccia
spiegarmi quali verbi si coniugano con "essere." (a-'vu-to)
(pre-tʃe-'dɛn-te) ('tʃɛr-to) (e-'sem-pi) (kom-'pjat-tʃa)

41. Il verbo ausiliare "essere" è impiegato con tutti i verbi passivi
ed anche con tutti i verbi riflessi. (ri-'flɛs-si)

42. Studii i verbi regolari con attenzione; li pratichi quanto più
può, per saperne recitare, se occorre, qualsiasi tempo o modo.
('stu-di) (at-ten-'tsjo-ne) ('pra-ti-ki) (re-tʃi-'ta-re) (ok-'kor-re)
(kwal-'si-a-si)

38. All active verbs and many neuter verbs are conjugated with "avere." The following, however, are conjugated with "essere."

> to go
> to stay, be, stand
> to enter
> to fall
> to leave, go away
> to come
> to return, come back
> to go out
> to arrive
> to go down
> to stay, remain

39. We also conjugate with "essere" the verbs "divenire," "per-venire," etc., which are derived from "venire," as well as "nascere," to be born, and "morire," to die. We say: "Where were you born? I was born in Paris." "He has died." "She died."

40. I think I understand this rule; we have had quite a number of examples in our previous lessons. But please explain to me which verbs are conjugated with "essere."

41. The auxiliary "essere" is used with all passive verbs and also with all reflexive verbs.

42. Study the regular verbs thoroughly and practice them as much as you can, so that you can give any tense or mood if necessary.

43. Non impari il quadro a memoria, ma pratichi un certo numero
di verbi regolari, finchè li sappia dire così: "Egli parla. Egli
avrebbe parlato. Che avrebbe pagato? Noi dobbiamo vendere
questa casa," ecc. (im-'pa-ri) ('sap-pja)

44. Ma devo partire, signore. Vedo che la lezione è finita. Han
suonato le undici in questo momento. (swo-'na-to) ('un-di-tʃi)
mo-'men-to)

45. Sì, sono le undici e cinque. Ebbene, per la prossima lezione,
scriva alcuni esercizi, delle frasi corte, ma usuali, osservando le
regole che le ho date[1]; studii anche i verbi regolari. ('skri-va)
(e-ser-'tʃi-tsi) ('kor-te) (u-su-'a-li) (os-ser-'van-do)

46. Farò quanto starà in me, signore. Desidero tanto possedere la
sua bella lingua.

47. Arrivederla, signore.

48. Arrivederci.

---

[1] The past participle with the auxiliary *avere* may agree or not with its direct
object. For further rules see Part X.

43. Do not learn the table by heart, but practice a number of regular verbs until you can say them like this: "He is speaking. He would have spoken. What would you have paid? We must sell this house, etc."

44. But I must go, sir. I see our lesson is over; it has just struck eleven.

45. Yes, it is five minutes past eleven. Well, write some exercises for our next lesson, short but practical sentences observing the rules I have given you, and study the regular verbs.

46. I shall do my best, sir. I want so much to master your beautiful language.

47. Good-bye, sir.

48. Good-bye.

118

VOCABOLARIO	VOCABULARY
Continuazione	*Continuation*

La Colazione / The Breakfast

La (prima) colazione	The (first) breakfast
La (seconda) colazione	The (second) breakfast; the luncheon
Il caffè	The coffee
Il tè	The tea
Una tazza di caffè	A cup of coffee
Una tazza di tè	A cup of tea
La cioccolata	The chocolate
Che cosa desidera per colazione? Caffè, tè o cioccolata?	What do you wish for breakfast? Coffee, tea or chocolate?
Io piglio caffè, ma mia moglie prende tè.	I drink coffee, but my wife takes tea.
Non le piace il tè?	Don't you like tea?
Preferisco il caffè.	I prefer coffee.
Ordinare, comandare	To order
Avete ordinato?	Did you order?
Che vuol ordinare, comandare?	What do you want to order?
La colazione	The breakfast
Ben cotto	Well done
Cameriere, portatemi una bistecca ed una tazza di caffè.	Waiter, bring me a steak and a cup of coffee.
La vuole ben cotta?	Do you want it well done?
No, poco cotta.	No, rare (=little cooked.)
La costoletta.	The mutton-chop, the cutlet.
La costoletta di vitello	The veal cutlet
La costoletta di maiale	The pork-chop

Patate	Potatoes
Patate fritte	Fried potatoes
Portatemi una costoletta e patate fritte.	Bring me a chop and fried potatoes.
Un uovo (masc.)	An egg
Uova (fem.)	Eggs
Uova bazzotte	Soft-boiled eggs
Uova dure, sode	Hard-boiled eggs
Uova fritte	Fried eggs
Uova affogate	Poached eggs
Uova strapazzate	Scrambled eggs
Uovo fritto	Fried egg
Uova fresche	Fresh eggs
Una frittata	An omelette
Come vuole le uova, bazzotte o dure (sode)?	How do you want the eggs, soft-boiled or hard?
Fatele bollire tre minuti.	Let them boil three minutes.
Il sale	The salt
Il pepe	The pepper
Lo zucchero	The sugar
Il latte	The milk
La crema, il fior di latte, la panna	The cream
L' aceto	The vinegar
L' olio	The oil
La mostarda	The mustard
La saliera	The salt-cellar
La zuccheriera	The sugar bowl
La caffettiera	The coffeepot

Il vaso da tè	The teapot
L' oviere	The egg cup
Mescere, versare	To pour out.
Per favore, versatemi una tazza di tè.	Please pour me out a cup of tea.
Acqua fresca	Fresh water
Un bicchier d' acqua	A glass of water
Mescetemi per piacere un bicchier d' acqua.	Please pour me out a glass of water.
Acqua fredda	Cold water
Acqua calda	Warm water
Acqua bollente	Boiling water
Acqua tiepida	Lukewarm water
Acqua minerale	Mineral water
Acqua ghiacciata	Ice water
Caraffa	Decanter

I Piatti — The Dishes

Apparecchiare la tavola	To lay the table
Apparecchiate la tavola.	Lay the table.
Un piatto	A plate
Netto, pulito	Clean
Favorite dare dei piatti netti.	Please serve clean plates.
La scodella	The soup-plate
Il piatto	The dish
Il cucchiaio	The spoon
Il cucchiaione	The large spoon
Il cucchiaino da tè	The teaspoon

Una cucchiaiata	A spoonful
La forchetta	The fork
Il coltello	The knife
I coltelli	The knives
Datemi un coltello pulito.	Give me a clean knife.
La tovaglia	The table-cloth
Il tovagliuolo	The napkin
Non m' avete dato il tovagliuolo.	You did not bring me a napkin.
La posata	The cover
Il bicchiere	The glass
Un bicchier d' acqua	A glass of water
Un bicchier di vino	A glass of wine
Un bicchiere da vino	A wine glass
Un bicchiere di birra	A glass of beer
Bere in un bicchiere	To drink out of a glass
La tazza	The cup
Il piattino	The saucer
Il cavaturaccioli (cavatappi)	The corkscrew
Mescete il caffè.	Serve the coffee.
Sparecchiate la tavola.	Clear the table.

Il Viaggio / The Journey

Fare un viaggio	To make a journey
Farà un viaggio?	Are you going to make a journey?
Sono in procinto di partire per l' Europa.	I am on the point of leaving for Europe.

Fare un viaggio; partire per; andare a	To make a journey; to leave for; to go to
Dove va?	Where are you going?
Parto per l'Italia.	I am leaving for Italy.
Andar fuori di città	To go out of town
Vado fuori di città domani.	I am going out of town to-morrow.
Il viaggio	The journey
Ha fatto buon viaggio?	Did you have a good journey?
Arrivederci; faccia buon viaggio. Buon viaggio! }	Good-bye, I wish you a pleasant journey.

La Ferrovia

The Railroad

Lo scalo	The dock, wharf
La stazione	The station
La stazione capolinea	The terminal
Da quale stazione parte?	From which station are you going?
Parto dalla stazione centrale.	I leave from the Central Station.

PART SIX

CONTENTS

"AVERE"

(*Continuazione*)

1. Favorisca darmi una regola sull' uso del verbo "avere" invece del verbo "to be" in inglese.

2. Con piacere. "Avere" vien impiegato nel senso di "to be" in inglese, quando esprime un desiderio o un sentimento. (e-'spri-me) (de-si-'dɛ-rjo) (sen-ti-'men-to)

3. Mi dispiace doverle dire che non comprendo molto bene quel che voglia dire. Per favore mi dia qualche esempio. ('vɔ-ʎa)

4. Lei ha ragione. Noi impariamo per mezzo della pratica e degli esempi. (ra-'dʒo-ne) ('mɛd-dzo)

5. Tale è pure il mio parere (la mia opinione), **or** così la penso anch' io. Il torto di quasi tutti i grammatici sta per l' appunto nel voler essere troppo astratti nell' esposizione delle loro regole. ('ta-le) (pa-'re-re) ('tɔr-to) ('kwa-si) (gram-'ma-ti-tʃi) (ap-'pun-to) (a-'strat-ti) (e-spo-si-'tsjo-ne) ('rɛ-go-le)

6. In breve (in due parole): il verbo "avere" si impiega invece del nostro verbo inglese "to be," quando è unito alle parole seguenti: fame, sete, freddo, caldo, sonno, vergogna, ragione, torto, voglia e paura. ('brɛ-ve) (in-'ve-tʃe) ('fa-me) ('se-te) ('fred-do) ('kal-do) ('sɔn-no) (ver-'gɔ-ɲa) (ra-'dʒo-ne) ('tɔr-to) ('vɔ-ʎa) (pa-'u-ra)

7. Ah! capisco benissimo, ma mi sarà malagevole (difficile) ricordarmi un sì gran numero di vocaboli isolati. (ma-la-'dʒe-vo-le) (ri-kor-'dar-mi) (vo-'ka-bo-li) (i-so-'la-ti)

8. Ci rammentiamo sempre difficilmente i vocaboli isolati, amico mio. Le parole sconnesse non formano una lingua, un idioma. Una persona può ben mandare a memoria il vocabolario intero e contuttociò essere perfettamente incapace di conversare. La natura c' insegna per mezzo di frasi e dobbiamo apprender frasi. (skon-'nɛs-se) (i-'djɔ-ma) (in-ka-'pa-tʃe) (kon-ver-'sa-re)

9. Ne son persuaso, e per questo Le sarei grato se potesse **farmi** alcune frasi con queste parole. (per-su-'a-so) ('gra-to)

"TO HAVE"

(*Continuation*)

1. Will you please give me a rule about the use of "avere" in place of the English verb "to be"?

2. With pleasure. "Avere" is used in the sense of "to be" in English when it expresses desire or sensation.

3. I regret to tell you that I cannot quite understand what you mean by this. Kindly give me some illustrations.

4. You are quite right. We learn by practice and through examples.

5. That is my opinion exactly. Grammarians generally make the mistake of being too abstract in their rules. (Lit.: Such is also my opinion, or, thus I think also. The wrong of nearly all grammarians consists precisely in their wanting to be too abstract in the expression of their rules.)

6. Briefly, (Lit.: in two words) "avere" is used in place of our English verb "to be" when it is connected with the following words: hunger, thirst, cold, warmth, sleep, shame, right, wrong, inclination and fear.

7. Ah, this I understand, but it will be quite difficult for me to remember such a large number of isolated words.

8. Isolated words, my friend, are always hard to remember. Disconnected words are not language. A person might learn the whole dictionary by heart and yet would not be able to carry on a conversation. Nature teaches by sentences, and sentences we will have to learn.

9. I am convinced of that and should feel obliged to you if you would form some sentences with these words for me.

10. Con piacere, ma per poter trarre il maggior vantaggio possibile dagli esempi che sto per darle, Lei dovrà provarsi di formare in casa un certo numero di frasi simili e portarmele perchè io le corregga. ('trar-re) (mad-'dʒor) (van-'tad-dʒo) (pro-'var-si) (kor-'rɛg-ga)

11. Lo farò. Impiegherò i verbi delle sue frasi in persone ed a tempi diversi. (di-'vɛr-si)

12. Benissimo! Ora cominciamo. Che ha? Lei non ha buona cera. ('tʃe-ra)

13. Formi ora una frase simile, facendo uso però del passato.

14. Ho incontrato Suo cugino che mi è parso molto ammalato. Che ha? (ɛ 'par-so) (am-ma-'la-to)

15. Benissimo! Formi una frase con "fame" e "sete," ma non la faccia troppo corta.

16. Da lunedì, quando mi son preso un forte raffreddore, non ho più appetito. Stamane ho preso solamente una tazza di caffè. Non ho potuto prender nulla a colazione. (lu-ne-'di) ('for-te) (raf-fred-'do-re) (ap-pe-'ti-to) ('tat-tsa) (kaf-'fɛ)

17. Ebbene, non ha fame adesso? Non farebbe una piccola colazione con me?

18. La ringrazio infinitamente; non ho affatto fame; mi sarebbe impossibile mangiare un boccone. Ma mi favorisca un bicchiere d' acqua. Ho gran sete. (rin-'gra-tsjo) (af-'fat-to) (bok-'ko-ne) (bik-'kjɛ-re)

19. Formi alcune frasi con "voglia," "vergogna" e "paura." Son curioso di vedere come impiegherà queste parole. ('vɔ-ʎa) (ver-'gɔ-ɲa) (pa-'u-ra)

20. Ho voglia di fare un viaggio in Corsica, ma, se devo dirle il vero, ho paura di non avere il tempo di farlo. ('kɔr-si-ka)

10. With pleasure, but in order to derive the full benefit of the examples which I am going to give you, you ought to try and form a number of similar sentences at home and bring them to me for correction.

11. I will do so. I shall put the verbs of your sentences into different tenses and persons.

12. Very well! Now let us begin. What is the matter with you? You do not look well. (Lit.: have good appearance).

13. Now, form a similar sentence, but using the past tense.

14. I met your cousin, and to me he seemed very ill. What is the matter with him?

15. Very well! Form a sentence with "hunger" and "thirst," but don't make it too short.

16. Since last Monday, when I took a violent cold, I have lost all appetite. This morning I took only a cup of coffee. I could not eat anything at breakfast.

17. Well, do you not feel hungry now? Would you not take a light lunch with me?

18. No, thank you very much; I am not at all hungry, and could not eat a mouthful. But may I trouble you for a glass of water? I feel very thirsty.

19. Form some sentences with "inclination," "shame," and "fear." I am curious to see how you will use these words.

20. I have a good mind to take a journey to Corsica, but the truth is, I am afraid I haven't the time for it.

21. Lei dovrebbe avere vergogna di perdere l' occasione di visitare una tanto storica isola, patria di Napoleone. Se lei ha fretta, può andarvi in aeroplano. ('i-so-la) ('pa-trja) (na-po-le-'o-ne)

22. Ora Lei ha degli esempi sull' uso idiomatico del verbo "avere." Spero che li comprenda benissimo.

23. Oh! perfettamente. Ma mi dica un po', non si usa il verbo "avere" in altre espressioni? (pɔ)

24. Sì, si usa. Noi l' impieghiamo per esempio parlando dell' età delle persone. Così noi diciamo: "Che età ha?"—"Che età può avere sua sorella?"—"Non so esattamente che età abbia, ma penso che avrà ventuno o ventidue anni."—"Non credo che sia così vecchia." (e-'ta) (so-'rɛl-la) (e-sat-ta-'men-te) ('ab-bja) ('si-a) ('vɛk-kja)

25. Questo modo d' esprimersi esiste pure in ispagnuolo. (e-'spri-mer-si) (e-'si-ste) (i-spa-'ɲwɔ-lo)

26. Precisamente. Parlando di dimensioni in italiano si può far uso dei due ausiliari "essere" ed "avere." Per esempio: (pre-tʃi-sa-'men-te) (di-men-'sjo-ni)

27. "Questo fiume ha ottanta metri di larghezza e cinquanta metri di profondità." Oppure: "Questo fiume è largo ottanta metri e profondo cinquanta." ('fju-me) (lar-'get-tsa) (pro-fon-di-'ta)

28. Quali dimensioni ha questa stanza? Credo che abbia venticinque piedi di lunghezza, su quindici di larghezza. Ossia: Credo che sia lunga venticinque piedi e larga quindici. (lun-'get-tsa) (os-'si-a)

29. Non ha questa casa circa sessanta piedi d' altezza? Ne ha per lo meno ottanta. Od anche: Non è alta sessanta piedi questa casa? È alta per lo meno ottanta. (al-'tet-tsa)

30. Troverò tutti gli idiotismi nella grammatica? Amico mio, coi soli proverbi toscani il Giusti ha riempito un intero volume. Ne potremmo riempire uno assai più grande cogli idiotismi. Non è dunque possibile rinchiuderli tutti in una grammatica, nè sarebbe prudente farlo. Dovremo contentarci dei più essenziali che Lei procurerà di rendersi famigliari. (pro-'vɛr-bi) (to-'ska-ni) ('dʒu-sti) (rin-'kju-der-li) (es-sen-'tsja-li) (pro-ku-re-'ra)

21. You ought to be ashamed of missing the opportunity to visit such a historic island, the native country of Napoleon. If you are in a hurry you could go by plane.

22. Now, here you have some examples of the idiomatic use of "avere." I hope you understand them thoroughly.

23. Oh, perfectly. But tell me, don't you use the verb "avere" in other expressions?

24. Oh, yes, it is used; we employ it, for instance, when speaking of people's age. Thus we say: "How old are you?" "How old may his sister be?" "I do not know exactly how old she is, but I think she is twenty-one or twenty-two." "I do not think she is as old as that."

25. This mode of expression exists also in Spanish.

26. Quite so. In speaking of dimensions Italians may use both "essere" and "avere." For instance:

27. This river is eighty metres broad and fifty metres deep.

28. What are the dimensions of this room? I think it may be twenty-five feet long by fifteen wide.

29. This house is about sixty feet high, isn't it? It is at least eighty.

30. Will I find all these idioms in the grammar? My friend, Giusti has filled a volume with Tuscan proverbs only. A much larger one could be filled with Italian idioms. It is impossible to put them all into one grammar, nor would it be advisable to do so. We will have, therefore, to be satisfied with the most important ones with which you will try to make yourself familiar.

130

FRASE PRINCIPALE

(Continuazione)

Perchè aspetto un mio amico da Boston e devo restare a New York finchè egli arrivi in piroscafo o in treno o in autobus.

perchè (per-'ke)
aspetto (as-'spɛt-to)
un mio amico (un 'mi-o a-'mi-ko)
da Boston
e devo (e 'de-vo)
restare (re-'sta-re)
a New York
finchè (fin-'ke)
egli ('e-ʎi)
arrivi (ar-'ri-vi)
in piroscafo (in pi-'rɔ-ska-fo)
o in treno (o in 'trɛ-no)
o in autobus (o in 'aw-to-bus)

IL TEATRO—IL CINEMA—IL CONCERTO

(te-'a-tro) ('tʃi-ne-ma) (kon-'tʃer-to)

1. Perchè rimane a Livorno? La città non è attraente; vi sono poche cose notevoli. (ri-'ma-ne) (li-'vor-no) (tʃit-'ta) (at-tra-'ɛn-te) (no-'te-vo-li)

2. Non mi fermo a Livorno per quel che c' è da vedere, ma bensì perchè aspetto una persona dall' America. ('fer-mo) (bɛn-'si)

3. Chi aspetta?

4. Una giovane signora che arriverà probabilmente col primo vapore. ('dʒo-va-ne) (ar-ri-ve-'ra) (va-'po-re)

5. Una giovane signora! Molto interessante! Io la credevo ammogliata. (in-te-res-'san-te) (kre-'de-vo) (am-mo-'ʎa-ta)

6. Sono ammogliato infatti. La signora di cui si tratta è una mia parente. È mia cugina. (in-'fat-ti) (pa-'rɛn-te) (ku-'dʒi-na)

7. Ah! è altra cosa. Mi perdoni lo scherzo. ('sker-tso)

MAIN SENTENCE
(Continuation)

For I expect a friend from Boston, and I must stay in **New York** till he arrives by steamer or by train or by bus.

For
(I) expect
a friend (of mine)
from Boston,
and (I) must
stay
in New York
till
he
may arrive
by steamer
or by train
or by bus

THE THEATRE—THE MOVIES—THE CONCERT

1. Why do you stay in Livorno? This town is not very interesting; there are but few sights.

2. I do not remain in Livorno on account of the sights, but because I expect someone from America.

3. Whom do you expect?

4. A young lady who will probably arrive by the next steamer.

5. A young lady! That is very interesting! I thought you were married.

6. Certainly I am married. The lady is related to me. She is my cousin.

7. Oh, that is different. Please excuse my joking.

8. Non occorre (non è necessario) scusarsi d' un simil piccolo scherzo. Livorno è alquanto monotona e non so come far passare il tempo. (ok-'kor-re) (sku-'sar-si) ('si-mil) ('pik-ko-lo) (al-'kwan-to) (mo-'nɔ-to-na)

9. Che! Lei s' annoia! Perchè non va al teatro od al cinematografo od a qualche concerto? (san-'nɔ-ja) (tʃi-ne-ma-'tɔ-gra-fo) (kon-'tʃer-to)

10. Mi piacciono molto il teatro ed il cinema, e sarei felicissimo di andarci, ma temo di non capir nulla. ('pjat-tʃo-no) (sa-'rɛj) (fe-li-'tʃis-si-mo)

11. Allora perchè non frequenta i concerti? C' è quì una sala di concerti. Forse non le piace la musica? (fre-'kwɛn-ta) ('for-se) ('mu-si-ka)

12. Anzi, ne vado pazzo ed a Chicago solevo assistere regolarmente ogni sabato ai concerti sinfonici. ('pat-tso) (so-'le-vo) (as-'si-ste-re) (re-go-lar-'men-te) (sin-'fɔ-ni-tʃi)

13. Benone! allora venga con me questo dopo pranzo al concerto. L' orchestra di Guglielmo Strauss è quì in questo momento. (be-'no-ne) (al-'lo-ra) ('dɔ-po 'pran-dzo) (or-'ke-stra) (gu-'ʎɛl-mo)

14. È egli parente del celebre "Re del Valzer"? (pa-'rɛn-te) ('tʃe-le-bre)

15. Come Lei sa, Giovanni Strauss è morto da lungo tempo. Questo Guglielmo Strauss appartiene ad un' altra famiglia. ('ko-me) ('mɔr-to) ('lun-go) ('tɛm-po) ('kwe-sto) (ap-par-'tjɛ-ne) (fa-'mi-ʎa)

16. Ne è proprio sicuro? Sa che il "Re del Valzer" ebbe un figlio, il compositore del "Pipistrello"? ('prɔ-prjo) (si-'ku-ro) ('fi-ʎo) (kom-po-si-'to-re) (pi-pi-'strɛl-lo)

17. Sì. Ma suo figlio non diede mai concerti e non fece altro che comporre musica. ('dje-de) (maj) ('fe-tʃe) (kom-'por-re)

18. Giovanni Strauss aveva anche un fratello. (fra-'tɛl-lo)

8. You need not ask my pardon on account of your little joke. Livorno is quite tiresome, and I do not know how to kill time.

9. What! Are you so bored? Why do you not go to the theatre, the movies or to some concert?

10. I am passionately fond of the theatre and the movies and would gladly go, but I am afraid I should not understand anything.

11. Then why don't you attend concerts? There is a concert hall here. But perhaps you are not fond of music?

12. On the contrary, I am crazy about it, and in Chicago I used to attend the symphony concerts regularly every Saturday.

13. Very well; then accompany me this afternoon to the concert. Wilhelm Strauss' orchestra is here just now.

14. Is he a relative of the celebrated "Waltz King"?

15. As you know, Johann Strauss died a long time ago. This Wilhelm Strauss belongs to another family.

16. Are you really sure of it? Do you know that the "Waltz King" had a son, the composer of "The Bat"?

17. Yes. But his son never gave any concerts, and did nothing but write music.

18. Johann Strauss also had a brother.

134

19. Lo so. Eduardo Strauss, splendido direttore d' orchestra. (e-du-'ar-do) ('splɛn-di-do) (di-ret-'to-re)

20. Eduardo Strauss molti anni fa venne in America con la sua orchestra e fece un giro negli Stati Uniti. ('ven-ne) ('dʒi-ro) (u-'ni-ti)

21. Ho sentito dire, infatti, che egli e la sua orchestra interpretavano la musica da ballo meglio di qualsiasi altro musicista. (in-'fat-ti) (in-ter-pre-'ta-va-no) ('bal-lo) (kwal-'si-a-si) (mu-si-'tʃi-sta)

22. Ma ho inteso ed ho letto che come uomo non riusciva simpatico al pubblico. (in-'te-so) ('lɛt-to) ('wɔ-mo) (ri-u-'ʃi-va) (sim-'pa-ti-ko) ('pub-bli-ko)

23. Perchè? Nelle fotografie che ho visto di lui mi parve un bell' uomo, molto attraente. (fo-to-gra-'fi-e) ('par-ve)

24. È vero, ma appunto per questo non piaceva. ('ve-ro) (ap-'pun-to)

25. È una contradizione! Come la spiega Lei? (kon-tra-di-'tsjo-ne) ('spjɛ-ga)

26. Ebbene, la cosa mi sembra abbastanza chiara. Era avvenente e, come qualche altro bell' uomo, era anche vano (era affettato). ('sem-bra) (ab-ba-'stan-tsa) ('kja-ra) (av-ve-'nɛn-te) ('kwal-ke) ('va-no) (af-fet-'ta-to)

27. Ha ragione. Gli uomini avvenenti sono spesso vani e fatui più delle donne. Un fatuo m' è assolutamente insopportabile. ('fa-tu-i) (in-sop-por-'ta-bi-le)

28. Non lo sono meno per me; un uomo affettato non piace neppure a me. ('pja-tʃe) (nep-'pu-re)

29. Ed Eduardo Strauss non piaceva al pubblico? (pja-'tʃe-va)

19. I know it; Edward Strauss, a splendid orchestra conductor.

20. Edward Strauss many years ago came to America with his orchestra and made a tour through the United States.

21. I heard, indeed, that he and his band played dance music better than any other musicians.

22. But I heard and read that as a man he was not liked by (Lit.: did not succeed sympathetic to) the public.

23. Why? In the photographs which I have seen of him, he appeared to me as a handsome and very attractive man.

24. He was, indeed, but that was exactly the reason why he was disliked.

25. But that is a contradiction. How do you explain it?

26. Well, the matter seems pretty obvious to me. He was handsome and, like some other handsome men, he was also conceited.

27. There you are right. Handsome men are frequently more vain and conceited than women, and a conceited man is absolutely unbearable to me.

28. They are no less so to me; a vain man does not appeal to me either.

29. And Edward Strauss did not appeal to the public?

30. Egli era antipatico a molti. Quando dirigeva l' orchestra ballava e smaniava come un saltamartino. (an-ti-'pa-ti-ko) (bal-'la-va) (sma-'nja-va) (sal-ta-mar-'ti-no)

31. A proposito, mi saprebbe spiegare la differenza che corre (che passa, che c' è) tra **vano**, aggettivo, e **vano**, sostantivo? (pro-'pɔ-si-to) (dif-fe-'rɛn-tsa) ('kor-re) (ad-dʒet-'ti-vo) (so-stan-'ti-vo)

32. No, non ne so niente. Queste due parole si pronunciano e si scrivono nello stesso modo. ('njɛn-te) (pro-'nun-tʃa-no) ('skri-vo-no) ('stes-so)

33. C' è la stessa differenza che si scorge tra **bello**, aggettivo, **e** **bello**, sostantivo. (tʃɛ) ('skor-dʒe)

34. Lo comprendo, ma vorrei vederne l' applicazione pratica. Io bramo sempre esser sicuro di quanto imparo. (ap-pli-ka-'tsjo-ne) ('pra-ti-ka) ('bra-mo)

35. È mera (pura, semplice) curiosità, od un desiderio vivo e sincero d' istruirsi? ('me-ra) ('sem-pli-tʃe) (ku-rjo-si-'ta) (de-si-'dɛ-rjo) (sin-'tʃɛ-ro) (i-stru-'ir-si)

36. No, non son curioso. (ku-'rjo-so)

37. Dice forse sua moglie lo stesso parlando di Lei? A mio parere (al parer mio) gli uomini sono curiosi quanto le donne. ('mo-ʎe) (pa-'re-re) ('wɔ-mi-ni) ('dɔn-ne)

38. Parlando in generale, Lei ha ragione; ma per ciò che mi spetta, non è certamente il caso. ('spɛt-ta)

39. Non c' è regola senza eccezione. (et-tʃet-'tsjo-ne)

40. È forse un proverbio francese? Mi piace più del nostro. (pro-'vɛr-bjo)

41. Sì, ha almeno più senso. Il proverbio inglese è una vera assurdità. Come mai l' eccezione può provare la regola? (as-sur-di-'ta) (maj)

30. He was distasteful to many. While leading the orchestra he danced and was as jittery as a jack-in-the-box.

31. By the way, could you explain to me the difference between "vano" used as an adjective, and "vano" used as a noun?

32. No, I don't know anything about it; these two words are pronounced and written in the same way.

33. There is exactly the same difference between them as between "bello" as an adjective and "bello" as a noun.

34. I understand, but I should like to see the practical application. I always like to be sure of what I learn.

35. Is it mere [pure, simple] curiosity, or a keen and sincere desire to learn?

36. No, I am not curious.

37. Does your wife say that, too, about you? In my opinion men are just as curious as women.

38. Generally speaking, you are right; but as far as I am concerned, it is really not true.

39. Well, there are exceptions to every rule.

40. Is that a French proverb? I like it better than ours.

41. Yes, there is at least more sense in it. The English proverb seems to be absolute nonsense. How can the exception prove the rule?

42. Non discutiamo se si tratti di un' assurdità o meno [o no]. Non mi piaccion le discussioni. Preferisco che mi dia degli esempi sulla parola "vano" usata aggettivamente e sostantivamente.

43. Le discussioni non piaccion molto nemmeno a me. A che approdano? (ap-'prɔ-da-no)

44. A nulla affatto nella maggior parte dei casi, specialmente quando la discussione si riferisce alla politica od alla religione. (ri-fe-'ri-ʃe) (po-'li-ti-ka) (re-li-'dʒo-ne)

45. Sono soggetti (argomenti) questi, che, come regola, meno si toccano meglio è. (sod-'dʒɛt-ti) (ar-go-'men-ti) ('tɔk-ka-no)

46. È così pure la mia opinione.

47. Sfortunatamente non tutti condividono il nostro punto di vista ed in certo modo molti godono a disputare su questi argomenti. (sfor-tu-na-ta-'men-te) ('tʃɛr-to) ('mɔ-do) ('gɔ-do-no) (di-spu-'ta-re)

48. Sarebbe meglio lasciare tali discussioni ai politicanti ed a coloro che hanno le responsabilità politiche dei paesi. (la-'ʃa-re) (po-li-ti-'kan-ti) (re-spon-sa-bi-li-'ta) (po-'li-ti-ke) (pa-'e-si)

49. Di certo. Se ognuno pensasse soltanto ai propri affari e si tenesse lontano da tutte le discussioni inutili, si potrebbero evitare molti fastidii e malintesi. (o-'ɲu-no) (pen-'sas-se) (af-'fa-ri) (te-'nes-se) (i-'nu-ti-li) (fa-'sti-di) (ma-lin-'te-si)

50. Debbo aggiungere che praticando simili principii rafforzeremmo quello spirito di reciproca tolleranza e comprensione, che è tanto consigliabile se desideriamo di vivere in pace e concordia con tutti. ('deb-bo) (ad-'dʒun-dʒe-re) (pra-ti-'kan-do) ('si-mi-li) (prin-'tʃi- pi) (raf-for-tse-'rem-mo) ('spi-ri-to) (re-'tʃi-pro-ka) (tol-le-'ran-tsa) (kom-pren-'sjo-ne) (kon-si-'ʎa-bi-le) (de-si-de-'rja-mo) ('vi-ve-re) ('pa-tʃe) (kon-'kɔr-dja)

42. Let's not argue whether it is nonsense or not. I am not fond of disputations. I prefer that you give me some examples on the word "vano" used as an adjective and as a noun.

43. I am not particularly fond of disputations myself. What do they lead to?

44. In most cases to nothing at all, especially when the dispute refers to politics or religion.

45. These are subjects about which, as a rule, the less said the better it is.

46. That is also my opinion.

47. Unfortunately all people do not share our viewpoint and in some way many enjoy arguing about such matters.

48. It would be better to leave such discussions to the politicians and those who have the political responsibilities of their countries.

49. Certainly. If everybody would only mind his own business and keep clear of all useless disputes, many troubles and misunderstandings would be avoided.

50. I must add that by applying such principles we would strengthen that spirit of mutual tolerance and understanding which is so highly desirable if we want to live in peace and harmony with everybody.

140

VOCABOLARIO	VOCABULARY
Il Biglietto	**The Ticket**
L' ufficio dei biglietti	The ticket office
Può dirmi dov' è l' ufficio dei biglietti?	Can you tell me where the ticket office is?
Per favore, dove posso ottenere il biglietto? Dove si prende (piglia) il biglietto?	Where do I get my ticket, please?
La seconda porta a destra	Second door right
Da questo lato, da questa parte	On this side
Dirimpetto; di faccia; dal lato opposto	Right opposite; straight before you; on the opposite side
Favorisca darmi un biglietto per Londra.	Please give me a ticket for London.
Un biglietto di prima classe	A first class ticket
Un biglietto di seconda classe	A second class ticket
Un biglietto di terza classe	A third class ticket
Vuole un biglietto di prima o di seconda?	Do you want a first or a second class ticket?
Il biglietto di ritorno; di andata e ritorno	The return ticket; the round trip ticket
Per quanto tempo valgono i biglietti di ritorno? Per quanto tempo son valevoli i biglietti di ritorno?	How long are return tickets good?
I biglietti circolari son valevoli per un mese.	Round trip tickets are good for a month.
Può darmi un biglietto per Parigi?	Can you give me a ticket for Paris?

Quanto costa un biglietto da quì a Berlino?	How much is a ticket from here to Berlin?
Il facchino, il portinaio	The porter, the doorman
Facchino, consegnate i miei bauli.	Porter, please check my baggage.
Quanti capi ha?	How many pieces have you?
Il baule	The trunk
La valigia	The bag
La cappelliera	The hat-box
Abbiate cura della mia cappelliera.	Be careful with my hat-box.
Lo scontrino	The baggage check
Favorisca darmi il suo biglietto; le porterò subito lo scontrino.	Please give me your ticket; I will bring you your baggage check at once.
Il bagaglio gratis	The free baggage
A quanti chili si ha diritto?	How much baggage is allowed free?
Le ferrovie italiane accordano solo cento cinquanta libbre.	Italian railroads allow only one hundred and fifty pounds of baggage free.
Il peso	The weight
Il soprappeso	The excess weight
Ho soprappeso?	Have I any excess weight?
Lei ha per mille lire di soprappeso.	You have one thousand lire excess weight.
Non si può viaggiare in Italia con molto bagaglio; costa troppo.	People cannot travel with much baggage in Italy; it is too expensive.

Scusi, dov' è la sala d' aspetto?	Pardon me, where is the waiting-room?
Le porte s' aprono dieci minuti prima della partenza del treno.	The gates open ten minutes before the train leaves.
Il buffè	The buffet

Fare un Viaggio (un Giro) in Ferrovia.	**To Take a Railway Trip**
Il viaggiatore	The traveler, the passenger
Partenza!	All aboard!
Il treno espresso, l' espresso Il treno diretto, il diretto	The express train
Il treno lampo	The lightning express
Il treno merci	The freight train
Il treno speciale	The special train
Il treno postale	The mail train
È l' espresso per Parigi?	Is this the Paris express?
Il conduttore	The conductor
Partire	To leave; to start
Il treno parte fra un minuto	The train leaves in a minute.
Montiamo; il treno sta per partire.	Let us get in; the train is going to leave.
È tempo di salire in vettura.	It is time to get in.
Il vagone, la vettura.	The railway car
Il compartimento	The compartment
Il posto	The seat

Per Pigliare un Posto	To Take a Seat
Posso montar quì?	Can I get in here?
Tutti i posti son presi.	All seats are taken.
Questo posto è preso.	This seat is engaged.
È libero questo posto?	Is this seat disengaged?
È libero questo posto? No, è preso.	Is this seat free? No, it is taken.
Mi serbi questo posto.	Retain this seat for me.
Ho riservato questo posto.	I reserved this seat.
Perdoni, questo è il mio posto.	Pardon me, this is my seat.
Dobbiam cambiare di posto?	Must we change seats?
Non può farsi in là un po'? Siam troppo stretti.	Can you move a little further? We are sitting very close.
Sono dispostissimo a cambiar di posto.	I am quite willing to change seats.
È seduta comodamente?	Are you comfortably seated?
C' è un posticino libero?	Is there a free spot?
Mi potrebbe dare tutt' un sedile per me solo, conduttore?	Can you give me a whole side (bench) to myself, conductor?
Vorrei poter dormire a mio bell' agio.	I should like to sleep comfortably.
Completo!	Quite full!
Tutto il compartimento è preso.	All the seats in this compartment are taken.
Scusi, ma c' è posto ancora per un' altra persona.	Pardon me, but there is still one seat vacant.

Non mi piacerebbe di dover rimaner indietro.

It would inconvenience me to stay behind.

Conduttore, questi signori non mi voglion lasciar entrare, eppure vi sono ancora due posti liberi, [disponibili].

Conductor, these gentlemen will not allow me to get in, and there are still two vacant seats.

Vi sono dei compartimenti per fumatori?

Are there smoking compartments?

Fumare, Il fumo

To smoke, the smoke

Fuma?

Do you smoke?

PART SEVEN

CONTENTS

FRASE PRINCIPALE

Lei non avrebbe dovuto uscire con questo tempo variabile senza le Sue soprascarpe. In conseguenza della sua trascuraggine Lei s' è raffreddata e sarà obbligata a restare in casa per qualche tempo prima di poter continuare il suo viaggio.

PRONUNCIA

Lɛj non a-'vreb-be do-'vu-to u-'ʃi-re kon 'kwes-to 'tɛm-po va-'rja-bi-le 'sɛn-tsa le 'su-e so-pra-'skar-pe. In kon-se-'gwɛn-tsa 'del-la 'su-a tra-sku-'rad-dʒi-ne lɛj sɛ raf-fred-'da-ta e sa-'ra ob-bli-'ga-ta a re-'sta-re in 'ka-sa per 'kwal-ke 'tɛm-po 'pri-ma di po-'ter kon-ti-'nwa-re il 'su-o 'vjad-dʒo.

Lei non avrebbe dovuto uscire con questo tempo variabile senza le sue soprascarpe.

Lei non avrebbe dovuto
uscire
con
questo tempo variabile
senza
le sue soprascarpe

1. Perchè è uscita con questo tempaccio senza le sue soprascarpe? Non avrebbe dovuto farlo. (tem-'pat-tʃo)

2. Non l' avrei fatto se non avessi creduto che il tempo si rischiari-rebbe. (kre-'du-to) (ri-skja-ri-'reb-be)

3. Come ha potuto crederlo? Il tempo è sempre stato così brutto in tutti questi giorni. ('brut-to)

4. Sì, quest' anno la stagione è stata abbastanza cattiva; ciò non ostante ho creduto che si schiarirebbe. (sta-'dʒo-ne) (skja-ri-'reb-be)

5. È un errore, mio caro signore. Lei non sa ancora quanto sia incostante il nostro clima. (er-'ro-re) (in-ko-'stan-te)

6. Ho sempre sentito dire che in Italia il clima era assai bello e secondo le previsioni ho creduto che certamente si volesse rasserenare. (pre-vi-'sjo-ni) (vo-'les-se) (ras-se-re-'na-re)

MAIN SENTENCE

You ought not to have gone out without your overshoes in this
changeable weather. In consequence of your carelessness you have
contracted a cold and will be obliged to remain at home for some
time before you are able to continue your journey.

You ought not to have gone out without your overshoes in this
    changeable weather.

You ought not to have
go out
with
this variable weather
without
your rubbers.

1. Why did you go out in this stormy weather without your overshoes? You ought not to have done that.

2. I would not have done so if I had not thought the weather
   would clear.

3. How could you have supposed such a thing? The weather has
   been fearful for days.

4. Yes, this year the season has been bad enough. Nevertheless I
   thought it would clear.

5. An erroneous supposition, my dear sir. You do not yet know how
   changeable is our climate.

6. I always heard that in Italy the climate was very fine, and,
   according to the weather reports, I supposed that it was surely
   going to clear.

7. Le previsioni? È pure Lei del numero di coloro che credono alle predizioni sul tempo? (pre-di-'tsjo-ni)

8. In generale non son credulo, ed in verità mi dispiace d' essermi lasciato ingannare questa volta dalle previsioni. ('kre-du-lo) (la-'ʃa-to)

9. Sì, Lei non avrebbe dovuto crederci. S' è lasciata ingannare. ('kre-der-tʃi) (in-gan-'na-re)

10. È probabile che resteremo in casa tutto il dopopranzo. Guardi come piove! (dɔ-po-'pran-dzo)

11. Sì, piove a catinelle. È inutile pensare ad uscire con questo tempo spaventevole. Questo tempo è noioso, è stucchevole. (ka-ti-'nɛl-le) (no-'jo-so) (stuk-'ke-vo-le)

12. Certamente! Che direbbe d' una giterella in automobile? (dʒi-te-'rɛl-la) (aw-to-'mɔ-bi-le)

13. Mi creda. Rimanga in casa. Veda come lampeggia! (lam-'ped-dʒa)

14. Sì, comincia a tuonare. Mio Dio, che scoppio di tuono! Deve aver colpito quì vicino. (two-'na-re) ('skɔp-pjo)

15. Che c' è? Un' automobile dinanzi alla nostra porta con questo tempo? Chi può essere?

16. Se non m' inganno (se non isbaglio, se non erro) è il Suo compatriotta, il signor N. (kom-pa-tri-'ɔt-ta)

17. Che cosa lo può condurre quì con questo tempo spaventevole? Ah, eccolo! (spa-ven-'te-vo-le)

18. Mio caro Luigi, che ti conduce quì con questo cattivo tempo? Sei bagnato (inzuppato) fino alla midolla. (ba-'ɲa-to) (in-tsup-'pa-to) (mi-'dol-la)

19. Non ho fatto altro che attraversare la via per prendere un tassì (per prendere a nolo, per noleggiare un tassì) ed in questi pochi momenti mi sono inzuppato fino alla midolla. (at-tra-ver-'sa-re) ('nɔ-lo) (no-led-'dʒa-re)

7. The weather reports? Do you belong to those who believe in weather prophecies?

8. Generally I am not credulous, and I only regret that this time I allowed myself to be misled by the forecasts.

9. Yes, you ought not to have believed them. You let yourself be misled.

10. Most likely we shall have to stay in all afternoon. Just look how it rains.

11. Yes, it is really pouring. It is useless to think about going out in this fearful weather. This weather is boring.

12. Certainly. What would you say about a short drive in a car?

13. Believe me. Stay at home. Just see how it lightens!

14. Yes, and now it's starting to thunder. Goodness, what a clap of thunder! That must have struck near by!

15. What is that? An automobile in this storm at our door! Who can that be?

16. If I am not mistaken, it is your fellow-countryman, Mr. N.

17. What can bring him here in this dreadful weather? Ah, here he is!

18. My dear Louis, what brings you here in this dreadful weather? And you are wet to the bone! (Lit.: marrow)

19. I only went across the street to get a taxi and in those few minutes I got wet through and through.

20. Tu dovresti mutar vestito immediatemente, se non vuoi arrischiare di cogliere una polmonite. (ar-ri-'skja-re) ('kɔ-ʎe-re) (pol-mo-'ni-te)

21. Vieni subito a spogliarti nella mia stanza. (spo-'ʎar-ti)

22. Venivo a portarti un invito. Il nostro comune amico, il signor P., ti manda i suoi saluti e . . . (por-'tar-ti) (in-'vi-to)

23. Perdonami se t' interrompo, ma la tua salute importa assai più d' un invito. Vieni prima a mutar vestito e mi dirai in seguito quel chi ti conduce qui. (in-ter-'rom-po) ('se-gwi-to)

24. Come vuoi. Non mi raffreddo così facilmente come lo credi. (raf-'fred-do)

25. Ecco tutto l'occorrente. Per fortuna abbiamo la medesima statura. Questi vestiti ti staranno a pennello. (ok-kor-'rɛn-te) (sta-'tu-ra) (pen-'nɛl-lo)

26. Togliti dunque subito i vestiti bagnati e mettiti i miei. Appena sarai vestito chiamerò il cameriere col campanello. Egli farà asciugare i tuoi vestiti. ('tɔ-ʎi-ti) ('dun-kwe) ('su-bi-to) (ap-'pe-na)

FRASE PRINCIPALE

(Continuazione)

In conseguenza della sua trascuraggine Lei s' è raffreddata.

In conseguenza della
sua trascuraggine
Lei s' è
raffreddata

1. Qual è il tema della lezione d' oggi? ('tɛ-ma)

2. Nella lezione d' oggi parleremo delle malattie e della salute; tema (soggetto) importantissimo. (ma-lat-'ti-e)

3. Assai probabilmente la conversazione ci condurrà ad impiegare (ad usare) nuove espressioni. (kon-dur-'ra)

20. You must change your clothes at once or you will catch pneumonia.

21. Come at once and undress in my room.

22. I come to bring you an invitation. Our mutual friend, Mr. P., sends his regards, and . . .

23. Pardon me for interrupting you, but your health is of greater importance than any invitation. First come and change your clothes, and then tell me what brings you here.

24. Just as you like. But I really do not take cold as easily as you imagine.

25. Here is everything you need. Fortunately we are of the same size and these clothes will fit you perfectly.

26. Take off your damp clothes at once and put on mine. As soon as you are dressed I will ring for the valet. He will see that your clothes are dried.

MAIN SENTENCE

(Continuation)

In consequence of your carelessness you have taken cold.

In consequence of
your carelessness
you have taken
cold.

1. What is the subject of to-day's lesson?

2. In today's lesson we will talk about diseases and health—a most important subject.

3. And the conversation will probably lead us to use many new expressions.

4. Senza dubbio. Orsù, cominciamo subito. Come sta oggi? (Come state oggi? Come stai oggi?) Lei mi sembra stanca e sofferente. ('stan-ka) (sof-fe-'rɛn-te)

5. Non sto troppo bene (non mi sento troppo bene). Credo d' essermi raffreddato ier sera nell' uscir di teatro. ('dɛs-ser-mi)

6. Sono spiacentissimo di sentir questo. Non aveva forse le soprascarpe? (spja-tʃen-'tis-si-mo)

7. Disgraziatamente no. Il tempo era così bello quando son partito per il teatro che non pensai nè a soprascarpe nè ad ombrello. (om-'brɛl-lo)

8. Lei ha un brutto raffreddore. Sembra proprio che abbia preso un brutto raffreddore. ('brut-to)

9. Infatti mi son preso un gran raffreddore. (in-'fat-ti)

10. Spero che sia solo un raffreddore. Sia prudente, porti vestiti pesanti, perchè nel nostro clima incostante un raffreddore può avere serie conseguenze. ('sɛ-rje)

11. È vero, in avvenire (d' ora in poi, d' ora innanzi) avrò maggior cura di me stesso. La gola mi fa male. ('go-la)

12. Se io fossi in Lei (nel suo caso) consulterei senza indugio (subito) un buon medico. La Sua voce è rauca. (in-'du-dʒo) ('raw-ka)

13. Un po' (poco) di raucedine non è niente, me ne libero facilmente, ma il mal di gola mi rende nervoso. (raw-'tʃɛ-di-ne)

14. Credo proprio che La sto rendendo nervosa, il che non era la mia intenzione. All' opposto, io desideravo solo avvertirla di non trascurare il suo raffreddore. ('prɔ-prjo) (av-ver-'tir-la)

15. Oh no! non divento nervoso così facilmente. Nondimeno seguirò il suo consiglio; consulterò un buon medico. (non-di-'me-no) (se-gwi-'rɔ)

4. Without doubt. Now let us begin at once. How are you to-day? It seems to me you are looking tired and ill.

5. I am not very well. I think I took cold last night on leaving the theatre.

6. I am very sorry indeed to hear that. Didn't you wear your over-shoes?

7. I am sorry to say I did not. The weather was so delightful when I started for the theatre that the thought of overshoes or umbrella never occurred to me.

8. You have a bad cold. You seem to have caught a really bad cold.

9. Yes, I have caught a miserable cold.

10. I trust it is nothing but a cold. Be sure to be careful and dress warmly, for a cold in our changeable climate may have serious consequences.

11. Quite true, and I will take better care of myself in future. My throat pains me.

12. If I were in your place, I would consult a good physician at once. Your voice is quite hoarse.

13. A little hoarseness is nothing, for I easily get rid of it; but the pain in my throat makes me uneasy.

14. I really believe I am making you nervous, which was not my intention. On the contrary, I only wished to warn you not to neglect your cold.

15. Oh, no, I do not get nervous as easily as that. Nevertheless I shall follow your advice and consult a good physician.

FRASE PRINCIPALE

(*Conclusione*)

Sarà obbligata a restare in casa per qualche tempo prima di poter continuare il suo viaggio.

Sarà obbligata a
restare in casa
per qualche tempo
prima di poter
continuare
il suo viaggio.

1. Vorrei consultarla, signor dottore. Da ier sera non mi sentɛ troppo bene, ed ho paura (temo) d' ammalarmi seriamente.

2. Che ha?

3. Ho creduto dapprima di avere un forte raffreddore. Ma da questɛ mattina sento dei dolori atroci nella gola e m' è difficile il respirare (dap-'pri-ma) (a-'trɔ-tʃi)

4. Ha osservato altri sintomi? ('sin-to-mi)

5. Mi sento tutte le membra rotte ed i miei piedi così pesanti da potermi a stento trascinare. ('mem-bra) (tra-ʃi-'na-re)

6. E la testa?

7. Mi sento la testa pesante, però non posso dire d' aver mal di capo.

8. E l' appetito?

9. Non ho appetito affato. Mi feci violenza per prendere un tazza di caffè, e non ho mangiato nulla oggi. (vjo-'lɛn-tsa)

10. Ha la tosse?—Ho cominciato a tossire un' ora fa. ('tos-se) (tos-'si-re)

11. Le fa male?

12. Sì, specialmente al petto, o piuttosto ai bronchi. (pjut-'tɔ-sto) ('bron-ki)

MAIN SENTENCE

(Conclusion)

You will have to keep to your room for some time before you can continue your journey.

You will be obliged to
stay in house
for some time
before you are able
to continue
your journey.

1. I would like to consult you, doctor. Since last evening I haven't felt too well, and I am afraid I shall be seriously ill.

2. What is the matter with you?

3. At first I fancied I had a bad cold. Since this morning, however, I feel violent pains in my throat, and my breathing has become troublesome.

4. Have you noticed any other symptoms?

5. I feel as if all my limbs were broken, and my feet feel so heavy that I can scarcely drag myself along.

6. And how is your head?

7. My head feels heavy, but cannot say I have a headache.

8. And your appetite?

9. I have no appetite at all. I really had to force myself to take a cup of coffee, and I have not eaten anything to-day.

10. Do you cough? I began coughing an hour ago.

11. Is it painful? (Lit.: Does it make pain to you?)

12. Yes, especially here in the chest, or rather in the bronchial tubes.

13. Si metta a sedere dinanzi alla finestra, affinchè possa esaminarla alla luce. (fi-'nɛ-stra) (af-fin-'ke) ('lu-tʃe)

14. Mi faccia vedere (mi mostri) la lingua; la metta fuori di più. ('lin-gwa) ('met-ta)

15. La sua lingua è molto carica (sporca, bianca). Quando s' è raffreddata? ('ka-ri-ka) ('spɔr-ka)

16. L' altra notte, credo. Sono andato dal teatro a casa mia senza sporascarpe nè soprabito.

17. Che! L' altra notte con quello spaventoso temporale? Come ha` potuto commettere una simile imprudenza?

18. Faceva un caldo soffocante nel teatro. La sala era affollata; non c' era un sol posto vacante. (sof-fo-'kan-te) (af-fol-'la-ta)

19. Fui ben felice di poter uscire all' aperto. Sentivo il bisogno di pigliare un po' fresco prima di rientrare. (di tornare a casa.) (ri-en-'tra-re)

20. Fu una vera imprudenza, di cui non l' avrei mai creduta capace. Perchè non ha preso un tassì? (ka-'pa-tʃe)

21. Volevo rinfrescarmi, come le ho detto.

22. Ella si mostrò molto imprudente. Favorisca levarsi il panciotto (il gilè). Voglio esaminarle i polmoni. (pan-'tʃɔt-to) (dʒi-'lɛ)

23. Ella mi fa paura (mi spaventa), dottore. Voglio sperare che i miei polmoni non siano intaccati (offesi). (spa-'vɛn-ta) (in-tak-'ka-ti)

24. Spero di no, ma devo esaminarli con gran cura. Vediamo, respiri fortemente.

13. Please take a seat in front of the window, so that I may have a good light for my examination. (Lit.: examine you in the light.)

14. Show me your tongue. Put it out a little further.

15. Your tongue is very much coated. When did you take cold?

16. The night before last, I think. I went home from the theatre without overshoes or overcoat.

17. What! The night before last in that frightful storm! How could you have been guilty of such indiscretion?

18. It was stiflingly hot in the theatre. The house was packed; not a single seat was vacant.

19. I was glad to get out in the fresh air. I felt the need of cooling off a little on my way home.

20. That was a piece of carelessness of which I really did not think you capable. Why did you not take a taxi?

21. I wanted to cool off, as I told you.

22. You were very careless. Please take off your vest. I want to examine your lungs.

23. You frighten me, doctor. I trust my lungs are not affected.

24. I hope not, but I have to examine them carefully. Now take a deep breath.

25. Oh! come mi duole (mi fa male)!—Dove? Mi faccia veder dove. ('dwɔ-le)

26. Bene, respiri un' altra volta; respiri il più profondamente che può.

27. Si volti, perchè le possa esaminare la schiena. ('skjɛ-na)

28. È cosa seria, dottore? ('sɛ-rja)

29. Glielo dirò fra un momento, appena avrò finito di esaminarla.

30. Come dorme?—Malissimo, non mi riposo.

31. Ha molta sete?—Sì, avevo molta sete ed ho bevuto molt' acqua. ('se-te)

32. Come è il polso?—Il Suo polso è molto agitato. Lei ha la febbre. ('pol-so) (a-dʒi-'ta-to)

33. Tenga quest' istrumento in bocca per alcuni minuti. Voglio sapere come è la Sua respirazione. (i-stru-'men-to)

34. Lei ha una bronchite. Ritorni a casa immediatamente e si corichi. È venuta a piedi? (bron-'ki-te) ('ko-ri-ki)

35. No, in tassì.—Voglio sperare che non fosse un tassì aperto?— Oh! no; era assai ben chiuso. ('kju-so)

36. Ha agito con senno. Eviti le correnti d' aria ed il freddo. Le darò una ricetta. Pigli regolarmente ogni due ore questa medicina. ('sen-no) ('ɛ-vi-ti) (ri-'tʃɛt-ta) ('pi-ʎi)

37. Non si fermi per via, ma ritorni a casa direttamente. ('fer-mi)

38. Devo mettermi a letto? ('lɛt-to)

25. Oh, how it hurts!—Where? Show me where.

26. Well, now take another breath; breathe as deep as you can.

27. And now turn around, so that I can examine your back.

28. Is it serious, doctor?

29. I will tell you in a few minutes, as soon as I am through examining you.

30. How do you sleep?—Badly; I get no rest.

31. Do you feel very thirsty? Yes, I have been quite thirsty, and have been drinking a great deal of water.

32. Let me feel your pulse. Your pulse is very fast. You have a fever.

33. Now keep this instrument for a few minutes in your mouth. I want to know how your respiration is.

34. You have an attack of bronchitis. Go home at once and go to bed. Did you walk here?

35. No, I came in a taxi.—Not in an open one, I trust.—Oh, no, it was tightly closed.

36. That was sensible. Avoid any draught or cold. I shall give you a prescription. Take this medicine punctually every two hours.

37. Do not stop on your way, but go home at once.

38. Do I have to go to bed?

39. Le ho già detto di coricarsi senza indugio. Dovrà starsene nella sua stanza per parecchi giorni, perchè le bronchiti nel nostro clima non son cose da nulla. (in-'du-dʒo) ('star-se-ne)

40. Allora sono seriamente ammalato?

41. Oh! non tanto. Ma La devo avvertire che deve rimanere in letto per una settimana almeno. (av-ver-'ti-re)

42. Quando potrò dunque continuare il mio viaggio? (po-'trɔ)

43. Dipenderà dalle circostanze. Anzi tutto deve sbarazzarsi (liberarsi) dalla febbre. In ogni modo deve far conto di rimaner quì almeno una quindicina. (kwin-di-'tʃi-na)

44. Quando verrà a trovarmi (a visitarmi)?

45. Adesso sono le dodici e un quarto. Ricevo visite fino alle due; ho tre ammalati, che non stanno bene, da visitare. (a-'dɛs-so)

46. Lei sembra molto occupata.—Sfortunatamente sì; al presente vi sono molti ammalati in città. (sfor-tu-na-ta-'men-te)

47. Quando posso sperare di rivederla?

48. Verrò senza fallo fra le quattro e le cinque. Frattanto pigli la medicina che le ho prescritto, una cucchiaiata ogni due ore. (kuk-kja-'ja-ta)

49. Abbia cura di avere sempre la stessa temperatura nella Sua stanza. Si faccia accendere il calorifero. (at-'tʃen-de-re) (ka-lo-'ri-fe-ro)

50. Si tenga al caldo ed eviti di raffreddarsi. Sarò da Lei fra le quattro e le cinque. Arrivederla, spero che starà presto meglio.

39. I told you already that you will have to go to bed at once. You will have to keep to your room for several days, for bronchitis in our climate is not to be trifled with.

40. Then I am seriously ill?

41. Not dangerously so. But I must tell you that you will have to stay in bed for a week at least.

42. When may I continue my journey?

43. That depends on circumstances. In the first place you must get rid of your fever. At any rate, you must be prepared to spend at least a fortnight here.

44. When will you call on me?

45. It is now a quarter past twelve. My office hours last till two. I have three patients to visit who are not well.

46. You seem to be very busy.—Unfortunately so. There is at present much sickness in town.

47. And when may I expect to see you again?

48. I will come between four and five, without fail. In the meanwhile, take the medicine I have prescribed for you; a spoonful every two hours.

49. Be careful always to have an even temperature in your room. Have them light the heater.

50. Keep yourself warm and avoid catching cold. I will be with you between four and five. Good-bye. I trust you will soon be better.

162

VOCABOLARIO	VOCABULARY
Mi permette d' accendere un sigaro?	Will you allow me to light a cigar?
Faccia il suo comodo, signore. Faccia, faccia pure, signore.	Go right ahead, sir.
Posso offrirle un sigaro?	May I offer you a cigar?
La disturba il fumo?	Does smoking bother you?
Il fumo mi è insopportabile.	I cannot endure tobacco-smoke
È permesso fumare?	Is smoking permitted?
Proibito di fumare.	Smoking is prohibited.
Mi farebbe una gran gentilezza se volesse rinunciare a fumare. Non posso sopportare il fumo.	You would greatly oblige me by leaving off smoking. I cannot endure the smell of tobacco

La Finestra	The Window
Apra la finestra.	Open the window.
Chiuda la finestra.	Shut the window.
La corrente d' aria	The draught
C' è una corrente d' aria.	There is a draught.
Sente la corrente d' aria quando apro la finestra?	Do you feel the draught when I open the window?
C' è una corrente d' aria assai forte; la lasci socchiusa.	There is a great draught here; leave it open just a little.
Il vento soffia da tutte le parti.	The wind blows from all sides.
Il sole risplende; abbasserò le cortine.	The sun is shining; I will lower the curtains.
La polvere	The dust

C' è molta polvere.

It is very dusty.

C' è tanta polvere; favorisca chiudere la finestra.

There is so much dust; please shut the window.

La Stazione

The Station

Che stazione è?

What station is this?

Ha inteso il nome che ha detto il conduttore?

Did you catch the name the conductor called out?

Conduttore, dove siamo?

Conductor, where are we?

È ancora molto lontana la prossima stazione?

Is it still very far to the next station?

A che stazione si può fare una buona colazione?

At what station is there a chance of getting a good breakfast?

Un vagone letto

A sleeping-car

Fermare

To Stop

Quanto tempo si ferma il treno quì?

How long does the train stop here?

Conduttore, quando ci fermiamo per pranzare?

Conductor, when do we stop for dinner?

Quanto ci fermeremo quì?

How long do we stop here?

Quanto tempo ci fermeremo alla prossima stazione?

How long do we stop at the next station?

Dove ci fermeremo un po' di più?

Where do we stop a little longer?

Perchè ci fermiamo?

Why are we stopping?

Quanto tempo ci fermeremo a Pisa?

How long do we stop at Pisa?

Milano! Ci fermeremo cinque minuti quì.

Milan! We stop five minutes here.

Cambiare di Vettura

Devo cambiare di vettura?

Mi mostri il suo biglietto, per favore.

No, Lei non cambia; questo treno va direttamente a Roma.

Lei dovrà cambiare a Firenze.

Questo treno ha coincidenza a Firenze?

Dove va? A Roma.

Dovrà aspettare quattro ore a Firenze.

Lei avrebbe dovuto cambiare a Milano; là hanno luogo le coincidenze.

Il treno ha mancato la coincidenza.

Il Confine

Abbiamo già passato il confine?

La dogana, il dazio

Dov' è la dogana?

Dove ha luogo la visita doganale?

È minuziosa la visita?

Si esaminano i bagagli sul battello, o a terra dopo lo sbarco?

Dove si devono portare i bagagli per la visita della dogana?

To Change Cars

Do I have to change cars?

Show me your ticket, please.

No, you do not change; this train goes directly to Rome.

You must change cars at Florence.

Does this train make connections in Florence?

Where are you going? To Rome.

You will have to wait four hours in Florence.

You should have changed at Milan; the trains make connections there.

The train has missed connection.

The Frontier

Have we already passed the frontier?

Customs, duties

Where is the Custom House?

Where does the customs examination take place?

Is the examination strict?

Will the baggage be examined on board or on shore after landing?

Where must I take my baggage for customs examination?

Che cosa va soggetto a dazio?	What is liable to duty?
Non credo d' avere nulla da dichiarare.	I do not think I have anything to declare.
Bisogna aprire i bauli?	Do the trunks have to be opened?
Bisogna metter fuori gli effetti?	Do the things have to be taken out?
Eccoci al confine. I doganieri italiani vengono.	Here we are at the frontier. Here come the Italian Custom House officers.
Avete articoli soggetti a dazio?	Have you anything dutiable with you?
Su quali articoli c' è dazio?	On which articles do you collect duties?
Sui sigari solamente.	On cigars only.
Non ho nè sigari nè sigarette; non fumo.	I carry neither cigars nor cigarettes; I do not smoke.
Favorisca aprire questo baule.	Open this trunk, please.
Che contiene questo baule?	What does this trunk contain?
Contiene solo vestiti, biancheria ed effetti personali.	It contains only clothing, linen and personal effects for my own use.

Arrivare

To Arrive

A che ora arriveremo a Parigi?	At what time shall we reach Paris?
Arriveremo presto a Parigi?	Shall we soon be in Paris?
Siamo ancora lontani da Parigi?	Are we still far from Paris?
Quante gallerie ci restano ancora da passare?	How many more tunnels do we still have to pass?
Abbiam già passato il Po?	Have we already crossed the Po?

Che fiume è questo?

What river is this?

Che montagna è questa?

What mountain is this?

Il treno ha dieci minuti di ritardo.

The train is ten minutes late.

Credo che saremo in ritardo.

I think we shall be late.

L'Arrivo

The Arrival

Facchino, andate a prendermi un tassì subito. Ecco il mio scontrino.

Porter, get a taxi for me, quick! Here is my baggage check.

Dove si ricevono i bagagli?

Where is the baggage delivered?

PART EIGHT

CONTENTS

168

CONVERSAZIONE

1. Ho fretta di raggiungere Roma. Che cosa mi consiglia? (rad-'dʒun-dʒe-re)

2. Se fossi in Lei andrei in automobile oppure volerei in aeroplano.

3. Mi piace l' idea. Ma non ho nè un' automobile nè un aeroplano. Perciò temo che dovrò andare in treno.

4. Non si preoccupi, signore. Lei può facilmente noleggiare un' automobile o un aeroplano. In questa città vi sono parecchie autorimesse pubbliche e due aerodromi di prim' ordine nei dintorni con molti apparecchi sempre pronti a partire. (pre-'ɔk-ku-pi) (aw-to-ri-'mes-se) (a-e-ro-'drɔ-mi) (ap-pa-'rek-ki)

5. Preferirei andare in aeroplano. (pre-fe-ri-'rɛj)

6. Ha mai volato prima d' oggi?

7. Sì, signore. Ho volato in tutti gli Stati Uniti. Sono infatti, aviatore licenziato. (a-vja-'to-re li-tʃen-'tsja-to)

8. Allora è cosa facile, purchè possa mostrare la Sua licenza d' aviatore alle autorità locali. (li-'tʃɛn-tsa)

9. Ho la licenza con me, ed essa prova che ho volato un totale di trecento cinquanta ore in aeroplano regolare ed in elicottero. (e-li-'kɔt-te-ro)

10. L' elicottero è una cosa nuova per me.

11. L' elicottero è una macchina per volare azionata da eliche che girano su assi verticali, ciò che consente di sollevarsi ed atterrare quasi perpendicolarmente. ('mak-ki-na) ('ɛ-li-ke)

12. Meraviglioso! Perchè immagino che un simile apparecchio non richieda che un piccolo spazio così per alzarsi come per atterrare.

CONVERSATION

1. I am in a hurry to reach Rome. What do you advise me to do?

2. If I were you I would either go by automobile or fly by airplane.

3. I like the idea. But I have no car or plane. Therefore, I am afraid that I must go by train.

4. Do not worry, sir. You can easily hire an automobile or an airplane. In this city there are many public garages and two first class airfields in the outskirts with many planes always ready to leave.

5. I would prefer to go by plane.

6. Did you ever fly before?

7. Yes, sir. I have flown all over the United States. I am, in fact, a licensed pilot.

8. Then it is an easy matter, provided that you can show your pilot's license to the local authorities.

9. I have the license with me and it proves that I have flown a total of 350 hours both in a regular plane and in a helicopter.

10. The helicopter is something new to me.

11. The helicopter is a flying-machine sustained by propellers turning on vertical axes, which allows one to rise and land almost perpendicularly.

12. Wonderful! Because I imagine that such a machine requires only a small space for both taking off and landing.

13. Precisamente. È come dice Lei. E allora andiamo immediatamente al più vicino campo di aviazione.

14. Come vuole, signore. Soltanto suggerirei che, per evitare il disturbo di pilotare Lei stesso l' aeroplano, si riservasse un posto **su** uno degli apparecchi commerciali che partono ogni giorno ad **una data ora.** (kom-mer-'tʃa-li)

15. Naturalmente mi costerebbe molto meno.

16. Certamente. Ma non so se troverà posto per oggi.

17. Communque informiamoci per telefono all' ufficio delle Aerolinee Commerciali. (in-for-'mja-mo-tʃi) (te-'lɛ-fo-no)

18. Mi dispiace, signore. Il mio telefono è guasto da ieri.

19. Non **sarà così** gentile da accompagnarmi all' ufficio delle Aerolinee?

20. Volentieri, signore. Ha fatto le valige?

21. Sì, le ho fatte.

LA CITTÀ ETERNA

1. Sono lieto di sapere che Lei visiterà Roma.

2. Mi è stato detto che Roma è divenuta una città **moderna,** e che invano vi si cercherebbero molte di quelle caratteristiche che la resero così cara ad artisti, pittori e poeti. (tʃer-ke-'reb-be-ro) **(ka-rat-te-'ri-sti-ke)**

3. Naturalmente, in seguito alla guerra, Roma ha assunto **un** aspetto completamente nuovo.

13. Exactly. That is as you say. Then let us go immediately to the nearest airport.

14. As you please, sir. Only I should suggest that in order to avoid the trouble of piloting yourself, you reserve a seat on one of the commercial planes leaving every day on scheduled time.

15. Of course it would cost me much less.

16. Certainly it would. But I do not know if you can secure a place for to-day.

17. Anyhow let us inquire of the Commercial Airlines by telephone.

18. I am sorry, sir, my telephone has been out of order since yesterday.

19. Will you be so kind as to accompany me to the Airlines office?

20. Gladly, sir. Have you packed your valises?

21. Yes, I have.

THE ETERNAL CITY

1. I am glad to know that you are going to visit Rome.

2. I have been told that Rome has become a modern city, and one would look in vain there for many of those characteristics which made it so dear to artists, painters and poets.

3. Of course, as a consequence of the war, Rome has taken on a completely new aspect.

4. Perciò la Città Eterna deve avere perduto molto della sua poesia e del suo fascino. (po-e-'si-a) ('fa-ʃi-no)

5. Non convengo con Lei, signore. Il turista può ancora ammirare il Vaticano con la sua meravigliosa basilica di San Pietro, il Colosseo, il Foro Romano ed un gran numero di altre belle ed interessanti vedute. (ba-'si-li-ka) (ko-los-'sɛ-o)

6. Sono particolarmente ansioso di vedere il Vaticano e la basilica di San Pietro.

7. Chi non desidererebbe vedere la residenza ufficiale del Papa?

8. Lei ha ragione. Il Vaticano riassume e simbolizza, nel pensiero dei Cristiani, tutto ciò che è connesso con la dignità, l' autorità e la potenza della Chiesa. (sim-bo-'lid-dza) (di-ɲi-'ta) ('kjɛ-sa)

9. Il solo pensiero che la splendida e maestosa basilica fu eretta sulla tomba del primo Papa, l' Apostolo Pietro, è affascinante. (a-'pɔs-to-lo) (af-fa-ʃi-'nan-te)

10. Inoltre è interessante sapere che la tomba di San Pietro è il solo oggetto rimasto intatto da secoli. (od-'dʒɛt-to) ('sɛ-ko-li)

11. Interessantissimo, davvero. Ma sa come quel prezioso e sacro cimelio ha potuto essere conservato per così lungo tempo? (tʃi-'mɛ-ljo)

12. Mi piacerebbe di apprenderlo.

13. Nel centro della basilica il colossale baldacchino di bronzo, disegnato dal Bernini, per ordine di Urbano VIII, sormonta l'altar maggiore. Sotto questo altare si trova la tomba di San Pietro. (bal-dak-'ki-no) ('bron-dzo)

14. Esposta al pubblico?

15. No, signore. E questo è importante. La tomba resta tuttora sepolta molto sotterra con l' aurea croce di Costantino e le lastre di bronzo onde fu ricoperta dai papi per proteggerla. ('tom-ba) ('law-re-a)

4. Therefore, the Eternal City must have lost much of its poetry and charm.

5. I do not agree with you, sir. The tourist may still admire the Vatican with its wonderful St. Peter's Cathedral, the Colosseum, the Roman Forum and a great number of other beautiful and interesting sights.

6. I am particularly anxious to see the Vatican and St. Peter's Cathedral.

7. Who would not like to see the official residence of the Pope?

8. You are right. The Vatican sums up and symbolizes, in the minds of Christians, all that is connected with the dignity, authority and power of the Church.

9. The mere thought that the splendid and majestic basilica was erected over the tomb of the first Pope, the Apostle Peter, is fascinating.

10. Moreover, it is interesting to know that St. Peter's Tomb is the only object which has remained intact for centuries.

11. Very interesting, indeed. But do you know how that precious sacred relic has been preserved for so long a time?

12. I would be pleased to hear about it.

13. In the center of the basilica the colossal bronze baldachin, designed by Bernini, by order of Urban VIII, surmounts the principal altar. Below this altar is the tomb of St. Peter.

14. Visible to the public?

15. No, sir. This is the point. The tomb still remains buried very deep in the earth with the golden cross of Constantine and the bronze slabs with which it had been covered by the Popes in order to protect it.

16. E c' è modo di osservare la tomba?

17. Sì, signore. Si può vederla attraverso l'unica apertura che sia rimasta ancora accessibile, circa cinque piedi al disotto della cripta.

18. Quando morì l'Apostolo Pietro?

19. Il martirio di San Pietro ebbe luogo nel 67 Dopo Cristo. I discepoli ne ottennero la salma e la tumularono sul colle del Vaticano, non lungi dal sito del martirio. ('lun-dʒì) (mar-'ti-rjo)

IL MUSEO DELLE MISSIONI

1. Quanti anni ha (a qual'epoca risale) la basilica di San Pietro? ('ɛ-po-ka)

2. Fu nell'anno 324 Dopo Cristo che l' imperatore Costantino I iniziò la costruzione d'una basilica, la quale non fu compiuta fino al 349. (i-ni-'tsjɔ) (kom-'pju-ta)

3. Allora l'attuale basilica ha circa 1600 anni!

4. No, signore. La basilica originale fu saccheggiata e devastata più volte dai barbari invasori. Nel quindicesimo secolo essa stava per rovinare e Papa Nicolò V decise che l'unico rimedio era di demolire la basilica di Constantino. (sak-ked-'dʒa-ta) ('bar-ba-ri)

5. Chi cominciò a costruire la nuova cattedrale?

6. Nel 1506 Giulio II pose la prima pietra della nuova basilica, secondo il piano del famoso architetto Bramante, nello stesso luogo della vecchia.

16. Is there any way to see the tomb?

17. Yes, sir. One may see it through the only opening which still remains unblocked, about five feet below the crypt.

18. When did the Apostle Peter die?

19. The martyrdom of St. Peter took place in A.D. 67. The disciples obtained possession of his body and buried it on Vatican Hill, not far from the site of his martyrdom.

THE MUSEUM OF MISSIONS

1. How old is St. Peter's Cathedral?

2. It was in the year A.D. 324 that Emperor Constantine I began the construction of a basilica, which was not completed until A.D. 349.

3. Then the present basilica is about 1600 years old!

4. No, sir. The original basilica was sacked and devastated several times by barbarian invaders. In the Fifteenth Century it was falling into ruins, and Pope Nicholas V decided that the only remedy was to demolish Constantine's basilica.

5. Who started to build the new cathedral?

6. In 1506 Julius II laid the first stone of the new basilica, according to the famous architect Bramante's plan, on the same site as the old one.

7. Di conseguenza la basilica che oggi tutti ammirano risale a quell'anno? (am-'mi-ra-no)

8. Precisamente. Nel 1546 il grande Michelangelo fu incaricato della direzione dei lavori da Paolo III. Quindi vi aggiunse la grandiosa cupola, da lui stesso disegnata. (mi-ke-'lan-dʒe-lo) (ad-'dʒun-se) ('ku-po-la)

9. Quanto tempo occorse ed erigere la monumentale cupola? (e-'ri-dʒe-re)

10. Essa fu finita nel 1590, dopo soli ventidue mesi di lavoro.

11. I palazzi papali ed i musei vaticani sono vicini alla basilica?

12. Sì, essi sono annessi alla cattedrale; e se Lei si reca là, presti particolare attenzione al Museo delle Missioni.

13. Che cosa sono queste Missioni di cui ho sempre sentito tanto parlare?

14. Alle Missioni è affidata la vasta e complessa opera di diffondere la dottrina del cristianesimo. (dif-'fon-de-re)

15. Quando fu fondato il Museo delle Missioni?

16. Nel 1925, da Papa Pio XI.

17. Che cosa si può vedere in questo Museo?

18. Esso è una meravigliosa esibizione storica e documentata dell'opera missionaria svolta da ordini religiosi e società. Quest'opera è sotto la suprema direzione del Papa e la sorveglianza della Congregazione "De Propaganda Fide." ('stɔ-ri-ka) ('ɔ-pe-ra) (sor-ve-'ʎan-tsa)

7. Consequently the basilica which nowadays everybody admires dates from that year?

8. Exactly. In 1546 the great Michelangelc was commissioned by Pope Paul III with the direction of the work. Afterwards he [Michelangelo] added the imposing dome, which he himself designed.

9. How long did it take to erect the monumental cupola?

10. It was completed in 1590, after only twenty-two months of work.

11. Are the papal palaces and Vatican museums close to the basilica?

12. Yes, they adjoin the cathedral, and if you go there, please pay special attention to the Musem of Missions.

13. What are these Missions of which I have always heard so much?

14. The Missions are entrusted with the vast and complex work of spreading the doctrine of Christianity.

15. When was the Museum of Missions established?

16. In 1925, by Pope Pius XI.

17. What can one see in this Museum?

18. It is a marvelous historical and documented exhibition of the missionary work carried on by religious orders and societies. This work is under the supreme direction of the Pope and the supervision of the Congregation "De Propaganda Fide."

VOCABOLARIO	VOCABULARY
Vi sono tre colli, facchino: questo baule, questo sacco da notte e questa cappelliera.	There are three pieces, porter: this trunk, this bag and this hat-box.
Portatemi tutto sul tassì numero 227.	Take them all to taxi No. 227.
Autista, datemi il vostro numero ed aspettate il mio bagaglio.	Driver, give me your number and wait for my baggage.
Mettete il baule presso l'autista.	Place the trunk on the driver's seat (near the driver).
Ecco, facchino, questo è per voi.	Here, porter, this is for you.
Conducetemi all' Albergo Continentale.	Drive me to the Continental Hotel.

L'Albergo Le Stanze La Mobilia	The Hotel The Rooms The Furniture
L' albergo	The hotel
Un albergo di primo ordine	A first-class hotel
Un albergo di seconda classe	A second-class hotel
Può raccomandarmi un albergo a Roma?	Can you recommend a hotel in Rome?
Qual'è il miglior albergo a Bologna?	Which is the best hotel in Bologna?
In che albergo si ferma?	At what hotel do you stop?
Bisogna prendere un tassì?	Is it necessary to take a taxi?
Le raccomando quest' albergo.	I can recommend this hotel.
La pensione	The board
Il proprietario	The proprietor
Il cameriere	The valet (bellboy)
La cameriera	The chambermaid
Nettate subito la mia stanza.	Please arrange my room at once.
Fate il mio letto, per favore.	Please make my bed.
L' ascensore	The elevator

La Stanza	The Room
La stanza, la camera	The room
Una stanza davanti	A front room
Una stanza di dietro	A back room
La camera da letto	The bed room

La sala di ricevimento	The reception room
Il salotto	The sitting room
Una stanza a pian terreno	A room on the ground floor
Una stanza al primo (piano), al secondo, al terzo	A room on the first, second, third floor
Posso avere una stanza?	Can I have a room?
Vi sono stanze disponibili?	Are there any rooms available?
Vorrei una stanza con un letto.	I should like a single bed room.
Vorrei un salotto e una stanza da letto con due letti.	I would like to have a sitting room and a bed room with twin beds.
A che piano?	On what floor?
Non vorrei trovarmi su troppo in alto.	I do not wish to be too far up.
C' è un ascensore?	Is there an elevator?
Potrei avere una stanza a pian terreno?	Could I have a room on the ground floor?
Desidererei una stanza al primo che domini il lago.	I wish to have a room on the first floor overlooking the lake.
Mette (dà, esce, guarda) questa stanza sulla via o sul cortile?	Does this room front on the street or the court?
La stanza non mi conviene; me ne faccia vedere un' altra.	I do not like this room, show me another.
La fermo (la prendo).	I will take it.
Mi fermerò per alcuni giorni. Quanto costa questa camera al giorno?	I shall stay several days. How much a day is this room?
Compreso il servizio?	Inclusive of service?
È troppo cara; potrei averne una a ottocento lire al giorno?	That is too dear. Could I have one for 800 lire a day?
Quanto fate pagare al giorno per la pensione, la stanza ed il servizio?	What is your charge for board, room, and service per day?

La Porta
The Door

Questa porta non si chiude.	This door will not shut.
Dove guarda (dà, mette, esce) questa porta?	Where does this door lead to?

Questa porta comunica colla sala di ricevimento.

This door communicates with the reception room.

La finestra

The window

Con una finestra; con due finestre

With one window; with two windows

Mi dia una stanza con una finestra.

Give me a room with one window.

No, voglio una stanza con due finestre; le stanze con una finestra sono troppo oscure.

No, I want a room with two windows; rooms with one window are too dark.

Il pavimento

The floor

Il tappeto

The carpet

Il tappeto davanti al letto

The bed-carpet; the mat

Non ha tappeti sul pavimento?

Have you no carpets on the floor?

Abbiamo solamente tappeti davanti al letto.

We have only mats before the beds.

Ben di rado si copre tutto il pavimento con tappeti in Italia.

One rarely finds carpets covering the whole floor in Italy.

Il soffitto

The ceiling

Il Letto—I Letti

The Bed—The Beds

Pulito, netto

Clean

Di bucato

Clean (newly washed)

La coperta

The blanket

Il capezzale

The bolster

Il materasso, la materassa

The mattress

Il materasso elastico

The spring mattress

Il lenzuolo, le lenzuola *or* i lenzuoli

The sheet, the sheets

Fate mettere lenzuola di bucato.

Have clean sheets put on.

Le lenzuola non sono molto pulite.

The sheets are not very clean.

Questa coperta non mi basta. Datemene un' altra.

This blanket does not keep me warm. Give me another.

Mi piace aver la testa alta. Datemi un altro guanciale.

I like my head to be high. Give me another pillow.

Dormire

To sleep

S' è riposata bene?

Did you rest well?

Di solito dormo benissimo, ma la notte scorsa (passata) ho dormito male.

Generally I sleep very well, but last night I slept badly.

Fare il letto

To make the bed

Per favore, fatemi subito il letto.

Please make my bed at once.

Sono molto stanco e voglio coricarmi subito.

I am very tired and wish to go to bed at once.

A che ora s' è coricato?

At what time did he go to bed?

S' è coricato alle dieci.

He went to bed at ten.

Non ho chiuso occhio in tutta la notte.

I have not slept a wink the whole night.

Svegliare, risvegliare

To awaken, to call

Svegliatemi per tempo, voglio partire col primo treno.

Call me early, I want to leave by the first train.

Voglio dormire fino ad ora avanzata. Non permettete a nessuno di disturbarmi domani mattina.

I want to sleep late. Do not allow anyone to disturb me to-morrow morning.

Non mi fate svegliare prima delle nove. Desidero di riposarmi per bene.

I am not to be called before nine o'clock. I wish to have a good night's rest.

La Tavola

The Table

Il tappeto da tavola	The table-cover
La sedia	The chair
La sedia a dondolo	The rocking chair
Il guardaroba, l'armadio	The wardrobe
Il canterano	The chest of drawers
Un canterano con tre cassetti	A bureau with three drawers
Lo specchio	The mirror
Il divano, il sofà, il canapè	The sofa, the divan, the couch
La lampadina elettrica	The electric lamp
Un paralume	A lamp shade
L'interruttore	The light switch
La candela	The candle
Il candelabro	The chandelier
La presa di corrente	The electric outlet
Accendere	To light
Spegnere	To put out

Girate l' interruttore	Turn on the switch
	Turn off the switch
Uno zolfanello (fiammifero, cerino)	A match
Fiammiferi, zolfanelli, cerini	Matches
Portatemi acqua fresca da bere.	Bring me fresh water to drink.
Portatemi acqua fresca per la toeletta.	Bring me fresh water to wash with.
Riempite la caraffa.	Fill the pitcher.
Dov' è il campanello?	Where is the bell?
A che ora si pranza?	At what hour is dinner?
Pulite questi vestiti, cameriere.	Brush these clothes, boy.
I miei vestiti ed i miei stivali sono umidi; fateli asciugare.	My clothes and boots are wet. Please dry them.
Accendete il fuoco.	Light a fire.
Procuratemi, per favore, un fattorino che sappia l' inglese, se è possibile.	Get me a messenger, one who speaks English, if possible.
Vi sono lettere per me?	Are there any letters for me?
Hanno chiesto (domandato) di me?	Did anyone inquire for me?
Se si domanda (chiede) di me, dite che sono andato dal signor Spinelli, dove mi si potrà trovare fino alle quattro.	If anyone inquires for me, tell them that I have gone to Mr. Spinelli's, where I can be found till four o'clock.
Se il sarto mi portasse il mio vestito, ditegli di ritornare domani mattina.	If the tailor should bring me my suit, tell him to call again to-morrow morning.
Se arrivassero dei pacchi per me, per favore fateli mettere nella mia stanza.	If any packages should come for me, please have them put in my room.
Posso scrivere alcune parole nell' ufficio (nello studio)?	Can I write a few words (lines) in the office?
Datemi l' occorrente per scrivere.	Please give me some writing materials.
Partirò domani col treno delle sei dalla stazione centrale. Posso valermi dell'omnibus dell'albergo?	I start to-morrow by the six o'clock train, Central Station. Can I use the hotel bus?

Fatemi chiamare a tempo.	Let me be called in time.
Noleggiate un tassì a tempo e fatemi portar giù i miei effetti.	Get me a taxi in good time and have my baggage brought down.
Dite di preparare il mio conto.	Have my bill made out.
Datemi il conto per piacere.	Please give me my bill.
Non ho avuto questo.	I have not had this.
È già pagato.	That has already been paid.
Trovo questo prezzo troppo alto.	I find this charge too high.
Svegliatemi domani mattina alle cinque. Bussate forte alla mia porta.	Call me at five to-morrow morning. Knock loudly at my door.
Mi spiacerebbe di perdere il treno.	I should be sorry to miss the train.

Il Vestito / The Dress

Il vestito	The suit
Un abito	A suit
Il soprabito	The overcoat
Un soprabito d' estate	A summer overcoat
Un soprabito d' inverno	A winter overcoat
La giacchetta	The coat
Il panciotto, il gilè	The waistcoat, the vest
Il panciotto bianco	The white waistcoat
Un paio di calzoni	A pair of trousers
Le bretelle	Suspenders
La tasca	The pocket
Il fazzoletto	The handkerchief
Il bottone	The button
Manca un bottone quì.	A button is off here.
Fatemi attaccare un bottone, ma ben solidamente.	Please have a button put on, but solidly.
Abbottoni il suo soprabito.	Button your overcoat.
Sbottoni la giacchetta.	Unbutton your coat.
L' occhiello	The buttonhole
L' occhiello è stracciato, rammendatelo.	The buttonhole is torn, please mend it.
La camicia	The shirt
La camicia da notte	The nightgown

Cambiar di camicia	To put on a clean shirt
Il davanti	The shirt-front
Il collo	The (shirt) collar
I manichini	The cuffs
La cravatta	The necktie
Legare, attaccare, annodare	To tie
Fare un nodo	To tie a knot
Il panciotto di flanella	The flannel waistcoat
Le mutande	The drawers, shorts, underwear
Le scarpe	The shoes
Un paio di scarpe	A pair of shoes
Un paio di stivali	A pair of boots
La camicetta	The blouse
La fascetta	The foundation
Il reggipetto	The brassière
I calzoncini corti	The shorts
Prendètemi la misura per un paio di stivali.	Measure me for a pair of boots.
Le pantofole	The slippers
Il vestito (da donna)	The dress
Il vestito da casa, l' abito da camera	The house dress
La gonnella, la gonna	The skirt
La biancheria	The linen
I guanti	The gloves
Un paio di guanti	A pair of gloves
Guanti di pelle	Kid gloves
La mantellina	The cloak
La pelliccia	The fur coat
Il manicotto	The muff

Dal Sarto | ## At The Tailor's

Può raccomandarmi un buon sarto?	Can you recommend a good tailor?
Lavora bene?	Is his workmanship good?
Fatemi vedere i vostri campioni.	Show me your patterns (or samples).

Voglio farmi fare un soprabito.	I want an overcoat made.
Prendetemi la misura per un vestito.	Measure me for a suit.
All' ultima moda	In the latest fashion
Non troppo stretto	Not too tight
Non troppo largo	Not too wide
Un po' più lungo	A little longer
Non così lungo	Not quite so long
A un petto	Single-breasted
A due petti	Double-breasted
La fodera	The lining
Per quando mi potete fare questo soprabito?	When can I have this overcoat?
Non prima?	Not before?
Non posso aspettar tanto. Mi abbisogna per martedì.	I cannot wait so long. I must have it by Tuesday.
Mandatemelo col conto saldato.	Send it to me C. O. D. (with a receipted bill).
Può raccomandarmi una casa d' abiti bell' e fatti?	Can you recommend a ready-made clothing store?
Fatemi vedere un vestito oscuro.	Show me a dark colored garment.
Come mi sta? Come mi va?	How does it fit?
Mi sta bene?	Does it fit?
Mi stringe troppo alla cintura.	It is too tight in the waist.
M' è troppo stretto sotto le braccia.	It is too tight under the arms.
Non sono troppo grandi le maniche?	Are not the sleeves too wide?
Mi piacciono i calzoni stretti.	I like my trousers to be close fitting.
Vi incaricate anche di riparazioni?	Do you also do repairs?
I calzoni sono logori in fondo. Rimboccateli un po'.	The trousers are worn at the bottom. Turn them up a little.
Riorlate il mio soprabito e cambiatevi i bottoni.	Rebind my overcoat and put on new buttons.
Rimovete queste macchie.	Remove those stains.

Una Sarta

Un sarto da donna
Vorrei farmi fare una veste.
Mostratemi dei campioni.
Fatemi vedere dei figurini di moda.
Fatemi il vestito su questo modello.
Prendetemi la misura.
Il davanti
Il di dietro
L' alto
Il basso
La vita
La gonna
Ci metterò la stoffa.
Quanti metri mi ci vorranno?
Quanto mi costerà la veste, tutto compreso?
È ancora di moda questo modello?
Desidero la veste corta (lunga).

Non la vorrei troppo stretta. Mi piace sentirmi comoda.
La guarnizione
Una veste col collo alto
Una veste scollata
Fatemi vedere dei campioni di nastri.
Mettetemi dei bottoni di avorio a questo mantello.
Vorrei avere la mia veste per sabato di buon' ora.
Quando dovrò venire a provarla?
Mi va bene alla vita?
La vita
Favorisca provarsi la vita.
La vita le sta benissimo.
Alterare

A Dressmaker

A ladies' tailor
I wish to have a dress made.
Show me some patterns.
Let me see some fashion plates.

Make the dress from this design.

Take my measure.
The front
The back
The top
The bottom
The body
The skirt
I shall supply my own materials.
How many yards will it take?
What will this dress cost complete?

Is this pattern still fashionable?
I wish to have a short (a long) skirt.
It must not fit too tightly. I like to feel comfortable.
The trimming
A high-necked dress
A low-necked dress
Show me some samples of ribbons.
Put ivory buttons on this cloak.

I should like my dress early on Saturday.
When shall I call to try it on?
Does it fit well in the waist?
The waist
Please try on the waist.
The waist fits you very well.
To change, to alter

Modificate questa vita; non mi va.

La spalla

La veste mi va male alle spalle. Per favore, alteratela.

Le maniche sono troppo strette (troppo larghe; troppo lunghe; troppo corte).

Far pieghe

La manica fa pieghe quì. Favorite alterarla.

Il collo è troppo basso.

Il collo non è alto abbastanza.

Quando sarà finito il mio vestito?

Il suo vestito sarà finito domani senza fallo.

Alter the waist, it does not fit.

The shoulder

The dress fits badly in the shoulders. Please alter it.

The sleeves are too narrow (too wide; too long; too short).

To wrinkle

The sleeve wrinkles right here. Change it, please.

The collar is too low.

The collar is not high enough.

When will my dress be done?

Your dress will be done to-morrow without fail.

La Toeletta

Abbigliarsi, vestirsi

Si veste, si sta vestendo.

Non è ancora vestita?

Non è ancora pronta?

Ella muta il vestito.

Egli si sveste.

Il gusto

Veste con molto gusto.

Questo cappello Le sta benissimo.

Le pare che mi stia bene questo cappello?

Mi pare che Le stia benissimo.

Il colore

Questo colore non mi torna bene.

La faccia, il volto

La carnagione, il colorito

Delicato

Roseo

Dressing

To dress

He is dressing.

Are you not dressed yet?

Are you not ready yet?

She is changing her dress.

He is undressing.

The taste

She dresses with a great deal of taste.

This hat is very becoming to you.

Do you think this hat is becoming to me?

I think it very becoming.

The color

This color is not becoming.

The face, the visage

The complexion, the coloring

Delicate

Rosy

Ella ha una carnagione delicata e rosea; non può portare un colore così stonante. Questo colore è troppo stonante. Ecco il vero colore.

She has a delicate, rosy complexion. She cannot wear such a vivid color. This color is too vivid. Here is the right color.

Lavare

To Wash

Vorrei lavarmi le mani.

I should like to wash my hands.

Vorrei lavarmi e pettinarmi.

I should like to wash and brush up.

Portatemi acqua, sapone e asciugamani.

Bring me some water, soap and towels.

C' è acqua corrente nella mia stanza?

Is there running water in my room?

Prima devo lavarmi.

First of all I must wash.

Il bacino

The wash-basin

La caraffa

The pitcher

Un pezzo di sapone

A cake of soap

La spugna

The sponge

L' asciugamani

The towel

Asciugare

To dry

Mi asciugo le mani.

I am drying my hands.

Si asciughi le mani con questo asciugamani.

Dry your hands with this towel.

Risciacquarsi la bocca

To rinse one's mouth

Mi risciacquo la bocca.

I am rinsing my mouth.

Il dente; i denti

The tooth; the teeth

Lo spazzolino da denti

The tooth-brush

Mi pulisco i denti collo spazzolino.

I am brushing my teeth.

La spazzola pei capelli

The hair-brush

La spazzolina da unghie

The nail-brush

Si spazzola i capelli.

He is brushing his hair.

Il pettine

The comb

Mi pettino

I am combing my hair.

La scriminatura

The part

La scriminatura è diritta.

The part is straight.

La scriminatura è storta.

The part is crooked.

L' olio

The oil

La pomata

The pomade

La lima	The file
Mi limo le unghie	I am filing my nails.
La polvere	The powder
La cipria	The toilet-powder
La polvere dentifricia	The tooth-powder
La scatola da polvere	The powder-box
La nappa da cipria	The powder-puff
S' è incipriata la faccia.	She powdered her face.
Bagnarsi	To bathe
Fare un bagno	To take a bath
Si sta bagnando; fa un bagno.	He is bathing; he takes a bath.
Radersi, farsi la barba	To shave
Mi rado, mi faccio sempre la barba da me solo.	I always shave myself.

Il Barbiere — The Barber

Vorrei farmi fare la barba. Mi faccia la barba.	I wish to be shaved. Give me a shave.
Fatemi la barba, per favore.	
Favorite farmi la barba, radermi.	Please shave me.
Radetemi tutta la barba.	Shave off all my beard.
Lasciatemi solo i baffi.	Leave only the mustache.
La barba	The beard
Radetemi il mento.	Shave the chin.
La mia barba è molto ruvida. Insaponatela di più.	My beard is very stubborn. Lather it more thoroughly.
Il vostro rasoio non è abbastanza tagliente (affilato).	Your razor is not sharp enough.
Il parrucchiere	The hair-dresser
Vorrei farmi tagliare i capelli.	I wish to have my hair cut.
Corti di dietro, un po' più lunghi sul davanti.	Short behind, a little longer in front.
Tagliate pochissimo, i miei capelli cadono.	Take off only a little, I am losing my hair.
Incanutisco; comincio a diventar grigio.	I am getting gray.

IL SALONE DI BELLEZZA

La parrucchiera, la pettinatrice
Per piacere, acconciatemi i capelli.
Vorrei avere i capelli ondulati con
le dita.
Desidererei avere un' ondulazione
permanente.
Vorrei lo sciampù.
Desidero il "manicure".
Favorite tagliarmi la pellicola
delle unghie.
Per favore, limatemi le unghie.
Per piacere, fatemi il massaggio
alla faccia.
Tingete i capelli?
Avete una tintura di buona
qualità?

THE BEAUTY PARLOR

The beautician, the hairdresser
Please have my hair set.
I would like to have a finger
wave.
I would like to have a permanent
wave.
I want a shampoo.
I wish a manicure.
Please cut my cuticle.

Will you file my nails?
Please give me a facial massage.

Do you dye hair?
Have you a good quality of
dye?

PART NINE

CONTENTS

ESERCIZI DI LETTURA[1] E DI TRADUZIONE

NOVELLINE[2] E RACCONTI[3]
Il Buon Fratellino

Carluccio aveva avuto da suo zio un bellissimo pomo.[4] Appena
giunto a casa, disse a Caterina, sua sorella: "Guarda[5] che bel pomo!
Vieni e mangiamolo insieme.[6]"—"Se fosse più grande," rispose la
sorella, "lo potremmo dividere, ma così piccolo com' è, mangialo pur
tu solo."—"Tant' è,[7]" soggiunse[8] Carluccio, "mangiamolo insieme, e
così mi sembrerà più saporito.[9]"

SALVATOR MUZZI

La Buona Figliolina[10]

Una povera fanciulla raccoglieva[11] delle mammole[12] presso una
siepe[13] e ne faceva un mazzolino.[14] Passò frattanto[15] un giovane e
le disse: "Dammi quel mazzolino, e ti do un soldo."—"Non posso,"
rispose la bimba,[16] "lo compongo per la mamma, chè[17] oggi è la sua
festa."—Ti do due soldi," proseguì l' altro.—"No!"—"Te ne do tre."
—"L' ho destinato alla mamma, e non lo darei per uno scudo."—
Il giovine commosso dall' amore di questa buona figliuola, le donò
una mezza lira, e le lasciò il mazzolino delle mammole.

LO STESSO

Aiuto Vicendevole[18]

Augusto andò con suo padre a vedere una pittura esposta nello
studio d' un artista.—"Chi è quel cieco[19]?" domandò a suo padre,

---

[1] lettura, reading
[2] novellina, short story
[3] racconto, tale
[4] pomo, apple
[5] guarda, see
[6] insieme, together
[7] tant' è, never mind
[8] soggiunse, replied
[9] saporito, tasty, sweet
[10] figliolina, little daughter
[11] raccoglieva, was gathering
[12] mammole, primroses
[13] siepe, hedge
[14] mazzolino, a small bouquet
[15] frattanto, meanwhile
[16] bimba, child
[17] chè instead of perchè, because
[18] vicendevole, mutual
[19] cieco, blind man

accennando[20] il dipinto.[21]—"È Belisario, antico soldato, pieno di
virtù e di disgrazie."—"E quel giovinetto che gli sta penzolone[22] sulle
spalle, chi è?"—"È la sua guida."—"Bella guida, che si fa portare!"
—"Non vedi il poverino com' è pallido e malato! eppure, mentre il
cieco lo porta, egli segna la strada sicura, e in questo modo si aiutano
con amicizia scambievole.[23]"—"Oh, babbo,[24] quanto voglio bene a
questi affettuosi amici!"—"Certamente deve piacere, perchè insegna[25]
virtù!"—"Sentimi, babbo, se farò il pittore, voglio dipingere sempre
dei fatti virtuosi."—"E così sarai un artista che adempirà il suo
dovere."   Lo stesso

L'Orfanello

Pierino[1] andava a passeggio[2] con sua madre, e favellando[3] con lei,
diceva queste parole: "Mi vorrai sempre bene,[4] mia cara mamma?"—
"Sì, davvero, figliuol mio," rispondeva la madre: "Ti amerò sempre
con un amore che tu non puoi ancora perfettamente intendere, ma che
supera[5] ogni amore terreno[6]!"—Passavano intanto dinanzi un
fanciullo mesto,[7] che li guardò sospirando,[8] e diede in un dirotto[9]
pianto.[10]—"Poverino, che hai?" gli chiese il piccolo Pietro; "perchè
piangi?"—"Iddio vi conservi la mamma e l' amor suo!" rispose il
fanciullo; "io l' ho perduta la mia buona genitrice,[11] e non ho alcuno
che rida meco,[12] che meco pianga; Iddio vi conservi la mamma e
l' amor suo!"—Pierino si mise a piangere[13] anch' egli, e fece la
limosina[14] a quello sventurato. E d' allora in poi sentì sempre vivis-
sima compassione dei poveri orfanelli.

                                                    Lo stesso

---

[20] accennando, pointing out
[21] dipinto, picture
[22] penzolone, hanging

[23] scambievole = vicendevole
[24] babbo, papa, father
[25] insegna, it teaches

---

[1] Pierino, little Peter
[2] passeggio, a walk
[3] favellando, conversing
[4] mi vorrai . . . bene, will you . . . love me
[5] che supera, that surpasses
[6] terreno, earthly
[7] mesto, sorrowful
[8] sospirando, sighing

[9] dirotto, excessive
[10] pianto, weeping
[11] genitrice, mother
[12] meco, teco, seco, with me, with you (familiar), with him
[13] si mise a piangere, began to cry, weep
[14] limosina, elemosina, alms

Amor Fraterno E Sincerità

Arrighetto[15] e Mariuccia dovevano andare col loro padre a visitare un bel giardino. Arrighetto si pose a saltellare[16] per gioia, e urtando in un vaso di porcellana,[17] lo fece cadere dal caminetto, e il vaso andò in pezzi. Mariuccia, dispiacente, corse a raccoglierne i cocci,[18] e intanto giunse il padre, che sorprendendola sul fatto, le disse: "Sgarbata[19] che sei! Hai rotto quel vaso che mi costava molto denaro; or bene, quest' oggi starai in casa."—"No, padre mio," disse Arrighetto, "il vaso l' ho rotto io e tocca[20] a me stare in casa."—Il genitore, commosso, abbracciò[21] allora i figlioletti, e disse loro amorevolmente: "Verrete meco ambedue, perchè ambedue siete buoni! tu, Mariuccia, sai soffrire e tacere; tu Arrighetto, sai prenderti la colpa che ti spetta, e ti mostri sincero. Abbracciatemi, ed amatevi sempre come ora fate, e amate pure tutti gli uomini, perchè tutti gli uomini sono vostri fratelli."

LO STESSO

Non Sa Dare Chi Tarda[1] Dare

Frettoloso[2] io avevo già attaccato il cavallo al barroccio[3] (così mi raccontò un mio amico), e stavo per salirvi, allorchè entrò nella corte[4] la Teresa, e: "Signor Ernesto, mi perdoni il disturbo. La mia povera madre mi manda a pregarla, se volesse favorirle un fiaschetto[5] di vin vecchio. Si sente così sfinita[6] di forze! e pregherà per Lei."

La madre della Teresa aveva un pezzo servito in casa nostra, ed io mi credevo in dovere di soccorrerla nella sua vecchiaia,[7] tanto più allora, che sentivasi aggravata dalla malattia. Ma ora avevo già il piede sul predellino[8]; ero involto nel mantello; mi rincrebbe cavar i guanti, tornar indietro, andare fino in cantina e perder tempo; onde dissi alla Teresa: "Vado solo fino a Monza e torno innanzi sera. Allora vi darò quanto volete."

---

[15] Arrighetto = Enrichetto, little Henry
[16] saltellare, to leap
[17] porcellana, porcelain
[18] coccio, piece
[19] sgarbata, awkward
[20] tocca a me, I ought to
[21] abbracciò, embraced

---

[1] tarda, delays
[2] frettoloso, hasty, quick
[3] barroccio, gig
[4] corte, yard
[5] fiaschetto, a small flask
[6] sfinita, exhausted
[7] vecchiaia, old age
[8] predellino, step

Io ravvisai[9] sul volto[16] della Teresa un' aria malinconica e morti-
ficata che mi andò al cuore. Pure me ne partii: spacciai[10] di fretta e
furia i miei negozii, e alle cinque ero già di ritorno. Smontato appena,
corro in cantina,[11] levo due fiaschetti del migliore, e vengo alla casa
della vecchia. Sulla soglia[12] trovo la Teresa, che col capo sulle ginocchia[13] piangeva. "Oh Teresa, come sta la mamma?"

Ella singhiozzò,[14] e senza rispondere mi additò[15] la camera. V' entrai, e vidi sua madre, spirata pochi minuti prima. Sul viso[16] della
morta mi parve leggere un severo rimprovero.[17] Forse quel bicchier di
vino le avrebbe prolungato d'un giorno la vita: forse sarebbe morta
più consolata, soddisfacendo quest' innocente voglia: forse spirò
malcontenta che il suo antico padroncino[18] le negasse un' ultima
domanda.

Dopo d' allora non mi viene mai innanzi una povera vecchia senza
ch' io provi un rimorso: per evitare il quale, io raccomando sempre che
"chi ha tempo non aspetti tempo."   CESARE CANTÙ

Rispetto Ai Genitori

Coriolano, celebre generale della repubblica romana, era sdegnato[1]
contro la patria,[2] perchè lo aveva trattato con ingratitudine[3]; ed
essendosi posto insieme coi nemici di Roma, aveva giurato[4] di com-
batterla e di distruggerla. Il senato, ossia i cittadini più vecchi e più
degni, che stavano al governo della repubblica, gli mandarono i
sacerdoti[5] stessi coi loro abiti sacri, per supplicarlo che scordasse[6]
l' ingiuria e perdonasse alla patria atterrita[7] da tanto pericolo. Ma
Coriolano era inflessibile, e pareva ormai[8] che i Romani non avessero
più alcuno scampo.[9] Allora Veturia, la vecchia madre di Coriolano,
andò a lui a rampognarlo[10] di così crudele sdegno, e a raccomandargli

---

[9] ravvisai, I perceived
[10] spacciai, I dispatched
[11] cantina, cellar
[12] soglia, threshold
[13] ginocchia, knees

[14] singhiozzò, she sobbed
[15] additò, pointed out with the finger
[16] viso (volto, faccia), face
[17] rimprovero, reproach
[18] padroncino, young master

---

[1] sdegnato, disgusted
[2] patria, fatherland, one's own country
[3] ingratitudine, ingratitude
[4] giurato, sworn
[5] sacerdoti, priests

[6] scordasse, should forget
[7] atterrita, dismayed, alarmed
[8] ormai = oramai, now
[9] scampo, escape
[10] rampognarlo, to scold him

la salvezza[11] della patria. Ed esso, tanto era amorevole e rispettoso
figliuolo, deposta la collera, si mostrò pacato[12] e pentito in faccia a
tutti: abbandonò il pensiero di muovere contro Roma; e si condannò
sè stesso ad esilio perpetuo, in pena d' aver preso le armi contro la
patria.   PIETRO THOUAR

Rispetto Ai Vecchi

Gli Spartani avevano in tanta venerazione i maggiori che tutti i
vecchi erano ugualmente rispettati dai giovani. Ai giuochi[13] pubblici,
che solevano[14] essere celebrati ogni quattro anni nella città d' Olimpia,
accorreva[15] gran folla[16] di popolo da ogni parte della Grecia. Una
volta un vecchio, essendo giunto degli ultimi, non trovava posto
da sedere sulle gradinate[17] dell' anfiteatro. Ma appena i giovani
Spartani, i quali erano tutti insieme, ebbero veduto questo vecchio,
si alzarono a gara[18] per fargli posto. La quale azione piacque tanto
alla moltitudine ivi raccolta, che tosto i giovani Spartani furono
salutati da applausi[19] generali.—Ai medesimi giuochi pubblici della
Grecia un giovine, per nome Trasibulo, essendo rimasto[20] vincitore
nella corsa dei carri, volle che invece del suo nome fosse pubblicato
quello di Senocrate padre suo, per meglio significare che se egli valeva
qualche cosa, tutto era venuto dalla buona educazione, ricevuta da
colui che gli aveva data la vita.—E i due figliuoli di Diagora, rimasti
vincitori anch' essi nei giuochi olimpici, appena ebbero ricevuto il
premio[21] della corona d' alloro,[22] la posero sulla fronte del padre, e poi
alzandolo sulle loro spalle, lo condussero in trionfo in mezzo agli
spettatori, i quali empivano l' aria d' applausi, e gettavano fiori su
qual padre avventurato.[23]   LO STESSO

---

[11] salvezza, safety
[12] pacato, appeased
[13] giuochi, games
[14] solevano, used to be
[15] accorreva, hastened to
[16] folla, crowd
[17] gradinate, flight of steps, tiers

[18] si alzarono a gara, vied with one
  another in their eagerness to rise
[19] applausi, applause
[20] rimasto, remained; rimasto vincitore,
  who was the winner, who won
[21] premio, prize, reward
[22] alloro, laurel
[23] avventurato, fortunate

Pietà[1] Vera

Non è passato gran tempo che nel Camaldoli[2] di S. Lorenzo morì
Michele, vecchio battilano,[3] il quale per aver tenuto vita onesta,
operosa ed utile al bene dei suoi vicini,[4] fu da essi compianto[5] con
affetto[6] filiale, e lasciò di sè onorata memoria. Egli fu buon padre di
famiglia, morigerato[7] e amorevole, e potè con savi portamenti[8]
indirizzarla al bene, nello stesso tempo che la moderazione nei desi-
derii, i risparmii[9] e il coraggio gli diedero modo di liberarla anche nei
giorni calamitosi dalle strettezze[10] del bisogno, che suole essere cagione
di tanti guai[11] . . .

I camaldolesi,[12] che tengono in molta venerazione San Rocco,
sogliono la sera della sua vigilia[13] far luminarie[14] nelle loro strade ai
tabernacoli ed alle case, ed imbandire[15] liete cene sull' uscio,[16] facendo
strage[17] di maccheroni, e talora chiudendo la veglia[18] con qualche
rissa,[19] cagionata dai vapori del vino. Due giorni prima che si dovesse
apparecchiare questa pia gozzoviglia,[20] morì, per esser caduto di sulla
fabbrica dov' ei lavorava, un falegname[21] del vicinato[22] di Michele,
giovine onesto e ben affetto a ciascuno, e lasciò desolata e povera la
moglie con quattro figliuoli. Michele deplorando la repentina[23] dis-
grazia di quella famiglia: "Io per me," diceva ad alcuni compagni,
"lasciamo stare che le cene non hanno nulla che fare con la divozione
a San Rocco, ma non potrò vedere tanta baldoria[24] e tanta allegria
pensando che quei tribolati[25] non hanno più chi li campi.[26] Si fa una
cosa, fratelli? Ci accordiamo noi a mettere assieme quel tanto che
si spenderebbe nei lumi alle finestra e nella cena, per poi donarlo

---

[1] pietà, compassion, pity
[2] Camaldoli, the name of a quarter of Florence
[3] battilano, wool-carder
[4] vicini, neighbors
[5] compianto, bewailed
[6] affetto, love
[7] morigerato, well-bred
[8] portamenti, behavior
[9] risparmii, savings
[10] strettezze, penury
[11] guai, woes
[12] camaldolesi, the inhabitants of the Camaldoli
[13] vigilia, eve
[14] luminarie, illuminations
[15] imbandire, to serve up
[16] uscio, door
[17] strage, slaughter, havoc
[18] veglia, the sitting up, the night feasting
[19] rissa, brawl
[20] gozzoviglia, guzzling, spree
[21] falegname, carpenter
[22] vicinato, neighborhood
[23] repentina, sudden
[24] baldoria, merriment
[25] tribolati, afflicted
[26] campi, maintains

alla vedova? Io non ricuso di pagare la mia tassa pe' lumi al taberna-
colo; ma ogni rimanente—a quella povera donna."—"Tu pensi bene,"
risposero ad una voce i compagni. "Ci stiamo anche noi[27]: "Detto
fatto[28]; ne parlarono con le loro mogli, che furono tosto del medesimo
sentimento; e il partito girando di bocca in bocca andò a genio[29] a
tutte le savie famiglie del vicinato, le quali deputarono Michele a
raccogliere le caritatevoli offerte per consegnarle alla vedova. Così
in quella strada non si videro illuminazioni alle case, nè tavole
apparecchiate sull' uscio, nè si udirono suoni o canti o schiamazzi[30]
di gente allegra.

I lumi[1] erano accesi[2] solamente alle immagini dei tabernacoli parati
con bell' assetto[3]; e le donne e i fanciullini recitavano il rosario[4] con
divozione consolata e tranquilla. Intanto la povera vedova del
falegname, benedicendo con le sue creaturine la buona ispirazione di
Michele, sopportava con più coraggio lo spasimo[5] d' aver perduto il
marito, e si confortava nel vedere assicurato per molti giorni il
campamento[6] della famiglia.

Lo stesso

Il Calzolaio Giudice d' Opere d' Arte

Soleva Apelle mettere le opere sue finite in pubblico,[7] estimando il
volgo[8] esser buon conoscitore[9] di molte cose; ed egli stava da parte
nascosto[10] per ascoltare[11] quello che dicesse, per poter poscia[12] emendare[13] le parti riprese. Avvenne che passando un calzolaio biasimò

---

[27] ci stiamo anche noi, we also are with
  you
[28] detto fatto, no sooner said than done

[29] andò a genio, pleased
[30] schiamazzi, noises, shouts

---

[1] lumi, lights
[2] accesi, lighted
[3] assetto, order
[4] rosario, rosary
[5] spasimo, shock
[6] campamento, necessities of life, food,
  maintenance

[7] mettere in pubblico, to exhibit to the
  public
[8] volgo, common people
[9] conoscitore, judge, connoisseur
[10] nascosto, hidden
[11] ascoltare, listen
[12] poscia, afterwards
[13] emendare, to amend, to correct

in una sua figura una pianella,[14] a cui non so che fibbia[15] mancava; la qual cosa conoscendo vera Apelle, la racconciò.[16] Ritornando poi l' altro giorno il calzolaio, e vedendo che il maestro aveva seguito il suo parere nella pianella, cominciò a voler dire sopra una gamba; onde Apelle sdegnato, uscì fuori dicendo; "Non conviensi[17] al calzolaio giudicar più su che la pianella"; il qual detto fu poi accettato per proverbio.

RAFFAELE BORGHINI

Proverbi

Cosa rara, cosa cara.

Chi t' accarezza[18] più di quel che suole,[19] o t' ha ingannato o ingannarti vuole.

La lode giova[20] al savio[21] e nuoce al matto.[22]

Cosa per forza non vale scorza.[23]

La lingua batte[24] dove il dente duole.[25]

Non è bello quel ch' è bello, ma è bello quel che piace.

Chi vuol vivere e star bene, pigli il mondo come viene.

Malinconia non paga debito.—Un carro di fastidii[26] non paga un quattrin[27] di debito.

Al bisogno si conosce l' amico.

Chi ama tutti non ama nessuno.

Val più un amico che cento parenti.[28]—Più vale il cuore[29] che il sangue.[30]

Lontan[1] dagli occhi, lontan dal cuore.

Con arte e con inganno,[2] si vive mezzo[3] l' anno; con inganno e con arte, si vive l' altra parte.

---

[14] pianella, slipper
[15] fibbia, buckle
[16] racconciare, to readjust, to improve
[17] non conviensi, it is not becoming (proper)
[18] accarezza, caresses
[19] suole, is wont, is accustomed
[20] giova, helps
[21] savio, sage
[22] matto, fool
[23] scorza, bark
[24] batte, strikes
[25] duole, pains
[26] fastidii, cares
[27] quattrin, farthing
[28] parenti, relatives
[29] cuore, heart
[30] sangue, blood

---

[1] lontano, far
[2] inganno, fraud, deceit
[3] mezzo, half

L' avaro[4] è come l' idropico: quanto più[5] beve, più ha sete.[6]

Le donne per parer[7] belle si fanno brutte.[8]

Una mano lava[9] l' altra, e tutt' e due lavano il viso.

A ogni uccello[10] il suo nido[11] è bello.

Casa mia, casa mia, per piccina[12] che tu sia, tu mi sembri[13] una badia.[14]

Meglio soli[15] che mal accompagnati.[16]

Comandi chi può[17] e obbedisca chi deve.[18]

Dio manda il freddo secondo i panni.[19]

Dal detto al fatto[20] c' è un gran tratto.[21]

Cane[22] che abbaia,[23] poco morde.[24]

Le parole son femmine, e i fatti son maschi.[25]

Meglio tardi[26] che mai.

Patti[27] chiari, amici cari.

Dagli amici mi guardi Dio, che dai nemici mi guardo io.

Un bel morir tutta la vita onora.

Il pane degli altri è troppo salato.[28]

Chi mal fa, mal pensa.

Non fu mai gloria senza invidia.[29]

Un conte senza contea[30] è come un fiasco senza vino.

Paese che vai, usanza[31] che trovi.

Chi dorme non piglia pesci.

Chi vuol, vada; e chi non vuol, mandi.

---

[4] avaro, miser
[5] quanto più, the more
[6] sete, thirst
[7] per parer, in order to look, to appear
[8] brutte, ugly
[9] lava, washes
[10] uccello, bird
[11] nido, nest
[12] per piccina, however small
[13] sembri, seem
[14] badia, mansion
[15] meglio soli, better alone
[16] mal accompagnati, ill assorted, evil companioned
[17] chi può, he who is able, who can
[18] chi deve, he who shall, who must
[19] secondo i panni, according to clothes
[20] dal detto al fatto, from word to deed
[21] c' è un gran tratto, is a long way off, "saying and doing are two things"
[22] cane, dog
[23] abbaia, barks
[24] morde, bites
[25] maschi, masculine
[26] tardi, late
[27] patti, conditions, agreement
[28] salato, salted (bitter)
[29] invidia, envy
[30] conte, count; contea, county
[31] usanza, use, custom

Chi s' aiuta[1] Iddio l' aiuta.

Chi si loda,[2] s' imbroda.[3]

Ogni pazzo[4] è savio quando tace.[5]

Bisogna distendersi quanto il lenzuolo[6] è lungo.

Anco tra le spine[7] nascono le rose.

Chi pecora[8] si fa, lupo la mangia.

La bugia ha le gambe[9] corte.—La verità vien sempre a galla.[10]

Chi troppo vuole niente ha.

Chi sta bene, non si muova.

Dalla "Raccolta[11] Di Proverbi Toscani"

[FATTA DA GIUSEPPE GIUSTI]

Il Miracolo Delle Noci[12]

—Sapete di quel miracolo delle noci, che avenne[13] molt' anni sono in quel nostro convento di Romagna?

—No, in verità, raccontatemelo un poco.

—Oh! dovete dunque sapere che in quel convento c' era un nostro padre, il quale era un santo, e si chiamava[14] il padre Macario. Un giorno d' inverno, passando per una viottola,[15] in un campo d' un nostro benefattore, uomo dabbene[16] anche lui, il padre Macario vide questo benefattore vicino a un noce,[17] e quattro contadini,[18] con le zappe[19] in aria, che principiavano a scalzar[20] la pianta, per metterne le radici[21] al sole.—"Che fate voi a quella povera pianta?" domandò il padre Macario.— "Eh! padre, son anni e anni che la non mi vuol far noci; e io ne faccio legna.[22]"—"Lasciatela stare," disse il padre, "sappiate che quest' anno la farà più noci che foglie.[23]" Il benefattore,

---

[1] s' aiuta, helps one's self
[2] loda, praises
[3] s' imbroda, soils one's self
[4] pazzo, fool
[5] tace, keeps silent
[6] lenzuolo, sheet
[7] spine, thorns
[8] pecora, sheep
[9] gambe, legs
[10] a galla, floating
[11] raccolta, collection
[12] noci, nuts

[13] avvenne, happened
[14] si chiamava, whose name was, literally, called himself
[15] viottola, narrow path
[16] dabbene, good, honest
[17] il noce, the nut-tree; la noce, the nut
[18] contadini, peasants
[19] zappe, hoes
[20] scalzar, to bare the root
[21] radici, roots
[22] legna, firewood
[23] foglie, leaves

che sapeva chi era colui che aveva detta quella parola, ordinò subito ai lavoratori,[1] che gettassero[2] di nuovo[3] la terra sulle radici; e, chiamato il padre, che continuava la sua strada: "Padre Macario," gli disse, "la metà della raccolta[4] sarà per il convento." Si sparse[5] la voce della predizione; e tutti correvano a guardare[6] il noce. In fatti a primavera, fiori a bizzeffe[7] e, a suo tempo, noci a bizzeffe. Il buon benefattore non ebbe la consolazione di bacchiarle[8]; perchè andò prima della raccolta a ricevere il premio della sua carità. Ma il miracolo fu tanto più grande come sentirete. Quel brav' uomo aveva lasciato un figliuolo di stampa[9] ben diversa. Or dunque alla raccolta, il cercatore[10] andò per riscuotere[11] la metà che era dovuta[12] al convento; ma colui se ne fece nuovo affatto,[13] ed ebbe la temerità di rispondere che non aveva mai sentito dire che i cappuccini sapessero far noci. Sapete ora cosa avvenne? Un giorno (sentite questa) lo scapestrato[14] aveva invitato alcuni suoi amici dello stesso pelo.[15] e, gozzovigliando, raccontava la storia del noce e rideva de'[16] frati. Que'[17] giovinastri[18] ebber voglia d' andar a vedere quello sterminato[19] mucchio[20] di noci; e lui li menò su in granaio.[21] Ma sentite: apre l'uscio, va verso il cantuccio[22] dov' era stato riposto il gran mucchio, e mentre dice: "Guardate," guarda egli stesso, e vede . . . che cosa? un bel mucchio di foglie secche di noce.—Fu un esempio questo!

ALESSANDRO MANZONI

---

[1] lavoratori, laborers
[2] gettassero, should throw
[3] di nuovo, anew
[4] raccolta, crop
[5] si sparse, was divulged, spread abroad
[6] a guardare, to look at, to observe
[7] a bizzeffe, abundantly, in plenty
[8] di bacchiarle, to beat them down (with a stick)
[9] stampa, nature
[10] cercatore, collector
[11] riscuotere, to receive

[12] dovuta, due
[13] se ne fece nuovo affatto, feigned to ignore
[14] lo scapestrato, rake, debauchee
[15] pelo, hair, nature
[16] de' = dei
[17] que' = quei
[18] giovinastri, bad young men
[19] sterminato, immense, enormous
[20] mucchio, heap, pile
[21] granaio, granary
[22] cantuccio, little corner

VOCABOLARIO

Biancheria di Bucato

Biancheria sporca, sudicia
Fate portare questa biancheria dalla lavanderia.
La nota; la lista c' è.
Quando potrò riaverla?
Mi occorre la biancheria per giovedì.
Non dimenticate di racconciare le camicie.
L' amido
Inamidare
Stirare
Non rendete i miei solini così duri.

Oggetti d' Acconciamento, di Ornamento, d' Abbigliamento

Dei gioielli
Dei diamanti
La perla, le perle
L' anello
L' anello con diamanti
Gli orecchini
Il braccialetto
La collana
L' orologio
La catena d' orologio
I bottoncini da camicia
I bottoni da polsini
Gli occhiali
L'occhialino
Miope
Presbite
Il binoccolo
Il bastone
Il parasole
L' ombrello
Il ventaglio

VOCABULARY

Clean Linen

Soiled linen
Send these clothes to the laundry.
The laundry list is there.
When can I have it back?
I must have the washing by Thursday.
Do not forget to mend the shirts.
The starch
To starch
To iron
Do not iron my collars so stiff.

Articles of Ornament in Dress

Jewels
Diamonds
The pearl, the pearls
The ring
The diamond ring
The earrings
The bracelet
The necklace
The watch
The watch-chain
The shirt-studs
The cuff-buttons
The spectacles
The eye-glass
Near-sighted
Far-sighted
The opera-glass
The cane
The parasol
The umbrella
The fan

Il Tempo / The Time

L' ora	The time; the hour
La misura	The time; the measure
Battere il tempo	To beat the time
Andare a tempo	To keep time
Perdere il tempo	To waste, lose time
Tre volte	Three times
Un' altra volta	Another time
Allora	Then; at that time
Oggi	Today; at the present time
Nel medesimo tempo	At the same time
Per molto tempo	For a long time
È un pezzo che non La vedo.	I have not seen you for a long time.
Questo si può fare in un batter d' occhio.	This can be done in no time.
Di buon' ora, per tempo; a tempo	In good time; early
Ai miei tempi	In my time
Per qualche tempo	For some time
Di tanto in tanto	From time to time
Venir a proposito	To come at the right time
Ciò viene molto a proposito.	That comes just at the right time.
Arriveremo a tempo?	Shall we be in time?
A che ora parte il treno per Venezia?	At what time does the train start for Venice?
Quanto tempo ci resta fino alla partenza?	How much time have we before the train starts?
Siamo a tempo per il treno?	Are we in time for the train?
Dove avremo tempo di mangiare qualche cosa?	Where shall we have time to eat something?
Avremo tempo abbastanza?	Shall we have enough time?
Ha tempo d'accompagnarmi?	Have you time to accompany me?
Non ho tempo.	I have no time.
Dia tempo al tempo.	Take your time.

L' Ora / The Time; The Hour; O'Clock

Che ora è? Che ore sono?	What time is it? What is the time?

Potrebbe dirmi che ora è?	Can you tell me the time?
È un' ora e mezzo.	It is half-past one.
Verso le cinque	About five o'clock
Son quasi le quattro.	It is nearly four.
Sono le quattro meno tre.	It is three minutes of four.
Stan per suonare le sei.	It is about to strike six o'clock
Le sei han suonato or ora.	It has just struck six.
Suona la mezza.	The half hour is striking.
Alle sette in punto	At seven sharp, at seven on the dot.
Dalle otto antimeridiane (dalle 8 antim.) alle tre pomeridiane (alle 3 pom.)	From 8 a. m. to 3 p. m.

La Divisione Del Tempo	**Division Of Time**
Oggi	To-day
Domani	To-morrow
Dopodomani	The day after to-morrow
Ieri	Yesterday
Ier l' altro	The day before yesterday
Stamane, Stamattina, questa mattina	This morning
Domani mattina, domattina	To-morrow morning
Domani a mezzodì,a mezzogiorno	To-morrow noon
Domani sera, domani a sera	To-morrow night
Ier sera, ier notte	Last night
La vigilia	The day before; the eve
La veglia	The sitting up, the watching, the evening party
Il domani; il giorno dopo; il giorno seguente	The morrow; the day after
Questa settimana	This week
La settimana prossima, **or** ventura, **or** che viene	Next week
La settimana passata **or** scorsa	Last week
Sette giorni	Seven days
Durante sette giorni	During a week
Per sette giorni	For a week
Dopo sette giorni	After a week

Fra otto giorni	In a week
Più di sette giorni	More than a week
Domani a otto	To-morrow week
Entro la settimana	In a week
Otto giorni fa	A week ago
Furono ieri quindici giorni	Two weeks ago yesterday
Quindici giorni, una quindicina	A fortnight

I Mesi	The Months
Gennaio	January
Febbraio	February
Marzo	March
Aprile	April
Maggio	May
Giugno	June
Luglio	July
Agosto	August
Settembre	September
Ottobre	October
Novembre	November
Dicembre	December

Il primo di dicembre, il primo dicembre	On the first of December
Il tre gennaio	On January third
Al principio di maggio, ai primi di maggio	At the beginning of May
In fin di maggio	At the end of May
Questo mese di giugno	This June
Nel prossimo giugno	Next June
Nel giugno passato, scorso	Last June
Questo mese	This month
Il mese venturo, prossimo, che viene	Next month
Il mese passato, scorso	Last month
Il primo del mese corrente, del corrente mese	The first instant
Alla fin del mese, negli ultimi del mese	At the end of this month
Tre mesi, un trimestre	A quarter of a year

Sei mesi, un semestre	A half year
Nove mesi	Three-quarters of a year
Un anno	A year
Nel mille quattrocento novanta-due	In 1492
Il giorno più lungo	The longest day
Il giorno più corto	The shortest day

Feste Religiose / Religious Feasts

L' Ognissanti	All Saints' Day
Il Giorno dei Morti	All Souls' Day
Il Mercoledì delle Ceneri	Ash Wednesday
Il Natale	Christmas
Pasqua	Easter
Il Venerdì Santo	Good Friday
La Quaresima	Lent
Mezza Quaresima	Mid-Lent
Il primo dell' anno, il capo d'anno	New Year's Day
La Domenica delle Palme	Palm Sunday
La settimana di Passione	Passion Week
La Settimana Santa	Holy Week
Il Martedì Grasso	Shrove Tuesday
La Pentecoste	Whitsuntide; Pentecost

Il Medico / The Physician

Non sto bene, faccia venire il medico. [Mandi a chiamare un medico.]	I am not well, send for a doctor.
Devo andar a cercare il medico? Devo andare a chiamare un medico?	Shall I go for the doctor? [go call a doctor?]
Che medico mi raccomanda?	What physician can you recommend?
C' è forse un medico americano quì?	Is there perhaps an American physician here?
Qual' è il suo onorario per una consultazione; per una visita?	What are his charges for a consultation; for a visit?
Quando riceve; a che ora riceve il dottore?	When does he receive; at what hour does the doctor receive?

Bisognerà aspettar molto?	Shall I have long to wait?
Soffro di ——.	I suffer from ——.
Ho la febbre.	I have a fever.
Ho alternativamente degli accessi di calore e dei brividi.	I have alternately fits of heat and of cold.
Non so nemmen io quel ch' io abbia.	I do not know myself what is the matter with me.
Mi sento un malessere generale.	I feel altogether uncomfortable.
Ho mal di testa, di denti, di gola, di petto, di ventre.	I have a headache; toothache; pain in the throat; in the chest; stomach-ache.
Ho mal di cuore.	I have heart trouble.
Mi fa male il piede.	I have a pain in my foot.
Mi duole il braccio.	My arm pains me.
Ho il fegato ammalato.	I am suffering from my liver.
Respiro con difficoltà.	I experience difficulty in breathing.
Non ho dormito in tutta la notte.	I have not slept all night long.
Passo molte notti insonni.	I pass many sleepless nights.
Credo d' avere un imbarazzo gastrico.	I think my stomach is out of order.
Non ho affatto appetito.	I have no appetite at all.
Mi può dare un rimedio contro ——?	Can you give me a remedy for ——?
Quante volte al giorno devo pigliare questo rimedio?	How many times a day must I take this medicine?
Devo stare a dieta?	Must I stay on a diet?
Che posso mangiare (bere)?	What may I eat (drink)?
Posso fumare?	Am I allowed to smoke?
Mi son fatto male in una caduta.	I have been injured by a fall.
Mi son rotto il braccio.	I broke my arm.
Mi son dato una storta alla caviglia.	I have sprained my ankle.
Mi sento un po' meglio.	I feel a little better.
Non sto ancora meglio.	I do not feel any better yet.
Mi sono raffreddato.	I have taken a cold.
Sono raffreddato.	I have a cold.
Mi son preso un raffreddore.	I have caught a cold.
Lei si raffredderà.	You are going to take cold.

Mi sono abbruciato.	I have burnt myself.
Ho la faccia gonfia.	My face is swollen.
È serio il mio caso; è seria la mia malattia?	Is my illness serious?
Può star tranquilla, non c' è niente.	You may rest easy—it is nothing.
Piglierà queste polveri.	Take these powders.
Quante ne devo pigliare al giorno?	How many do I have to take a day?
Ne pigli tre.	Take three of them.
Per favore, mi dica quanto le devo.	Please tell me how much I owe you.

PROVERBI

La superbia andò a cavallo, e tornò a piedi.

La troppa familiarità genera disprezzo.

Lauda la moglie e tienti donzello.

Muor giovane colui ch' al cielo è caro.

Ne ammazza più la gola che la spada.

Necessità non ha legge.

Odi, vedi, e taci, se vuoi vivere in pace.

Ogni cane è leone a casa sua.

Ognun sa navigar per il buon tempo.

Onor di bocca assai giova e poco costa.

Quattrino risparmiato due volte guadagnato.

Saggio fanciullo è chi conosce il suo vero padre.

Se occhio non mira, cuor non sospira.

Una rondine non fa primavera.

PROVERBS

Pride set out on horseback and came back on foot.

Too much familiarity breeds contempt.

Praise married life but remain single.

Whom the gods love dies young.

Gluttony kills more than the sword.

Necessity knows no law.

Listen, see, and keep silent, if you wish to live in peace.

Every dog is a lion at home.

Everybody can steer the ship when the sea is calm.

Fair words go for much and cost but little.

A penny saved is doubly earned.

He is a wise child who knows his own father.

What the eye does not see the heart does not grieve for.

One swallow does not make a summer.

PART TEN

CONTENTS

THE DEFINITE ARTICLE

1. There are only two Genders in the Italian language, viz: the masculine and the feminine.

This distinction of Gender applies both to persons and inanimate objects, and is indicated by the Definite Article prefixed to Substantives.

Il, lo, l' are the various forms of the masculine Definite Article; **la, l'** are the feminine forms.

2. In the singular masculine Nouns beginning with consonants, except the **impure s** (s impura), take **il**; while feminine Nouns beginning with a consonant, the **impure s** included, require **la**.

EXAMPLES

MASCULINE	FEMININE
il padre, the father	la madre, the mother
il figlio, the son	la figlia, the daughter
il fratello, the brother	la sorella, the sister
il cugino, the cousin	la cugina, the cousin
il cognato, the brother-in-law	la cognata, the sister-in-law
il suocero, the father-in-law	la suocera, the mother-in-law
il nipote, the nephew	la nipote, the niece
il nonno, the grandfather	la nonna, the grandmother
il nipotino, the grandchild	la nipotina, the grandchild

3. Masculine Nouns beginning with an **s impura**, that is, with an **s** followed by another consonant, as: **sb, sc, sd, sf, sg,** etc., take **lo,** in order to avoid the disagreeable meeting of three consonants. Examples: **lo sbaglio,** the mistake; **lo sdegno,** the anger; **lo specchio,** the mirror. Whenever a Substantive beginning with **s impura** is preceded by a Preposition ending with a consonant, as **in, per, con,** etc., an **i** may be prefixed to the Substantive. Thus: **In Isvezia** (to avoid **in Svezia**), **con isdegno,** with anger, etc. Masculine Nouns beginning with **z** also take **lo,** as: **lo zio,** the uncle. Words beginning with either **sce** or **sci,** which sound like **shey** or **shee,** are also preceded by **lo,** as: **lo scettro,** the scepter, etc.

4. **L** with the apostrophe, (**L'**), indicating that either **o** or **a** has been dropped, is used before masculine and feminine Nouns beginning with a vowel.

EXAMPLES

MASCULINE	FEMININE
l' amico, the friend	l' amica, the friend
l' amore, the love	l' abitudine, the custom, habit

THE INDEFINITE ARTICLE

5. The Indefinite Article before masculine Nouns beginning with a consonant, except **s impura,** or with a vowel, is **un.** Nouns with **s impura** take **uno.** Feminine Nouns beginning with a consonant take **una,** and those beginning with a vowel **un'.** Masculine Nouns beginning with **sce, sci,** or **z,** take **uno.**

EXAMPLES

MASCULINE	FEMININE
un libro, a book	una penna, a pen
un tavolo, a table	una casa, a house
uno stato, a state	un' amica, a friend
uno zio, an uncle	una zia, an aunt

The Plural of the Article

6. **Il** is changed into **i** in the plural, **lo** and **l'** masculine into **gli,** **la** and **l'** feminine into **le.**

EXAMPLES

MASCULINE

il padre, i padri, the father, the fathers
lo stato, gli stati, the state, the states
l' amico, gli amici, the friend, the friends

FEMININE

la madre, le madri, the mother, the mothers
l' amica, le amiche, the friend, the friends

7. Nouns beginning with **sce, sci,** or **z,** take in the singular **lo,** and in the plural **gli.**

EXAMPLES

lo zio, gli zii, the uncle, the uncles
lo scettro, gli scettri, the scepter, the scepters

8. **Gli** may be changed into **gl'** before an **i,** and **le** into **l'** before any vowel, but this practice is somewhat antiquated.

EXAMPLES

gli infelici or gl' infelici, the unhappy ones
le amiche or l' amiche, the (female) friends

CONTRACTION OF PREPOSITIONS WITH THE DEFINITE ARTICLE

9. The prepositions **di** (of), **a** (to), **da** (from, by, at the house of), **in** (in), **con** (with), **su** (on), **per** (for, through), contract with the seven forms of the definite article (**il, la, lo, l', i, gli, le**) in accord with the following scheme:

	il	la	lo	l'	i	gli	le
di	del	della	dello	dell'	dei	degli	delle
a	al	alla	allo	all'	ai	agli	alle
da	dal	dalla	dallo	dall'	dai	dagli	dalle
in	nel	nella	nello	nell'	nei	negli	nelle
con	col	colla	collo	coll'	coi	cogli	colle
su	sul	sulla	sullo	sull'	sui	sugli	sulle
per	pel				pei		

10. These contractions are compulsory for **di, a, da, in, con,** optional for **su, per.**

del padre, of the father
della madre, of the mother
dello zio, of the uncle
dell' anima, of the soul
dei padri, of the fathers

dallo zio, from the uncle
dalla madre, from the mother
dall' uomo, from the man
nei libri, in the books
nelle pagine, in the pages

delle madri, of the mothers
degli zii, of the uncles
al padre, to the father
agli zii, to the uncles
alle donne, to the women

sul muro, on the wall
sulle mura, on the walls
coi libri, or *con i libri*, with the books
colle mani, or *con le mani*, with the hands
pel padre, or *per il padre*, for the father
pei genitori, or *per i genitori*, for the parents

11. The Prepositions are not contracted with the Indefinite Article. **Di** commonly becomes **d'** before a vowel, as:

> *un padre*, a father; *d' un padre*, of a father;
> *una madre*, a mother; *d' una madre*, of a mother

Da is never apostrophized, and instead of **a,** for the sake of euphony, **ad** is preferred.

> *da un padre*, from a father; *ad una madre*, to a mother

USE OF THE ARTICLE

12. In general, the Article is more frequently used than in English. The learner should be careful to observe the following rules:

I. The Definite Article is used:

a. After the verb **avere**, if particular qualities of an **organic** body are mentioned, as:
Francesca ha I *denti bianchi*, GLI *occhi azzurri*, I *capelli biondi e* LE *labbra vermiglie.*
Frances has white teeth, blue eyes, fair hair and red lips.
Questo ragazzo ha LA *testa rotonda.*
This boy has a round head.

b. Before **di cui** (also **cui**), whose, as:
L' uomo LA *di cui (la cui) riputazione è perduta, è sfortunato.*
The man whose reputation is lost is unhappy.

c. Before **abstract notions,** when taken in their whole extent, as:
L' occupazione è il miglior rimedio contro LA *noia.*
Occupation is the best remedy for ennui.

d. Before the names of **countries, provinces,** etc., as: **L' Italia,** Italy; **L' Austria,** Austria; **il Belgio,** Belgium; **il Perù,** Peru; except when used in the possessive and as an equivalent for an Adjective derived from the name of a nation, as: **Il parlamento**

d' Inghilterra, The English Parliament; **l' ambasciatore di Francia,** the French ambassador. The names, too, of countries or provinces the capital of which has the **same name,** are used **without** the Article, as: **Napoli,** Naples; **Parma,** etc.

e. With the two names **Charlemagne** and **Alexander the Great,** no Article is placed before the Adjective **magno,** thus: **Carlomagno, Alessandro Magno.** This is also the case in the expression **Maria Vergine,** Mary The Virgin. But it is used in **La Vergine Maria.**

f. Before celebrated family names, as: **L' Ariosto,** Ariosto; **il Tasso,** Tasso, etc. But not when they are preceded by Christian names, as: **Dante Alighieri, Michelangelo Buonarotti.**

g. Before several names of towns: **il Cairo, la Mirandola, la Bastia, La Spezia, l' Aia,** The Hague; **la Mecca.**

h. Before names of females in familiar conversation, as: **la Cristina, la Fiammetta,** etc.

i. In expressions like: **alla turca,** after the Turkish fashion; **all' inglese,** after the English fashion, etc.

l. Before words implying **higher rank, dignity,** or **profession,** as: **il conte Pallavicini,** Count Pallavicini; **il principe Eugenio,** Prince Eugene; **l' arcivescovo Turpino,** Archbishop Turpin; **il dottor Bianchi,** Dr. Bianchi; **l' avvocato Saivati,** Attorney Salvati, and before the words **signore, signora,** and **signorina** (provided they are not used in direct address).

m. The French forms **madama, madamigella,** are sometimes used instead of **signora, signorina,** which should then be followed by the article, as in French, as: **Madamigella la Contessa** (Mademoiselle la Comtesse), Countess; **Madama la Baronessa** (Madame la Baronne), Baroness.

n. Before Proper Nouns accompanied by Adjectives or by some expression that restricts their meaning, as: **Il giusto Iddio,** the just God; **il Dio d' Abramo, d' Isacco,** the God of Abraham, of Isaac; **il povero Giobbe,** poor Job.

o. Before Proper Nouns used in the plural, as: **i Demosteni, i Plutarchi, gli Ambrogi.**

p. Before Proper Nouns used to indicate the work of a painter, a sculptor, etc., as: **Il Mosè** di Michelangelo, **la Gerusalemme** del Tasso, **il Guglielmo Tell** di Rossini.

q. Before the names of mountains, rivers, seas, lakes, oceans, as: **il Monviso, il Po, il Mediterraneo, l' Atlantico.**

r. In many expressions like: **Imparare o sapere il francese, l' italiano,** etc., to learn or to know French, Italian; **suonare il pianoforte,** to play the piano; **giuocare alle carte, al biliardo,** to play at cards, at billiards; **sia il benvenuto!** welcome, sir! **domandare l' elemosina,** to ask for charity; **entrò (il) pel primo, (la) per la prima,** he (she) entered first; **verso le sei,** towards six o'clock; **la settimana scorsa, l' anno scorso,** last week, last year; **dare del tu, del voi, del lei,** to address a person with "thou," "you."

II. The Definite Article is omitted:

a. Before the names of the months, as: **gennaio,** January; **il mese di marzo,** March. But the Article is used, when these names are followed by some other word denoting **time,** etc., as: **nell' ottobre dell' anno scorso,** in October of last year.

b. Before Ordinal Numbers, when used with the names of sovereigns, as: **Carlo decimo,** Charles X; **Enrico quarto,** Henry IV.

c. If **Santo (San)** precedes a Proper Name, the Article is omitted, as: **San Carlo,** St. Charles. Before an Appellative Noun the construction is as in English, as: **la Santa Cena,** the Lord's Supper, the Holy Eucharist; **il Santo Padre,** the Holy Father.[1]

d. Before the days of the week, as in English: **Vi andrò lunedì o martedì,** I shall go there on Monday or Tuesday; except when the **same day** of each consecutive week is meant, as:

Il vapore per Corfù parte da Trieste il martedì ed il venerdì.
The steamer to Corfu starts from Trieste *every* Tuesday and Friday.

e. After the Verb **essere,** to be; **divenire, diventare,** to become; **fare,** to make; **nascere,** to be born as; **morire,** to die as; **parere, sembrare,** to seem; **essere creduto, riputato,** to be believed, to be taken for; **ritornare,** to come back; **essere dichiarato,** to be declared; **proclamare,** to proclaim; **mostrarsi,** to show one's self, etc., if these Verbs are followed by a Substantive implying dignity, rank, nation, etc. Examples: **Sono Italiano,** I am an Italian. **Luigi Napoleone venne eletto imperatore,** Louis Napoleon was elected Emperor. **Egli nacque principe,** he is a prince by birth.

---

[1] *Santo* before a vowel is shortened into *Sant';* before a consonant, except *S impura,* into *San,* and before *S impura* it does not change, thus: *Sant' Agostino, San Gregorio, Santo Stefano.*

Davide fu proclamato re d' Israele, David was proclaimed King of
Israel.[1]

f. When speaking of much frequented places, as: **andare a
scuola,** to go to school; **essere in chiesa,** to be at church.

g. In a great many phrases, as: **sotto pretesto,** under pretext;
dopo pranzo, after dinner; **essere d' avviso,** to be of the opinion;
chiudere occhio, trovar modo di, andare a caccia, etc.

h. The Definite Article is further omitted before Substantives
implying **dignity** when they are preceded by a Possessive Adjective,
as: **Sua Santità,** Your Holiness; **Vostra Maestà,** Your Majesty,
etc. But it is said: **La Santità Sua, La Maestà Vostra,** etc.[2]

l. Before the title names **fra** or **frate,** friar: **monsignore; donna,
madonna,** madam; **suora,** sister, and **Santo,** when followed by
some other Noun, as: **fra Cristoforo, monsignore Della Casa,
donna Luisa, madonna Laura, madama Margherita, suora Marta,
Santo Stefano.**

m. The Definite Article may be omitted also before Nouns used
in a general sense, as: **Pane, vino, olio, legna sono le cose più
necessarie in una famiglia,** bread, wine, oil, and wood are the most
necessary things in a family; before Nouns indicating relationship,
as: **padre, madre, fratello, sorella,** when they are preceded only by
an Adjective Possessive in the singular: **tuo padre,** your father;
mia sorella, my sister; but **l'ottimo tuo padre,** your excellent
father; **la virtuosa tua sorella,** your virtuous sister; **il mio caro
padre,** my dear father; **i tuoi fratelli,** your brothers.

III. The Indefinite Article is omitted:

a. After the Verb **essere.** (See above rule II., *e.*)

b. In **apposition,** which in English generally requires the
Indefinite Article, as: **L' Avaro, commedia di Molière,** The Miser,
a comedy by Molière.[3]

c. In such cases where the notion is quite indefinite, as: **Se
assiso in sì gran teatro** (poetically), if sitting in so large a theatre.

---

[1] Except when used with *ecco* (there is, here is) or if an *attribute* is added to the
substantive, as: *ecco un inglese,* here is an Englishman. *Il signor N. è un medico
di merito,* Mr. N. is a physician of merit. The noun *Re,* king, when followed by a

d. In many expressions like: **far segno,** to make sign; **far regalo, far dono,** to make a present; **dar principio,** to begin; **mettere fine,** to make an end; **dare** or **attaccare battaglia,** to engage in battle; **prestare servizio,** to do a service, to be of use; **far piacere,** to give pleasure.

13. The two languages agree:

a. In many proverbial expressions, as: **Vivere insieme come cane e gatto,** to lead a cat-and-dog life; **povertà non è onta,** poverty is no disgrace.

b. Where similar words are rapidly enumerated and finally comprehended in a general expression, like **tutto, niente, nulla,** etc., as: **Vecchi, giovani, donne, fanciulli, tutti furono trucidati,** old and young men, women and children, all were killed.

c. Headings in books: **atto primo,** first act; **scena terza,** third scene; **libro quinto,** fifth book.

d. After **nè—nè,** neither—nor, and **mai,** never; **nè preghiere nè minacce potevano muoverlo,** neither prayers nor threats could move him; **mai predizione ebbe un compimento sì pronto,** never was a prediction so promptly fulfilled.

e. After the Prepositions **con, senza, per, di, a, da,** etc., when these particles form **adverbial expressions** with the following Substantives, as: **con pazienza,** with patience (= patiently); **con piacere,** with pleasure; **con permesso,** with permission; **con cura,** carefully; **senza denaro,** without money; **senza cerimonie,** without ceremony; **per ordine,** by order; **sotto pena di morte,** on pain of death; **di notte,** by night; **di giorno,** by day; **da galantuomo,** as an honest man; **per anno,** a year, per annum; **per mese,** monthly; **per terra,** by land; **per mare,** by sea, etc.

---

proper noun, generally takes the Article, as: *il re Salomone.* But *Papa,* Pope, rejects it usually, as: *Papa Innocenzo.*

[2] In the plural these nouns always require the Article, whether the possessive adjective precedes or follows: *Le loro signorie* or *le signorie loro.*

[3] In English the Definite Article is occasionally used with the Noun in apposition, as: *the lion, the king of beasts.* When such an apposition is to be taken in *quite a general sense,* and expresses *a fact known by everybody,* the Definite Article is used in Italian as in English. Example: *Il leone, il re degli animali. Dante e Petrarca, i più grandi poeti d' Italia,* Dante and Petrarch, the greatest poets of Italy.

220

f. After a great many verbs that require the Prepositions **di, a** or **da,** if the following noun is employed in a general sense, as: **Colmare di benefici,** to overwhelm with benefits; **vivere di pane,** to live on bread; **scendere da cavallo,** to dismount, to alight; **essere a cavallo,** to be on horseback; **morire di noia,** to die of ennui, etc.

g. Finally, in many expressions like the following, where the Verb together with the Substantive suggest but one idea, for instance: **rendere grazie,** to thank; **prestare fede,** to believe. Such expressions are: **aver fame,** to be hungry; **aver motivo,** to have a reason; **aver sete,** to be thirsty; **far paura,** to frighten; **aver cura,** to take care; **far caso di,** to heed; **aver compassione,** to pity; **far menzione,** to mention; **aver vergogna,** to be ashamed; **aver voglia,** to have a mind; **aver ragione,** to be right; **aver bisogno,** to want; **aver torto,** to be wrong; **prendere parte,** to participate; **prendere piede,** to settle; **rendere grazie,** to thank; **prendere moglie,** to take a wife; **rendere conto,** to account for; **correre rischio,** to run the risk; **far mostra,** to feign; **chiedere perdono,** to beg pardon; **correre fortuna,** to risk.[1]

Special Rules On The Use Of The Article

14. When the article is given to a Noun followed by others of the same Gender and Number, these Nouns may each take or reject it. For instance:

Niuna cosa è tanto in grazia degli uomini, quanto la virtù, la bontà e l' onestà.—L' umanità, continenza e modestia nei giovani è molto lodata.

Nothing pleases men so much as virtue, goodness and honesty.— Humanity, continence and modesty are praiseworthy in young people.

15. Whenever an Article precedes a Noun followed by other Nouns of a different Gender or Number, each of them must take it, too. Example:

L' ingegno, il giudizio, la memoria, la ragione, il consiglio, e l' altre potenze in noi non ci sono date per non adoperarle.

---

[1] NOTE.—All these words, when used in a definite sense, require the Article as in English. Example: *Senza il denaro che mi avete promesso,* without the money you have promised me.

Talent, judgment, memory, reason, prudence, and the other
faculties were not given to us to be left idle.

16. Various Nouns of the same Gender and Number, but expressing
qualities that cannot be found in the same Subject, must, each of
them, be accompanied by the Article, Example:

Ama gli amici e i nemici.
Thou shalt love friends and foes.

17. Of two or more Nouns referring to the same Subject, only the
first one will take the Article. Example:

*Il legislatore e condottiero del popolo ebreo non entrò nella terra
promessa.*
The lawgiver and leader of the Hebrews did not enter the Promised
Land.

THE PARTITIVE ARTICLE

18. In English the words **some, any** often precede a Substantive
taken in an indefinite sense, as: **some** wine, **some** bread, **any** money.

In Italian, as in French, this relation is expressed by **di** plus the
Definite Article.

Thus, while **the** wine, **the** beer, **the** oil are rendered by **il vino,
la birra, l' olio**; **some** wine, **some** beer, **some** oil are expressed by
del vino, **della** birra, **dell'** olio.

19. Whenever such words are used in quite an **indefinite, and
general sense,** both languages agree, and no Article precedes the
Substantive. Example: He sells paper, pencils, and ink, **egli vende
carta, matite ed inchiostro.** In negative sentences, the Partitive
Article is generally omitted. Thus: We have no flowers, **Non abbiamo
fiori.** You have neither money nor friends, **Non avete nè denaro nè
amici.**

20. The Partitive is of frequent occurrence. The Article is entirely
omitted and **di** takes its place before the Substantive, and is generally
governed by another word implying **measure, weight, number** or
quantity, as: **Una bottiglia di vino,** a bottle of wine; **un bicchiere d'
acqua,** a glass of water; **dieci libbre di carne,** ten pounds of meat;
una quantità di zucchero, a quantity of sugar.

21. English Compound Substantives are often rendered by this
use of the preposition **di**: **Il maestro di scuola,** the schoolmaster;
il mercante di vino, the wine-merchant.

22. Adjectives denoting the material of which a thing is made are rendered by a Substantive with **di**, as: **Un anello d' oro,** a gold ring; **una tavola di legno,** a wooden table.

23. It is used after expressions of **quantity,** as: **Niente di buono,** nothing good; **qualche cosa di grande,** something great.

NOUNS
Formation Of The Plural
GENERAL RULES

24. All masculine Nouns ending in unaccented **a, e, o,** and all feminine Nouns ending in unaccented **e, o,** form their plural by changing these terminations into **i,** as: **il profeta, il dottore, il maestro, la siepe, la mano,** the prophet, the doctor, the teacher, the fence, the hand; **i profeti, i dottori, i maestri, le siepi, le mani,** the prophets, the doctors, the teachers, the fences, the hands.

25. All feminine Nouns ending in an unaccented **a,** form their plural by changing it into **e,** as: **la pera, la mela, la rosa,** the pear, the apple, the rose; **le pere, le mele, le rose,** the pears, the apples, the roses.

26. Masculine and feminine Nouns ending in **i,** as: **il barbagianni, l' ipotesi, la diocesi,** the owl, the hypothesis, the diocese; in an accented vowel, as: **l' infermità, la virtù,** the infirmity, the virtue; or of **one single** syllable, as: **il re, la gru,** the king, the crane, retain the same termination in the plural as in the singular.

EXCEPTIONS

27. **Dio** (God), **gli dei and dii; l' uomo** (man), **gli uomini; il bue** (ox), **i buoi; la moglie** (wife), **le mogli; mille** (a thousand), **mila** (thousands).

Special Rules for the Plural of Nouns

28. Masculine Nouns ending in **ca** and **ga,** as: **il patriarca,** the patriarch; **il monarca,** the monarch; **il duca,** the duke; **il collega,** the colleague, end in the plural in **chi** and **ghi : i patriarchi, i monarchi, i duchi, i colleghi. Il Belga,** the Belgian, however, has **i Belgi.**

29. The feminine Nouns in **ca** and **ga,** as: **la fatica,** fatigue; **l'ortica,** nettle; **la ruga,** wrinkle; **la spiga,** ear of corn, are in the plural: **le fatiche, le ortiche, le rughe, le spighe.**

30. Nouns ending in **cia, gia,** as: **la ciancia,** idle talk; **lancia,** spear;

scheggia, splinter; **pioggia,** rain, end in the plural in either **ce, ge,** or in **cie, gie : ciance; lance; schegge; piogge.**[1]

31. Nouns of two syllables ending in **co, go,** as: **baco,** worm, silkworm; **fico,** fig; **spago,** thread; **luogo,** place, generally end in the plural in **chi, ghi : bachi, fichi, spaghi, luoghi.**[2]

32. Some Nouns of three, four or more syllables ending in **co, go,** have in the plural **chi, ghi,** and others **ci, gi. Stomaco** (stomach), **stomachi; castigo** (punishment), **castighi; amico** (friend), **amici; asparago** (asparagus), **asparagi.** Also, some Nouns take both terminations; as: **mendico** (beggar), **mendici** and **mendichi; astrologo** (astrologer), **astrologi** and **astrologhi; teologo** (theologian), **teologi** and **teologhi.**

33. Nouns ending in **io,** with an accented **i,** as: **lavorio,** work; **mormorio,** murmur, change the final **o** into **i,** and become: **lavorii, mormorii.**

34. Nouns ending in **io,** with an unaccented **i,** as: **arancio,** orange; **ciliegio,** cherry-tree; **rosaio,** rose-bush; **finocchio,** fennel; **tiglio,** linden-tree; **vizio,** vice, simply drop the **o** to form the plural, thus: **aranci, ciliegi, rosai, finocchi, tigli, vizi.**

35. Nouns in **io** form their plural regularly, that is with double **ii,** by changing **o** into **i,** whenever they might be mistaken for other words with a different meaning. Thus: it is necessary to distinguish **atrio** (atrium, vestibule), **atrii,** from **atro** (dark, dreadful), **atri; benificio,** (benefit, benefice, profit), **beneficii,** from **benefico,** (beneficent), **benefici; maleficio** (ill action or deed, crime), **maleficii,** from **malefico** (maleficent), **malefici; odio** (hatred), **odii,** from **odi** (thou hearest); **principio** (principle), **principii,** from **principe** (prince), **principi; assassinio** (murder), **assassinii,** from **assassino** (murderer), **assassini; augurio** (augury, wish), **augurii,** from **auguri** (thou wishest), etc.

Other Nouns in **io** require **ii** in the plural simply because this sounds better to Italian ears, as in **astio** (invidiousness, wrath), **astii; olio** (oil), **olii.**

---

[1] NOTE.—It is necessary to use *cie* and *gie* wherever the other terminations may cause a misapprehension, as: *camicie* (shirts), *cámice* (alb, a priest's vestment); *fallacie* (fallacies), *fallace* (fallacious); *torcie* (torches), *torce* (he twists).

[2] NOTE.—*Mago* becomes *Magi* to indicate the Three Wise Men of the East, and *maghi* to indicate magicians or sorcerers. *Greco* is changed into *greci. Porco* (swine), is changed into *porci. Stoico* (Stoic), is changed into *stoici.*

Nouns With More Than One Ending

36. Some Nouns have more than one termination either in the singular or in the plural, or even in both Cases, and are, therefore, **irregular.**

The following Nouns have in the plural a masculine ending in **i** and a feminine one in **a**:

Singular	Plural
l' anello, the ring	gli anelli or le anella
il braccio, the arm	i bracci or le braccia
il budello, the gut	i budelli or le budella
il calcagno, the heel	i calcagni or le calcagna
il ciglio, the eyelash	i cigli or le ciglia
il sopracciglio, the eyebrow	i sopraccigli or le sopracciglia

And in the same way **il corno,** the horn; **il dito,** the finger; **il filo,** the thread; **il fondamento,** the foundation; **il ginocchio,** the knee; **il labbro,** the lip; **il lenzuolo,** the bed-sheet; **il membro,** the limb; **il muro,** the wall; **l' osso,** the bone; **il riso,** the laugh, the rice, etc.

37. The following feminine Nouns have two endings in the singular, **a** and **e,** which are correspondingly changed into two terminations, **e** and **i**:

Singular	Plural
l' ala, l' ale, the wing	le ale, le ali
l' arma, l' arme, the weapon	le arme, le armi
la sementa, la semente, the seed	le semente, le sementi

38. Some Nouns have in the singular a masculine termination in **o** and a feminine termination in **a,** the first being changed into **i** for the plural, and the other into **e,** as:

Singular		Plural	
MASC.	FEM.	MASC.	FEM.
il bisogno	la bisogna, the need, the task	i bisogni	le bisogne
il briciolo	la briciola, the crumb	i bricioli	le briciole
il canestro	le canestra, the basket	i canestri	le canestre
il cesto	la cesta, the basket	i cesti	le ceste
il gocciolo	la gocciola, the drop	i goccioli	le gocciole
il midollo	la midolla, the marrow	i midolli	le midolle
l' orecchio	l' orecchia, the ear	gli orecchi	le orecchie
il nuvolo	la nuvola, the cloud	i nuvoli	le nuvole

39. Further, a final **o** for the masculine, and a final **a** for the feminine in the singular, the former being changed into **i**, and the latter into **e** or **a** in the plural, are the termination of the few nouns below:

Singular		Plural	
MASC.	FEM.	MASC.	FEM.
il cervello	la cervella, the brain	i cervelli	le cervella
il frutto	la frutta, the fruit	i frutti	le frutta
il gesto	la gesta, the gesture, exploit	i gesti	le gesta
il legno	la legna, the wood	i legni	le legna
il vestigio	the vestige	i vestigi	le vestigia

REMARK.—Some of these Irregular Nouns change their meaning in changing their termination. Thus we may say:

Il frutto, la frutta, i frutti, le frutta di quest'albero, the fruit, the fruits of this tree; but we can only say: **Il frutto, i frutti della terra, dell' ingegno, della virtù,** the fruit, the fruits of the earth, of talent, of virtue.

I membri, le membra del corpo, the limbs of the body; but only **i membri di una famiglia, di un' accademia,** the members of a family or of an academy.

I muri, le mura di una casa, the walls of a house; but only **le mura d' una città,** the walls of a city.

I fondamenti, le fondamenta di una casa, the foundations of a house; but only **i fondamenti della religione, di una scienza,** the foundations of religion, of a science.

Gli ossi, le ossa del corpo degli animali, the bones of the body of animals; but only **gli ossi delle ciliegie, delle pesche,** the pits of cherries, of peaches.

Legna da ardere, firewood; but only **legni** to signify vehicles or ships.

Bisogno, bisogni, needs; while **bisogna, bisogne,** mean business, affairs, task.

Le gesta, exploits; **i gesti,** the movements of the body or gestures of the hand.

40. The following masculine Nouns have two terminations for the singular and one for the plural:

Singular	Plural
il consigliero or consigliere, the counselor, adviser	i consiglieri
il destriero or destriere, the war-horse, steed	i destrieri
lo scolaro or scolare, the pupil	gli scolari
lo stilo or stile, the style	gli stili
il vomero or vomere, the ploughshare	i vomeri

41. The plural of Compound Nouns is formed in accordance with the rules below:

  a. The first part of a Compound Noun does not change if it is a truncated word, or a word of Latin or Greek extraction, or a Verb or an invariable word by nature.

Singular	Plural
il melarancio, the orange-tree	i melaranci
il malcontento, a discontented person	i malcontenti
il granduca, the Grand Duke	i granduchi
il Paternostro, the "Our Father" or the Lord's Prayer	i Paternostri
l' Avemaria, the "Hail Mary!"	le Avemarie
l' antropofago, the cannibal	gli antropofagi
lo spazzacamino, the chimney-sweeper	gli spazzacamini

  b. The following Nouns form their plural by changing the endings of both parts or only that of the second one. Thus:

Singular	Plural
il capolavoro, the masterpiece	i capolavori
il capomastro, the master mason	i capimastri
il bassorilievo, the bas relief	i bassorilievi or bassirilievi
il melogranato, the pomegranate	i melogranati or meligranati
il capoverso, the beginning of a verse	i capoversi or capiversi
il pannolino, the handkerchief, linen	i pannolini or pannilini
la cassapanca, the locker	le cassapanche
il verdebruno, dark green, olive color	i verdebruni or verdibruni
il verdegiallo, a color between green and yellow, apple-green	i verdegialli or verdigialli

  c. The second part of a Compound Noun is generally invariable in the plural if the Preposition **di** has been understood between the two parts. Thus:

Singular	Plural
il capoparte (capo di parte), the leader of a faction	i capiparte (capi di parte)
il capopopolo (capo di popolo), the head of the people	i capipopolo (capi di popolo)
il caposcuola (capo di scuola), the head of a school	i capiscuola (capi di scuola)

42. Proper compound family Nouns form their plural in the following ways:

Singular	Plural
Acquaviva	gli Acquaviva or Acquavivi
Casanova	i Casanova or Casanovi
Fortebraccio	i Fortebraccio or Fortebracci

Modifying Suffixes

43. The richness of the Italian language lies in its power of developing new terms by adding syllables not generally recognizable as separate words. This method of word-making is one of the most conspicuous features of the language, and one of the most difficult to master in all its details.

These derivatives usually indicate size or importance greater or less than normal, and are called respectively Augmentatives and Diminutives, though the force of those called Augmentatives is often extended to express ugliness, grotesqueness, coarseness, etc., while Diminutives frequently become terms of endearment, or imply insignificance or contemptibility.

These secondary values sometimes supplant the original meanings; but as the forms are the same it will be convenient to treat all mere modifying terminations as Augmentatives and Diminutives. They are added to Nouns, Adjectives, and occasionally to Adverbs.

Augmentative Suffixes

44. The terminations **one, ona** indicate large size, or an increased degree of a quality, and sometimes add the idea of clumsiness and grotesqueness. Feminine Nouns frequently assume the masculine termination **one,** but may also take the feminine ending **ona.**

libro, librone, book, large book.
porta, portone or **portona,** door, large door.

scala, **scalone** or **scalona,** stair.
donna, **donnone** or **donnona,** woman, big woman.
ricco, **riccone** or **riccona,** rich, very rich.
bene, **benone,** well, very well.

45. **Otto, otta** express strength and bigness.

giovane, **giovanotto,** young man, strong, smart young man.
contadina, **contadinotta,** country woman, strong countrywoman.

46. **Accio, accia; astro, astra; azzo, azza** are merely depreciative, expressing the poor quality of what is represented by the Noun, or contempt or disdain for it.

dottore, **dottoraccio,** doctor, bad, ignorant doctor.
donna, **donnaccia,** woman, a very bad woman.
medico, **medicastro,** physician, a quack.

Diminutive Suffixes

47. **Ino, ina; etto, etta; ello, ella;** convey the idea of pretty, sweet, dear, nice, etc., as well as **little;** but size is sometimes left out of account.

povero, **poverino,** poor, my dear poor boy.
mano, **manina,** hand, nice little hand.
vecchio, **vecchietto,** old man, little old man.
conte, **contino,** count, young count.
contessa, **contessina,** countess, young countess.

48. **Uolo, olo, uccio, uzzo, ola, uzza,** denote diminution and at the same time contempt or disdain; but they do not always exclude the idea of endearment.

casa, **casuccia,** house, a miserable little house.

49. For the sake of euphony a letter or a syllable is often inserted before these terminations, as: **rete,** net; **reticella,** little net; **testa,** head; **testolina,** little head; **pazzo,** fool; **pazzerello,** little fool.

50. Other terminations of this kind are:

aglia, as: **plebaglia,** populace.
icciolo, icciola, as: **terricciola,** little village; **resticciolo,** little remainder.
iccio, igno, ognolo, as: **giallognolo,** yellowish; **verdiccio,** greenish; **asprigno,** somewhat harsh.
uto, as: **nasuto,** long-nosed; **corpacciuto,** stout.

51. Not every word having one of these terminations is an Augmentative or a Diminutive word, as: **scodella,** dish.

Nor can these terminations be used indifferently. There are Substantives which are never found, *e. g.,* with **ella** or **ello,** etc., whereas they admit **etto** or **etta.** Thus **casella,** from **casa,** is seldom or never used, the usual form being **casetta,** etc.

Formation of Feminine Nouns

52. Many Nouns ending in **o** or **e** change this termination into **a,** as: **servo, serva,** man-servant, maid-servant; **signore, signora,** gentlemen, lady; **padrone, padrona,** master, mistress.

Others change their termination **tore** into **trice,** as: **imperatore, imperatrice,** emperor, empress; **pittore, pittrice,** painter, female painter.

Some Nouns in **a** or in **e** change these endings into **essa,** as: **poeta, poetessa,** poet, poetess; **oste, ostessa,** host, hostess.

Others change the entire name, as: **il padre, la madre,** the father, the mother; **il fratello, la sorella,** the brother, the sister, etc.

53. Others have a double termination, as: **rivenditore,** broker, a seller of second-hand articles, **rivenditrice** or **rivenditora; traditore,** traitor, has **traditrice** and **traditora; dottore,** doctor, makes **dottora** and **dottoressa.**

GENDER OF NOUNS ACCORDING TO TERMINATIONS

54. Nouns in **o** are generally masculine, as: **fuoco,** fire; **libro,** book; **ferro,** iron.[1]

55. Nouns in **a** are generally feminine, as: **favilla,** spark; **fiamma,** flame.[2]

56. Nouns ending in **e** or **i** are some masculine and some feminine, and others of both genders, as: **il pane,** bread; **il latte,** milk; **il brindisi,** the toast; **la neve,** the snow; **la siepe,** the hedge; **la voce,** the voice; **il** or **la carcere,** the prison; **il** or **la fonte,** the spring; **il** or **la fronte,** the front, the forehead; **il** or **la trave,** the beam.

---

[1] REMARK.—*Imago,* image; *propago,* layer of a vine or tree; *vorago,* abyss; *testudo,* tortoise (poetical forms), and *mano,* hand, are feminine.

[2] EXCEPTIONS.—Nouns in *ma* of Greek origin, as: *aroma, assioma, clima, emblema, enigma, idioma, poema,* etc.

57. The names of the letters of the alphabet are either masculine or feminine except the foreign letter **k,** which is always masculine: **il k (il cappa).**

58. Any other part of speech used substantively is of the masculine Gender, as: **il bello, il ridere, il perchè, il quando, il dove.**

Gender Of The Names Of Plants

59. Names of plants, flowers, or fruits in **o, e** or **u** are masculine, those in **a** are feminine, as: **il frassino,** the ash-tree; **il salice,** the willow-tree; **il lampone,** the raspberry plant; **il bambù,** the bamboo; **la quercia,** the oak; **la rosa,** the rose; **l' uva,** the grape.[1]

60. Whenever the tree has the same name as the fruit, the former takes the masculine termination **o,** and the latter the feminine termination in **a.**

il ciliegio, the cherry-tree; **la ciliegia,** the cherry
il pero, the pear-tree; **la pera,** the pear[2]

Gender Of The Names of Cities, Countries, and Rivers

61. Names of cities in **a** are feminine, as:

I vestigi dell' antica Roma adornano ancora la nuova.
The traces of ancient Rome still adorn new Rome.

Names of cities in **e, i, o,** or **u,** as: **Firenze, Milano, Napoli, Corfù,** are of both genders.

62. Names of countries or rivers in **a** are feminine, and masculine if they end in any other vowel: **la Francia, la Dora, il Portogallo, il Piemonte, il Friuli, il Perù, l' Arno, il Tevere, il Tamigi.**[3]

---

[1] REMARK.—*La vite,* the vine; *la noce,* the nut; *la querce,* the oak, are feminine; while *abete,* fir-tree; *elce,* holm oak; *rovere,* the male oak, *noce,* nut-tree, are of both genders.

[2] REMARK.—*Arancio* is used for both fruit and tree, while *arancia,* orange, is employed only to indicate the fruit, while *il cedro, il cedrato,* and *il fico* denote both the lemon-tree and the lemon, the cedrate lemon-tree and the cedrate lemon, the fig-tree and the fig, without changing the gender.

[3] REMARK.—*Mella, Volga,* rivers' names, are always masculine, while *Adda, Brenta,* are of both genders.

Auxiliary Verbs—Verbi Ausiliari

Essere—To Be	Avere—To Have

Modo Indicativo
Presente

Essere	Avere
sono, I am	ho, I have
sei, you are (f.s.)	hai, you have (f.s.)
è, he is	ha, he has
siamo, we are	abbiamo, we have
siete, you are	avete, you have
sono, they are	hanno, they have

Imperfetto

Essere	Avere
ero, I was	avevo, I had
eri, you were (f.s.)	avevi, you had (f.s.)
era, he was	aveva, he had
eravamo, we were	avevamo, we had
eravate, you were	avevate, you had
erano, they were	avevano, they had

Passato Remoto

Essere	Avere
fui, I was	ebbi, I had
fosti, you were (f.s.)	avesti, you had (f.s.)
fu, he was	ebbe, he had
fummo, we were	avemmo, we had
foste, you were	aveste, you had
furono, they were	ebbero, they had

Futuro Semplice

Essere	Avere
sarò, I shall be	avrò, I shall have
sarai, you will be (f.s.)	avrai, you will have (f.s.)
sarà, he will be	avrà, he will have
saremo, we shall be	avremo, we shall have
sarete, you will be	avrete, you will have
saranno, they will be	avranno, they will have

Modo Condizionale
Presente

Essere	Avere
sarei, I should be	avrei, I should have
saresti, you would be (f.s.)	avresti, you would have (f.s.)
sarebbe, he would be	avrebbe, he would have
saremmo, we should be	avremmo, we should have
sareste, you would be	avreste, you would have
sarebbero, they would be	avrebbero, they would have

Tempi Composti—Compound Tenses
Passato Prossimo

(I have been, etc.)
  sono stato-a
  sei stato-a
  è stato-a
  siamo stati-e
  siete stati-e
  sono stati-e

(I have had, etc.)
  ho avuto
  hai avuto
  ha avuto
  abbiamo avuto
  avete avuto
  hanno avuto

Trapassato Prossimo

(I had been, etc.)
  ero stato-a
  eri stato-a
  era stato-a
  eravamo stati-e
  eravate stati-e
  erano stati-e

(I had had, etc.)
  avevo avuto
  avevi avuto
  aveva avuto
  avevamo avuto
  avevate avuto
  avevano avuto

Trapassato Remoto

(I had been, etc.)
  fui stato-a
  fosti stato-a
  fu stato-a
  fummo stati-e
  foste stati-e
  furono stati-e

(I had had, etc.)
  ebbi avuto
  avesti avuto
  ebbe avuto
  avemmo avuto
  aveste avuto
  ebbero avuto

Futuro Anteriore

(I shall have been, etc.)
  sarò stato-a
  sarai stato-a
  sarà stato-a
  saremo stati-e
  sarete stati-e
  saranno stati-e

(I shall have had, etc.)
  avrò avuto
  avrai avuto
  avrà avuto
  avremo avuto
  avrete avuto
  avranno avuto

Modo Condizionale
Passato

(I should have been, etc.)
  sarei stato-a
  saresti stato-a
  sarebbe stato-a
  saremmo stati-e
  sareste stati-e
  sarebbero stati-e

(I should have had, etc.)
  avrei avuto
  avresti avuto
  avrebbe avuto
  avremmo avuto
  avreste avuto
  avrebbero avuto

sii (sia), be (f.s.)
non essere, be not (f.s.)
sia, be (polite form)
siamo, let us be
siate, be (you)
siano, let them be

abbi, have (f.s.)
non avere, have not (f.s.)
abbia, have (polite form)
abbiamo, let us have
abbiate, have
abbiano, let them have

Modo Soggiuntivo
Presente

(That I be, etc.)
  che sia
  che sii, *or* sia
  che sia
  che siamo
  che siate
  che siano

(That I may have, etc.)
  che abbia
  che abbi *or* abbia
  che abbia
  che abbiamo
  che abbiate
  che abbiano

Imperfetto

(That I were, etc.)
  che fossi
  che fossi
  che fosse
  che fossimo
  che foste
  che fossero

(That I had, etc.)
  che avessi
  che avessi
  che avesse
  che avessimo
  che aveste
  che avessero

Passato

(That I have been, etc.)
  che sia stato-a
  che sii *or* sia stato-a
  che sia stato-a
  che siamo stati-e
  che siate stati-e
  che siano stati-e

(That I have had, etc.)
  che abbia avuto
  che abbi *or* abbia avuto
  che abbia avuto
  che abbiamo avuto
  che abbiate avuto
  che abbiano avuto

Trapassato

(That I had been, etc.)
  che fossi stato-a
  che fossi stato-a
  che fosse stato-a
  che fossimo stati-e
  che foste stati-e
  che fossero stati-e

(That I had had, etc.)
  che avessi avuto
  che avessi avuto
  che avesse avuto
  che avessimo avuto
  che aveste avuto
  che avessero avuto

Modo Infinito

essere, to be   avere, to have

Gerundio

essendo, being   avendo, having

Participio Presente

essente (seldom used), being   avente, having

Participio Passato

stato, been   avuto, had

Remarks on "Essere" and "Avere"

63. The Compound Tenses of **essere** are formed with itself, as: **io sono stato,** I have been (Lit.: I am been): **io sarò stato,** I shall have been. The Past Participle **stato** always agrees in Gender and Number with the Subject, as **ella è stata,** she has been; **noi siamo stati,** we have been; **esse sono state,** they have been.

If I had, if he had, etc., must be rendered by the **imperfetto del soggiuntivo: se io avessi, se egli avesse;** and if I had been, if we had had, by the **trapassato del soggiuntivo: Se io fossi stato, se noi avessimo avuto.**

64. When in English, after **if,** the Indicative Mood is used, the same mood stands in Italian after **se.** After this latter even the Future Tense can be used in Italian, if the action is a future one, just as after **when** (as soon as) in English. Example:

Se egli non ha libri, non è contento.
If he has no books, he is not contented.
Se avrò denaro, comprerò una casa.
If I shall have money, I shall buy a house.

65. As has been stated before, the Italian verb does not always require the personal pronouns **io, tu, egli,** etc., the persons being sufficiently marked by the terminations of the Verb. For example: **Avete?** have you? **Avrete?** will you have? etc.

66. **Avere** also means **to receive, to get,** as: **Avrò del danaro,** I shall get some money.

67. The second person singular of the Imperative is expressed by the Infinitive whenever it is employed negatively, as: **Non essere impaziente,** do not be impatient.

68. The words **è, era, fu, sia, fosse,** etc., are occasionally employed instead of **sono, erano, furono, siano, fossero,** etc., in the sense of "there are," "there were," etc., as:

C' è uomini di tal fatta che nella foggia del vestire pongono il merito della persona.

There are men who put the merit of a person into the manner of [his] dressing.

69. **Ha, aveva, ebbe, abbia** are sometimes elegantly used instead of **è, era, fu, sia.** Example:

Non vi ha cosa che mi dispiaccia di più.

There is nothing that displeases me more.

70. The words **è, ha** are sometimes contracted into one word with **mi, ti, si, ci, vi,** whose initial consonant is then doubled, thus:

Il tempo è breve ed ecci (ci è) necessario a molte cose. Havvi degli uomini (vi ha degli uomini) sfaccendati che si mostrano occupatissimi a tutte le ore.

Time is brief and we need it for many things.

There are idle men who seem to be always very busy.

This usage is purely literary.

Regular Verbs—Verbi Regolari

71. There are in Italian three regular Conjugations:

The First Conjugation with the Infinitive Mood ending in **are,** as: **Amare,** to love.

The Second Conjugation with the Infinitive Mood ending in **ere,** as: **Temere,** to fear.

The Third Conjugation with the Infinitive Mood ending in **ire,** as: **Partire,** to leave.

These Verbs are called Regular, because their root never changes throughout the entire Conjugation, and their terminations are always formed in accordance with a fixed rule.

Coniugazione dei Verbi Regolari

1.ª Am-are—To Love	2.ª Tem-ere—To Fear	3.ª Part-ire—To Leave

Modo Indicativo
Presente

(I love, etc.)	(I fear, etc.)	(I leave, etc.)
am-o	tem-o	part-o
am-i	tem-i	part-i
am-a	tem-e	part-e
am-iamo	tem-iamo	part-iamo
am-ate	tem-ete	part-ite
am-ano	tem-ono	part-ono

Imperfetto

(I loved, etc.)	(I feared, etc.)	(I left, etc.)
am-avo	tem-evo	part-ivo
am-avi	tem-evi	part-ivi
am-ava	tem-eva	part-iva
am-avamo	tem-evamo	part-ivamo
am-avate	tem-evate	part-ivate
am-avano	tem-evano	part-ivamo

Passato Remoto

(I loved, etc.)	(I feared, etc.)	(I left, etc.)
am-ai	tem-ei	part-ii
am-asti	tem-esti	part-isti
am-ò	tem-è	part-ì
am-ammo	tem-emmo	part-immo
am-aste	tem-este	part-iste
am-arono	tem-erono	part-irono

Futuro Semplice

(I shall love, etc.)	(I shall fear, etc.)	(I shall leave, etc.)
am-erò	tem-erò	part-irò
am-erai	tem-erai	part-irai
am-erà	tem-erà	part-irà
am-eremo	tem-eremo	part-iremo
am-erete	tem-erete	part-irete
am-eranno	tem-eranno	part-iranno

REMARK.—The vowel preceding the syllable *re* is characteristic of the whole Conjugation. The inflexions after these characteristic vowels are nearly alike in all three Conjugations. Some terminations are even always the same; they are:

The second person singular ending in *i*.
The first person plural ending in *mo*.
The second person plural ending in *te*.

Condizionale
Presente

(I should love, etc.)	(I should fear, etc.)	(I should leave, etc.)
am-erei	tem-erei	part-irei
am-eresti	tem-eresti	part-iresti
am-erebbe	tem-erebbe	part-irebbe
am-eremmo	tem-eremmo	part-iremmo
am-ereste	tem-ereste	part-ireste
am-erebbero	tem-erebbero	part-irebbero

Imperativo

am-a, love (f.s.)	temi, fear (f.s.)	parti, leave (f.s.)
non amare, don't love (f.s.)	non temere, don't fear (f.s.)	non partire, don't leave (f.s.)
am-i, let him love	tema, fear (polite form)	parta, leave (polite form)
am-iamo, let us love	temiamo, let us fear	partiamo, let us leave
am-ate, love (you)	temete, fear (you)	partite, do (you) leave
am-ino, let them love	temano, fear (polite form)	partano, leave (polite form)

Modo Soggiuntivo
Presente

(that I love, etc.)	(that I fear, etc.)	(that I leave, etc.)
che io am-i	che tem-a	che part-a
che tu am-i	che tem-a	che part-a
che egli am-i	che tem-a	che part-a
che noi am-iamo	che tem-iamo	che part-iamo
che voi am-iate	che tem-iate	che part-iate
che essi am-ino	che tem-ano	che part-ano

Imperfetto

(if I loved, etc.)	(if I feared, etc.)	(if I left, etc.)
se io am-assi	se tem-essi	se part-issi
se tu am-assi	se tem-essi	se part-issi
se egli am-asse	se tem-esse	se part-isse
se noi am-assimo	se tem-essimo	se part-issimo
se voi am-aste	se tem-este	se part-iste
se essi am-assero	se tem-essero	se part-issero

Infinito

am-are, to love	tem-ere, to fear	part-ire, to leave

Participio Presente

am-ante, loving	tem-ente, fearing	part-ente, leaving

Participio Passato

am-ato, loved   tem-uto, feared   part-ito, left

Gerundio

am-ando, loving   tem-endo, fearing   part-endo, leaving

Tempi Composti—Compound Tenses
Passato Prossimo

(I have loved, feared, etc.)   (I have left, etc.)
  ho amato, temuto   sono partito-a
  hai amato, temuto   sei partito-a
  ha amato, temuto   è partito-a
  abbiamo amato, temuto   siamo partiti-e
  avete amato, temuto   siete partiti-e
  hanno amato, temuto   sono partiti-e

Trapassato Prossimo

(I had loved, feared, etc.)   (I had left, etc.)
  avevo amato, temuto   ero partito-a
  avevi amato, temuto   eri partito-a
  aveva amato, temuto   era partito-a
  avevamo amato, temuto   eravamo partiti-e
  avevate amato, temuto   eravate partiti-e
  avevano amato, temuto   erano partiti-e

Trapassato Remoto

(I had loved, feared, etc.)   (I had left, etc.)
  ebbi amato, temuto   fui partito-a
  avesti amato, temuto   fosti partito-a
  ebbe amato, temuto   fu partito-a
  avemmo amato, temuto   fummo partiti-e
  aveste amato, temuto   foste partiti-e
  ebbero amato, temuto   furono partiti-e

Futuro Anteriore

(I shall have loved, feared, etc.)   (I shall have left, etc.)
  avrò amato, temuto   sarò partito-a
  avrai amato, temuto   sarai partito-a
  avrà amato, temuto   sarà partito-a
  avremo amato, temuto   saremo partiti-e
  avrete amato, temuto   sarete partiti-e
  avranno amato, temuto   saranno partiti-e

Condizionale
Passato

(I should have loved, feared, etc.)
  avrei amato, temuto
  avresti amato, temuto
  avrebbe amato, temuto
  avremmo amato, temuto
  avreste amato, temuto
  avrebbero amato, temuto

(I should have left, etc.)
  sarei partito-a
  saresti partito-a
  sarebbe partito-a
  saremmo partiti-e
  sareste partiti-e
  sarebbero partiti-e

Modo Soggiuntivo
Passato

(That I have loved, feared, etc.)
  che io abbia amato, temuto
  che tu abbi amato, temuto
  che egli abbia amato, temuto
  che noi abbiamo amato, temuto
  che voi abbiate amato, temuto
  che essi abbiano amato, temuto

(That I have left, etc.)
  che io sia partito-a
  che tu sii partito-a
  che egli sia partito-a
  che noi siamo partiti-e
  che voi siate partiti-e
  che essi siano partiti-e

Trapassato

(That I had loved, feared, etc.)
  che io avessi amato, temuto
  che tu avessi amato, temuto
  che egli avesse amato, temuto
  che noi avessimo amato, temuto
  che voi aveste amato, temuto
  che essi avessero amato, temuto

(That I had left, etc.)
  che io fossi partito-a
  che tu fossi partito-a
  che egli fosse partito-a
  che noi fossimo partiti-e
  che voi foste partiti-e
  che essi fossero partiti-e

Remarks On Some Regular Verbs

72. Verbs ending in **ciare, giare, sciare,** as: **cominciare, mangiare, lasciare,** retain the **i** before **a, o,** as: **comincia,** he begins; **mangio,** I eat; **lascio,** I leave. They usually reject it before an **e,** as: **cominceremo,** we shall begin; **mangerai,** you will eat; and they are never written with double **i,** as: **cominci,** you (fam. sing.) begin; **lasci,** you leave etc.

73. Verbs in **care, gare,** as: **giudicare, pregare,** take an **h** whenever **c** or **g** are followed by either an **i** or an **e,** as in **giudichiamo,** we judge; **giudicherò,** I shall judge; **preghiamo,** we pray; **pregherei,** I should pray.

74. Verbs ending in **iare,** as: **inviare,** to send; **obliare,** to forget; **traviare,** to lead astray, take the double i in the second person of the Present of the Indicative Mood, in the third person of the Imperative, in the singular of the Present of the Subjunctive, in the third person plural of the Imperative and the Subjunctive; if in the first person of the Present Tense of the Indicative the accent falls on the same i that precedes the termination, as: **invio,** I send; and hence **tu invii, oblii,** etc.

75. If the stress in the first person of the Present Tense of the Indicative is not on the i of **iare,** as in **io consiglio, cambio, macchio,** said Verbs will be written with but one **i,** as: **tu consigli, cambi, macchi,** you (f.s.) advise, change, stain.[1]

76. In the first person of the Imperfect Tense of the Indicative Mood, the Verb in the older, more literary language, could also end in **a,** as: **io amava, temeva, partiva,** I loved, feared, left.

77. Verbs of the Second and Third Conjugation may drop in the Imperfect of the Indicative the **v** of the terminations **va, vano,** as: **temea, temeano** instead of **temeva, temevano; sentia, sentiano** instead of **sentiva, sentivano.**

78. The Past Participle of the First Conjugation is sometimes abridged by changing **ato** into **o,** as **tronco** instead of **troncato.**

79. The Verbs **sentire, dissentire, consentire** have an Irregular Present Participle: **senziente, dissenziente, consenziente.**

80. The greater number of the Verbs of the Third Conjugation are Irregular in the Present Tense of the Indicative, the Imperative, and the Subjunctive Moods in the following way:

INDICATIVE

finisco, I finish
finisci, you finish (f.s.)
finisce, he finishes
finiamo, we finish
finite, you finish
finiscono, they finish

---

[1] REMARK.—But several Verbs in *iare,* as: *alleviare,* to alleviate; *variare,* to vary; *odiare,* to hate; *accoppiare,* to couple, etc., take double *i* in such cases in order not to be mistaken for some other Verbs or to give the *i* the right intonation. Example: *Bisogna che l' uomo si umilii, e faccia umili operazioni,* man must humiliate himself and perform humble things.

IMPERATIVE	SUBJUNCTIVE
finisci, finish (f.s.)	che finisca, that I finish
finisca, let him finish	che finisca, that you finish (f.s.)
finiamo, let us finish	che finisca, that he finish
finite, finish	che finiamo, that we finish
finiscano, let them finish	che finiate, that you finish
	che finiscano, that they finish

The Passive Verb

81. The Passive Verb is formed in Italian in three ways:

a. By means of the Auxiliary Verb **essere,** to be, with the Past Participle of the Active Verb. Example:

La felicità è cercata da tutti.

Happiness is sought by all.

b. By means of the simple Tenses of the Verb **venire,** with the Past Participle of the Verb to be conjugated. Example:

La felicità vien cercata da tutti.

Happiness is sought by all.

c. By the third person of the Active Verb preceded by the Pronoun **si.** Example:

La felicità si cerca, si è cercata, si cercherà sempre da tutti.

Happiness is sought, has been sought, and will always be sought by all.

d. There are other expressions found after the English or Latin fashion, as:

Dicono che avremo la guerra.

They say that we shall have war.

Mi danno del denaro.

They give me money.

Raccontano che il re voglia abdicare.

They say that the king will abdicate.

e. The Pronoun **si** may precede or follow the Verb—(The latter usage is literary). In this latter case it is contracted into one word with the Verb.

Coniugazione Passiva

Essere Amato, Venire Amato, Amarsi—To Be Loved

Modo Indicativo

Presente

io sono amato, vengo amato	I am loved
tu sei amato, vieni amato	you are loved (f.s.)
egli è amato, viene amato, si ama	he is loved
noi siamo amati, veniamo amati	we are loved
voi siete amati, venite amati	you are loved
essi sono amati, vengono amati, si amano	they are loved

Imperfetto

io ero amato, venivo amato	I was loved
tu eri amato, venivi amato	you were loved (f.s.)
egli era amato, veniva amato, si amava	he was loved
noi eravamo amati, venivamo amati	we were loved
voi eravate amati, venivate amati	you were loved
essi erano amati, venivano amati, si amavano	they were loved

Passato Remoto

io fui amato, venni amato	I was loved
tu fosti amato, venisti amato	you were loved (f.s.)
egli fu amato, venne amato, si amò	he was loved
noi fummo amati, venimmo amati	we were loved
voi foste amati, veniste amati	you were loved
essi furono amati, vennero amati, si amarono	they were loved

Futuro Semplice

io sarò amato, verrò amato	I shall be loved
tu sarai amato, verrai amato	you will be loved (f.s.)
egli sarà amato, verrà amato, si amerà	he will be loved
noi saremo amati, verremo amati	we shall be loved
voi sarete amati, verrete amati	you will be loved
essi saranno amati, verranno amati, si ameranno	they will be loved

Condizionale

Presente

io sarei amato, verrei amato	I should be loved
tu saresti amato, verresti amato	you would be loved (f.s.)
egli sarebbe amato, verrebbe amato, si amerebbe	he would be loved
noi saremmo amati, verremmo amati	we should be loved
voi sareste amati, verreste amati	you would be loved
essi sarebbero amati, verrebbero amati, si amerebbero	they would be loved

Imperativo

sii or sia amato (tu), vieni amato (tu)	be loved (f.s.)
non essere amato, non venire amato	don't be loved (f.s.)
sia amato egli, venga amato egli, si ami	let him be loved
siamo amati noi, veniamo amati noi	let us be loved
siate amati voi, venite amati voi	be (you) loved
siano amati essi, vengano amati essi, si amino	let them be loved

Modo Soggiuntivo

Presente

che io sia amato, venga amato	that I be loved
che tu sii amato, venga amato	that you be loved (f.s.)
che egli sia amato, venga amato, si ami	that he be loved
che noi siamo amati, veniamo amati	that we be loved
che voi siate amati, veniate amati	that you be loved
che essi siano amati, vengano amati, si amino	that they be loved

Imperfetto

se io fossi amato, venissi amato	if I were loved
se tu fossi amato, venissi amato	if you were loved (f.s.)
se egli fosse amato, venisse amato, si amasse	if he were loved
se noi fossimo amati, venissimo amati	if we were loved
se voi foste amati, veniste amati	if you were loved
se essi fossero amati, venissero amati, si amassero	if they were loved

244

Indicativo, Tempi Composti—Compound Tenses

Passato Prossimo

io sono stato amato	I have been loved
tu sei stato amato	you have been loved (f.s.)
egli è stato amato, si è amato	he has been loved
noi siamo stati amati	we have been loved
voi siete stati amati	you have been loved
essi sono stati amati	they have been loved

Trapassato Prossimo

io ero stato amato	I had been loved
tu eri stato amato	you had been loved (f.s.)
egli era stato amato, si era amato	he had been loved
noi eravamo stati amati	we had been loved
voi eravate stati amati	you had been loved
essi erano stati amati, si erano amati	they had been loved

Trapassato Remoto

io fui stato amato	I had been loved
tu fosti stato amato	you had been loved (f.s.)
egli fu stato amato, si fu amato	he had been loved
noi fummo stati amati	we had been loved
voi foste stati amati	you had been loved
essi furono stati amati, si furono amati	they had been loved

Futuro Anteriore

io sarò stato amato	I shall have been loved
tu sarai stato amato	you will have been loved (f.s.)
egli sarà stato amato, si sarà amato	he will have been loved
noi saremo stati amati	we shall have been loved
voi sarete stati amati	you will have been loved
essi saranno stati amati, si saranno amati	they will have been loved

Condizionale

Passato

io sarei stato amato	I should have been loved
tu saresti stato amato	you would have been loved (f.s.)
egli sarebbe stato amato	he would have been loved
noi saremmo stati amati	we should have been loved
voi sareste stati amati	you would have been loved
essi sarebbero stati amati	they would have been loved

Soggiuntivo

Passato

che io sia stato amato	that I have been loved
che tu sii stato amato	that you have been loved (f.s.)
che egli sia stato amato, si sia amato	that he has been loved
che noi siamo stati amati	that we have been loved
che voi siate stati amati	that you have been loved
che essi siano stati amati, si siano amati	that they have been loved

Trapassato

che io fossi stato amato	that I had been loved
che tu fossi stato amato	that you had been loved (f.s.)
che egli fosse stato amato, si fosse amato	that he had been loved
che noi fossimo stati amati	that we had been loved
che voi foste stati amati	that they had been loved
che essi fossero stati amati, si fossero amati	that you had been loved

Modo Infinito—Infinitive Mood

Presente

essere amato, venire amato, amarsi, to be loved

Passato

essere stato amato, essersi amato, to have been loved

Participio Passato

amato, loved

Gerundio Semplice

essendo amato, venendo amato, amandosi, being loved

Gerundio Composto

essendo stato amato, essendosi amato, having been loved

Reflexive Verbs

82. They are called Reflexive, Reflective, Reciprocal, or Pronominal Verbs, because the action proceeding from the Subject returns upon it.

83. Italian Reflexive Verbs are conjugated with the Auxiliary **essere** in the Compound Tenses.

84. This reflexive form is very frequently met with in Italian, while in English most of these Verbs are employed as Neuter Verbs, as: **io mi rallegro,** I rejoice.

Reflexive Conjugation

Rallegrarsi—To Rejoice

Modo Indicativo

Presente

AFFIRMATIVE	INTERROGATIVE
mi rallegro, I rejoice	mi rallegro (io)?
ti rallegri, you rejoice (f.s.)	ti rallegri (tu)?
si rallegra, he rejoices	si rallegra (egli)?
ci rallegriamo, we rejoice	ci rallegriamo (noi)?
vi rallegrate, you rejoice	vi rallegrate (voi)?
si rallegrano, they rejoice	si rallegrano (essi)?

NEGATIVE	INTERROGATIVE AND NEGATIVE
non mi rallegro	non mi rallegro (io)?
non ti rallegri	non ti rallegri (tu)?
non si rallegra	non si rallegra (egli)?
non ci rallegriamo	non ci rallegriamo (noi)?
non vi rallegrate	non vi rallegrate (voi)?
non si rallegrano	non si rallegrano (essi)?

And so on throughout the entire Conjugation, except in the Imperative, the Past Participle and Gerund, which see below:

Imperativo

AFFIRMATIVE

rallegrati, rejoice (f.s.)
si rallegri, rejoice (polite form) *or* let him rejoice
rallegriamoci, let us rejoice
rallegratevi, rejoice (you)
si rallegrino, let them rejoice

NEGATIVE

non ti rallegrare, do not rejoice (f.s.)
non si rallegri, do not rejoice (polite form) *or* do not let him rejoice
non ci rallegriamo, do not let us rejoice
non vi rallegrate, do not (you) rejoice
non si rallegrino, do not let them rejoice

Gerundio

rallegrandomi
rallegrandoti
rallegrandosi
rallegrandoci $\Big\}$ rejoicing
rallegrandovi
rallegrandosi

Participio Passato

rallegratosi
rallegratasi
rallegratisi $\Big\}$ having rejoiced
rallegratesi

Ricordarsene—To Remember It

Modo Indicativo

Presente

me ne ricordo, I remember it
te ne ricordi, you remember it (f.s.)
se ne ricorda, he remembers it
ce ne ricordiamo, we remember it
ve ne ricordate, you remember it
se ne ricordano, they remember it

Compound Tense

Passato Prossimo

me ne sono ricordato-a	I have remembered it
te ne sei ricordato-a	you have remembered it (f.s.)
se ne è ricordato-a	he has remembered it
ce ne siamo ricordati-e	we have remembered it
ve ne siete ricordati-e	you have remembered it
se ne sono ricordati-e	they have remembered it

Imperativo

ricordatene, remember it (f.s.)
se ne ricordi, remember it (polite form), let him remember it
ricordiamocene, let us remember it
ricordatevene, remember (you) it
se ne ricordino, let them remember it

Gerundio

ricordandomene
ricordandotene
ricordandosene
ricordandocene } remembering it
ricordandovene
ricordandosene

Participio Passato

ricordatosene, having remembered it

REMARKS

85. As has been seen, the Reflexive Pronouns precede the Verb except in the Infinitive, Imperative, Gerund and Past Participle, when they follow, and are contracted into one word with the Verb.

The Pronouns **mi, ti, si, ci, vi,** are changed into **me, te, se, ce, ve,** whenever followed by some other Personal Pronoun.

The second person singular, the first and second person plural constitute the real Imperative, the third person, singular and plural, being borrowed from the Subjunctive. Hence the Reflexive Pronouns, or any other Pronouns representing the Object, precede the Verb in this latter case.

It has already been remarked that these Reflexive Pronouns frequently follow the Verb even in other Tenses than the aforesaid; but such usage is literary and archaic.

Impersonal Verbs—Verbi Impersonali

86. Verbs are either real Impersonal Verbs, that is, they are only used in the third person singular, as: **piove,** it rains, **nevica,** it snows; **tuona,** it thunders; or they are used as Impersonals, as: **sembra,** it seems; **comincia,** it begins, etc.

a. The following are real Impersonal Verbs:

piove, it rains
lampeggia, it lightens
tuona, it thunders
grandina, it hails
gela, ghiaccia, it freezes
nevica, it snows

sgela, it thaws
albeggia, it is twilight, it dawns
abbuia, it gets dark
annotta, it becomes night

And others formed with **fare, essere,** etc., as:

fa caldo, it is warm	c' è della nebbia, it is foggy
fa freddo, it is cold	tira vento, it is windy
fa bel tempo, it is good weather	è umido, it is damp
fa cattivo tempo, it is bad weather	

Used as Impersonal Verbs are:

bisogna, it is necessary
conviene, it is proper, it behooves
occorre, it is necessary
basta, it is enough
pare, sembra, it seems
s' intende, of course
piace, it pleases
mi rincresce, I am sorry
avviene, accade, succede, it happens

87. The English Verbs **must, to be obliged, etc.,** are rendered by either **dovere,** or the Impersonal **bisognare,** followed by the Infinitive, as: **devo andare, bisogna andare,** I must go.

88. In case the Subject is a Noun or a Pronoun, the Subjunctive must follow, as:

Bisogna che i soldati ubbidiscano ai loro superiori.

Soldiers must obey their superiors.

89. Sometimes **must** is rendered by **aver da,** or by **convenire,** as:
Ho da tacere? must I be (have I to be) silent?

A tale scongiuro convenne bere.

At such entreaty it behooved him to drink.

90. Transitive Verbs used impersonally, as **tirare,** to draw, are conjugated with **avere** in the Compound Tenses:

Ha tirato vento tutta la notte.

The wind blew the whole night.

Essere is used with really Impersonal Verbs: **E accaduto,** it (has) happened.

91. There is, there are, etc., are rendered by **c' è (ci è),** or **v' è (vi è), ci sono,** or **vi sono,** and also by **vi ha, v' ha,** or **havvi;** but the latter forms are literary and archaic.

Defective Verbs

92. Verbs that are not used in the entire conjugation are called Defective Verbs. Many of them are not in common spoken use

today, though they appear frequently in the older literary works.
These are met most frequently:

Calere, to matter, to be important, to care, a reflexive verb, has
ónly: Pres., **mi cale;** Imperf., **mi caleva;** Pass. Rem., **mi calse;**
Subj. Pres., **che mi caglia;** Imperf., **se mi calesse;** Condiz., **mi
carrebbe;** P. P., **caluto;** Ger., **calendo. Mettere in non cale,** to neglect,
is about the only phrase used in common language.

Gire, to go, to walk: Pres. Ind., **gite,** you go; Imperf., **io giva,
tu givi, egli giva** or **gia, noi givamo, voi givate, essi givano** or **giano;**
Fut., **giro, girai, girà, giremo, girete, giranno;** Imperat., **giamo noi,
gite voi;** Sogg. Pres., **giamo, giate;** Imperf., **gissi, gissi, gisse, gis-
simo, giste, gissero;** Condiz., **girei, giresti, girebbe, giremmo,
gireste, girebbero.** This verb is archaic, though largely used today in
the dialects.

Ire, to go: Pres. Ind., **voi ite;** Imperf., **io iva, egli iva, essi ivano;**
Pass. Rem., **tu isti, voi iste;** Fut., **iremo, irete, iranno;** Imperat.,
ite; Sogg., Imperf. **egli isse, voi iste, essi issero;** P. P., **ito.** It is
generally used only in Compound Tenses, as: **Io sono ito, tu sei ito,**
etc. Also archaic and dialectal.

Redire or **riedere,** to return: Ind. Pres., **io riedo, tu riedi, egli
riede, essi riedono;** Imperf., **rediva, redivi,** etc., Pass. Rem., **redii,
redisti, redì, redimmo, rediste, redirono;** Imperat., **riedi, rieda,
riedano;** Sogg. Pres., **rieda, riedano;** Imperf., **redissi, redissi,** etc.,
Condiz., **redirei.** (Archaic)

Licere: Ind. Pres., **lice;** P. P., **lecito.** (Archaic, save in the past
participle).

Serpere, to wind: Ind. Pres., **serpo, serpi, serpono;** Imperf.,
serpeva; Imperat., **serpa, serpiano, serpano;** Pres. Part., **serpente;**
Ger., **serpendo.** (Archaic).

Solere, to use, to be accustomed: Ind. Pres., **soglio, suoli, suole,
sogliamo, solete, sogliono;** Imperf., **soleva, solevi, soleva, solevamo,
solevate, solevano;** Pass. Rem., **solei, solesti;** Sogg. Pres., **soglia,
sogliamo, sogliate, sogliano;** Imperf., **solessi, solessi, solesse, soles-
simo, soleste, solessero;** Ger., **solendo;** P. P., **solito.** The compound
forms are preferred to the simple ones, as: **io sono solito,** I use, I am
accustomed; **io ero solito,** I used, I was accustomed.

Esimere, to free, to exempt. It has no Past Participle, and hence no
Compound Tenses can be formed (note, however, **essere esente,**
to be exempt: **esente da tasse,** tax-exempt).

Fervere, to boil. It has only **ferve, fervono, ferveva, ferva, fervessi, fervessero.**

Lucere, to shine: **Luce** and **lucente.**

Verbs Conjugated With "Avere" or "Essere"

93. Transitive Verbs are conjugated with **avere: Ho comperato un libro,** I bought a book.

94. The following Verbs are also conjugated with **avere: cenare,** to sup; **desinare** or **pranzare,** to dine; **passeggiare,** to walk; **peccare,** to sin; **dormire,** to sleep; **ridere,** to laugh; **tossire,** to cough, and all those expressing the sounds made by animals, as: **abbaiare,** to bark, etc.

95. The following Verbs take **essere: andare,** to go; **venire,** to come; **stare,** to stay; **entrare,** to enter; **uscire,** to go out; **cadere,** to fall; **salire,** to ascend; **arrivare,** to arrive; **partire,** to leave; **riuscire,** to succeed.

96. **Vivere,** to live; **dimorare,** to dwell; **volare,** to fly; **giovare,** to be useful; **correre,** to run, are conjugated with either one.

97. The Verbs **dovere,** to be obliged, and **potere,** to be able, take the Auxiliary required by the Verb which they govern: **è dovuto andare,** he had to go; **ha dovuto fare,** he had to do.

IRREGULAR VERBS

98. Those Verbs are called Irregular which undergo some change either in the Root or in the Termination.

Irregular Verbs of the First Conjugation

99. There are four Irregular Verbs in **are**
(Regular Tenses are omitted)

Andare, to go

Ind. Pres.: Vo *or* vado, vai, va, andiamo, andate, vanno
Futuro Sem.: Andrò *or* anderò, andrai *or* anderai, etc.
Imperat. Pres.: Va, vada, andiamo, andate, vadano
Sogg. Pres.: Che io vada, tu vada, egli vada, andiamo, andiate, vadano
Condiz. Pres.: Andrei *or* anderei, etc.
Participii: Andante, andato
Gerundio: Andando

Dare, to give

Ind. Pres.: Io do, dai, dà, diamo, date, danno
Imperfetto: Davo, davi, dava, davamo, davate, davano
Pass. Rem.: Diedi *or* detti, desti, diede *or* dette, demmo, deste, diedero *or* dettero
Futuro Sem.: Darò, darai, etc.
Imperat.: Da, dia, diamo, date, diano
Sogg. Pres.: Dia, dia, dia, diamo, diate, diano
Imperfetto: Dessi, dessi, desse, dessimo, deste, dessero
Condiz. Pres.: Darei, daresti, etc.
Part. Pass.: Dato
Gerundio: Dando

Fare, to do, to make

Ind. Pres.: Fo *or* faccio, fai, fa, facciamo, fate, fanno
Imperfetto: Facevo, facevi, etc.
Pass. Rem.: Feci, facesti, fece, facemmo, faceste, fecero
Futuro Sem.: Farò, farai, etc.
Imperat.: Fa, faccia, facciamo, fate, fanno
Sogg. Pres.: Faccia, faccia, etc.
Imperfetto: Facessi, facessi, etc.
Condiz. Pres.: Farei, faresti, etc.
Participii: Facente, fatto
Gerundio: Facendo

Stare, to stay, to remain

Ind. Pres.: Sto, stai, sta, stiamo, state, stanno
Imperfetto: Stavo, etc.
Pass. Rem.: Stetti, stesti, stette, stemmo, steste, stettero
Futuro Sem.: Starò, etc.
Imperat.: Sta, stia, stiamo, state, stiano
Sogg. Pres.: Stia, stia, stia, etc.
Imperfetto: Stessi, etc.
Condiz. Pres.: Starei, etc.
Participii: Stante, stato
Gerundio: Stando

Remarks

100. **Dà,** he gives; **ridò,** I give again; **ridà,** he gives again, from **ridare;** as well as **mi addò, si addà,** I perceive, he perceives, take the **accento grave.**

101. **Fa,** he makes, does not take the accent, but **soddisfà,** he satisfies, and **disfà,** he undoes, may have it.

102. The Verbs **ostare,** to oppose; **restare,** to remain, are conjugated regularly like **amare.**

Sovrastare or **soprastare,** to stand over, to tarry, may be conjugated either like **amare** or **stare,** and makes **sovrasta** or **sovrastà, essi sovrastano** or **sovrastanno, io sovrastai** or **sovrastetti.**

Contrastare, to contrast, is conjugated usually like **amare. Contrasto, contrasta.**

Irregular Verbs of the Second Conjugation

103. Of the Verbs of the Second Conjugation some are irregular only in the **Passato Remoto;** many in the **Passato Remoto,** and in the **Participio Passato,** and several in the **Passato Remoto,** the **Participio Passato,** and in other Tenses, too. The **Passato Remoto** of the Irregular Verbs has three Irregular and three Regular persons, as:

Singular	Plural
1st, Irregular, **lessi**	1st, Regular, **leggemmo**
2nd, Regular, **leggesti**	2nd, Regular, **leggeste**
3rd, Irregular, **lesse**	3rd, Irregular, **lessero**

104. Irregular only in the **Passato Remoto:**

Conoscere, to know, to be acquainted with: **Conobbi, conoscesti, conobbe, conoscemmo, conosceste, conobbero.**

Crescere, to grow: **Crebbi, crescesti, crebbe, crescemmo, cresceste, crebbero.**

Piacere, to please: **Piacqui, piacesti, piacque, piacemmo, piaceste, piacquero.**

Piovere, to rain: **Piovvi, piovesti, piovve, piovemmo, pioveste, piovvero.**

105. Irregular in the **Passato Remoto** and in the **Participio Passato:**

Accendere, to light: **Accesi, accendesti, accese, accendemmo, accendeste, accesero;** P. P., **acceso.**

Ardere, to burn: **Arsi, ardesti, arse, ardemmo, ardeste, arsero;** P. P., **arso.**

Chiedere, to ask: **Chiesi, chiedesti, chiese, chiedemmo, chiedeste, chiesero;** P. P., **chiesto.**

Chiudere, to close: **Chiusi, chiudesti, chiuse, chiudemmo, chiudeste, chiusero;** P. P., **chiuso.**

Cingere, to grid: Cinsi, cingesti, cinse, cingemmo, cingeste, cinsero; P. P., cinto.

Dividere, to divide: Divisi, dividesti, divise, dividemmo, divideste, divisero; P. P., diviso.

Figgere, to fix, to put in: Fissi, figgesti, fisse, figgemmo, figgeste, fissero; P. P., fisso.

Espellere, to expel, to drive out: Espulsi, espellesti, espulse, espellemmo, espelleste, espulsero; P. P., espulso.

Incutere, to inspire, to infuse: Incussi, incutesti, incusse, incutemmo, incuteste, incussero; P. P., incusso.

Invadere, to invade: Invasi, invadesti, invase, invademmo, invadeste, invasero; P. P., invaso.

Leggere, to read: Lessi, leggesti, lesse, leggemmo, leggeste, lessero; P. P., letto.

Mettere, to put: Misi or messi, mise or messe, misero; P. P., messo.

Muovere, to move: Mossi, movesti, mosse, movemmo, moveste, mossero; P. P., mosso.

Nascere, to be born: Nacqui, nascesti, nacque, nascemmo, nasceste, nacquero; P. P., nato.

Piangere, to weep: Piansi, piangesti, pianse, piangemmo, piangeste, piansero; P. P., pianto.

Porgere, to offer, to give, to reach: Porsi, porgesti, porse, porgemmo, porgeste, porsero; P. P., porto.

Rompere, to break: Ruppi, rompesti, ruppe, rompemmo, rompeste, ruppero; P. P., rotto.

Stringere, to press, to squeeze: Strinsi, stringesti, stinse, stringemmo, stringeste, strinsero; P. P., stretto.

Ungere, to anoint: Unsi, ungesti, unse, ungemmo, ungeste, unsero; P. P., unto.

Vivere, to live: Vissi, vivesti, visse, vivemmo, viveste, vissero; P. P., vissuto.

106. Verbs having two terminations in the **Passato Remoto** or in the **Participio Passato,** or in both:

Assistere, to assist: Assistei or assistetti, assistè or assistette, assisterono or assistettero; P. P., assistito.

Cedere, to cede, to give in: Cedei or cedetti, cedè or cedette, cederono or cedettero.

Cernere, to select: **Cernei** or **cernetti, cernè** or **cernette, cernerono** or **cernettero; P. P., cernuto.**

Connettere, to connect: **Connettei** or **connessi, connettè** or **connesse, connetterono** or **connessero; P. P., connesso.**

Credere, to believe: **Credei** or **credetti, credè** or **credette, crederono** or **credettero; P. P., creduto.**

Fendere, to cleave, to split: **Fendei** or **fendetti, fendè** or **fendette, fenderono** or **fendettero; P. P., fenduto** or **fesso.**

Rilucere, to shine, to glitter: **Rilucei** or **rilussi, rilucè** or **rilusse, rilucerono** or **rilussero;** no **P. P.**

Risolvere, to resolve: **Risolvei** or **risolvetti** or **risolsi, risolvè** or **risolvette** or **risolse, risolverono** or **risolvettero** or **risolsero; P. P., risoluto** or **risolto.**

107. Verbs Irregular in the **Passato Remoto** and other tenses:

Addurre, to bring, to convey, to produce

Ind. Pres.: Adduco, adduci, adduce, adduciamo, adducete, adducono
Imperf.: Adducevo, etc.
Pass. Rem.: Addussi, adducesti, addusse, adducemmo, adduceste, addussero
Futuro: Addurrò, addurrai, addurrà, addurremo, addurrete, addurranno
Imperat.: Adduci, adduca, adduciamo, adducete, adducano
Sogg. Pres.: Adduca, adduca, adduca, adduciamo, adduciate, adducano
Condiz. Pres.: Addurrei, addurresti, addurrebbe, addurremmo, addurreste, addurrebbero
Part. Pass.: Addotto

Cadere, to fall

Ind. Pres.: Cado, cadi, cade, cadiamo, cadete, cadono
Imperf.: Cadevo, etc.
Pass. Rem.: Caddi, cadesti, cadde, cademmo, cadeste, caddero
Futuro: Cadrò, cadrai, cadrà, cadremo, cadrete, cadranno
Condiz. Pres.: Cadrei, cadresti, cadrebbe, cadremmo, cadreste, cadrebbero

Bere or bevere, to drink

Ind. Pres.: Bevo, bevi, beve, beviamo, bevete, bevono
Imperfetto: Bevevo, etc.
Pass. Rem.: Bevvi, bevei *or* bevetti, bevesti, bevve, bevè *or* bevette, bevemmo, beveste, bevvero, beverono *or* bevettero
Futuro: Berrò *or* beverò, and so on throughout the tense
Imperat.: Bevi, beva, beviamo, bevete, bevano

Sogg. Pres.: Beva, etc., beviamo, beviate, bevano
Condiz. Pres.: Berrei *or* beverei, and so on
Part. Pass.: Bevuto

Cogliere, to cull, gather, reap

Ind. Pres.: Colgo, cogli, coglie, cogliamo, cogliete, colgono
Imperfetto: Coglievo, etc.
Pass. Rem.: Colsi, cogliesti, colse, cogliemmo, coglieste, colsero
Futuro: Coglierò, coglierai, etc.
Imperat.: Cogli, colga, cogliamo, coglieto, colgano
Sogg. Pres.: Colga, colga, colga, cogliamo, cogliate, colgano
Condiz. Pres.: Coglierei, coglieresti, coglierebbe, coglieremmo, cogliereste, coglierebbero
Part. Pass.: Colto

Cuocere, to cook

Ind. Pres.: Cuocio, cuoci, cuoce, cociamo, cocete, cuociono
Imperfetto: Cocevo *or* cuocevo, etc.
Pass. Rem.: Cossi, cocesti, cosse, cocemmo, coceste, cossero
Imperat.: Cuoci, cuocia, cociamo, cocete, cuociano
Sogg. Pres.: Cuocia, cuocia, cuocia, cociamo, cociate, cuociano
Condiz. Pres.: Cocerei, etc., *or* cuocerei, etc.
Futuro: Cocerò, etc., *or* cuocerò, etc.
Part. Pass.: Cotto. (When *cuocere* is used instead of *scottare,* to scorch, its past participle is *cociuto.*)[1]

Dovere, must, to be necessary

Ind. Pres.: Devo *or* debbo, devi, deve, dobbiamo, dovete, devono *or* debbono
Imperfetto: Dovevo, etc.
Pass. Rem.: Dovetti *or* dovei, dovesti, dovette *or* dovè, dovemmo, doveste, dovettero
Futuro: Dovrò, dovrai, dovrà, dovremo, dovrete, dovranno
Sogg. Pres.: Debba, debba, debba, (*or* deva, deva, deva), dobbiamo, dobbiate, debbano (*or* devano)
Condiz. Pres.: Dovrei, dovresti, dovrebbe, dovremmo, dovreste, dovrebbero
Part. Pass.: Dovuto[2]

---

[1] Remark.—*Cuocere* (to cook), and *nuocere* (to hurt, to prejudice), may drop *u* whenever the stress of the voice is on the following vowel, as in *coceva,* etc., and must do so when the diphthong would be followed by two consonants, as in *cossi,* I cooked.

[2] Note.—This verb changes *o* into *e* whenever the prosodic accent is on the first syllable, as: *deve, devono.*

Nuocere, to hurt, to prejudice

Ind. Pres.: Nuoco *or* noccio, nuoci, nuoce, nociamo, nocete, nuocono *or* nocciono
Imperfetto: Nocevo, etc.
Pass. Rem.: Nocqui, nocesti, nocque, nocemmo, noceste, nocquero
Futuro: Nocerò, etc.
Imperat.: Nuoci, nuocia, nociamo, nociate, nuociano
Sogg. Pres.: Nuocia, nuocia, nuocia, nociamo, nociate, nuociano
Condiz. Pres.: Nocerei, noceresti, etc.
Part. Pass.: Nociuto

Parere, to seem, to appear

Ind. Pres.: Paio, pari, pare, paiamo, parete, paiono
Pass. Rem.: Parvi, paresti, parve, paremmo, pareste, parvero
Futuro: Parrò, parrai, etc.
Imperat.: Pari, paia, pariamo, parete, paiano
Sogg. Pres.: Paia, paia, paia, pariamo, pariate *or* paiate, paiano
Condiz. Pres.: Parrei, etc.
Part. Pass.: Parso (seldom paruto)

Note.—Forms ending in *iamo, iate,* may either retain or drop *r;* thus: *pariamo,* or *paiamo; pariate,* or *paiate.*

Porre, to put

Ind. Pres.: Pongo, poni, pone, poniamo, ponete, pongono
Imperfetto: Ponevo, etc.
Pass. Rem.: Posi, ponesti, pose, ponemmo, poneste, posero
Futuro: Porrò, porrai, etc.
Imperat.: Poni, ponga, poniamo, ponete, pongano
Sogg. Pres.: Ponga, ponga, ponga, poniamo, poniate, pongano
Condiz. Pres.: Porrei, porresti, etc.
Part. Pass.: Posto

Potere, can, to be able

Ind. Pres.: Posso, puoi, può, possiamo, potete, possono
Pass. Rem.: Potei, potesti, potè, potemmo, poteste, poterono
Futuro: Potrò, etc.
Sogg. Pres.: Possa, possa, possa, possiamo, possiate, possano
Condiz. Pres.: Potrei, etc.
Part. Pass.: Potuto

Rimanere, to remain

Ind. Pres.: Rimango, rimani, rimane, rimaniamo, rimanete, rimangono
Pass. Rem.: Rimasi, rimanesti, rimase, rimanemmo, rimaneste, rimasero
Futuro: Rimarrò, etc.
Imperat.: Rimani, rimanga, rimaniamo, rimanete, rimangano
Sogg. Pres.: Rimanga, rimanga, rimanga, rimaniamo, rimaniate, rimangano
Condiz. Pres.: Rimarrei, etc.
Part. Pass.: Rimasto

Sapere, to know

Ind. Pres.: So, sai, sa, sappiamo, sapete, sanno
Pass. Rem.: Seppi, sapesti, seppe, sapemmo, sapeste, seppero
Futuro: Saprò, etc.
Imperat.: Sappi, sappia, sappiamo, sappiate, sappiano
Sogg. Pres.: Sappia, sappia, sappia, sappiamo, sappiate, sappiano
Condiz. Pres.: Saprei, etc.
Part. Pass.: Saputo

Scegliere, to choose, to select

Ind. Pres.: Scelgo, scegli, sceglie, scegliamo, scegliete, scelgono
Pass. Rem.: Scelsi, scegliesti, scelse, scegliemmo, sceglieste, scelsero
Futuro: Sceglierò, etc.
Imperat.: Scegli, scelga, scegliamo, scegliete, scelgano
Sogg. Pres.: Scelga, scelga, scelga, scegliamo, scegliate, scelgano
Condiz. Pres.: Sceglierei, etc.
Part. Pass.: Scelto

Sedere, to sit down

Ind. Pres.: Siedo *or* seggo, siedi, siede, sediamo, sedete, siedono *or* seggono
Pass. Rem.: Sedei *or* sedetti, sedesti, sedè *or* sedette, sedemmo, sedeste, sedettero
Futuro: Sederò, etc.
Imperat.: Siedi, sieda *or* segga, sediamo, sedete, siedano *or* seggano
Condiz. Pres.: Sederei, etc.
Part. Pass.: Seduto

Spegnere, to put out, to extinguish

Ind. Pres.: Spengo, spegni, spegne, spegniamo, spegnete, spengono
Imperf.: Spegnevo, etc.
Pass. Rem.: Spensi, spegnesti, spense, spegnemmmo, spegneste, spensero
Futuro: Spegnerò, etc.
Imperat.: Spegni, spenga, spegniamo, spegnete, spengano

Sogg. Pres.: Spenga, spenga, spenga, spegniamo, spegniate, **spengano**
Cond. Pres.: Spegnerei, etc.
Part. Pass.: Spento[1]

Svellere, to uproot, to tear up

Ind. Pres.: Svello *or* svelgo, svelli, svelle, svelliamo, svellete, svellono *or* svelgono
Pass. Rem.: Svelsi, svellesti, svelse, svellemo, svelleste, svelsero
Futuro: Svellerò, etc.
Imperat.: Svelli, svella *or* svelga, svelliamo, svellete, svellano *or* svelgano
Sogg. Pres.: Svella *or* svelga, svelliamo, svelliate, svelgano *or* svellano
Cond. Pres.: Svellerei, etc.
Part. Pass.: Svelto

Tenere, to hold

Ind. Pres.: Tengo, tieni, tiene, teniamo, tenete, tengono
Pass. Rem.: Tenni, tenesti, tenne, tenemmo, teneste, tennero
Futuro: Terrò, etc.
Imperat.: Tieni, tenga, teniamo, tenete, tengano
Sogg. Pres.: Tenga . . ., teniamo, teniate, tengano
Condiz. Pres.: Terrei, etc.
Part. Pass.: Tenuto

Trarre, to draw, to drag

Ind. Pres.: Traggo, trai, trae, traiamo, *or* traggiamo, traete, traggono
Imperf.: Traevo, etc.
Pass. Rem.: Trassi, traesti, trasse, traemmo, traeste, trassero
Futuro: Trarrò, etc.
Imperat.: Trai, tragga, traiamo *or* traggiamo, traete, traggano
Sogg. Pres.: Tragga, traiamo *or* traggiamo, traiate *or* tragghiate, traggano
Condiz. Pres.: Trarrei, etc.

Valere, to be worth

Ind. Pres.: Valgo, vali, vale, vagliamo, *or* valiamo, valete, valgono
Pass. Rem.: Valsi, valesti, valse, valemmo, valeste, valsero
Futuro: Varrò, etc.
Imperat.: Vali, valga, vagliamo *or* valiamo, valete, valgono
Sogg. Pres.: Valga *or* vaglia . . ., valiamo *or* vagliamo, valiate *or* vagliate, valgano *or* vagliano

---

[1] NOTE.—This verb, as may be seen, requires *g* after *n* before the vowels *a, o;* and retains the *n* after *g* before *e, i.*

Condiz. Pres.: Varrei, etc.
Part. Pass.: Valso *or* valuto

Vedere, to see

Ind. Pres.: Vedo *or* veggo, vedi, vede, vediamo, vedete, vedono *or* veggono
Pass. Rem.: Vidi, vedesti, vide, vedemmo, vedeste, videro
Futuro: Vedrò, etc.
Imperat.: Vedi, veda *or* vegga, vediamo, vedete, vedano *or* veggano
Sogg. Pres.: Veda *or* vegga . . ., vediamo, vediate, vedano *or* veggano
Condiz. Pres.: Vedrei, etc.
Part. Pass.: Veduto *or* visto

Volere, to will

Ind. Pres.: Voglio, vuoi, vuole, vogliamo, volete, vogliono
Pass. Rem.: Volli, volesti, volle, volemmo, voleste, vollero
Futuro: Vorrò, etc.
Sogg. Pres.: Voglia . . ., vogliamo, vogliate, vogliano
Condiz. Pres.: Vorrei, etc.
Part. Pass.: Voluto[1]

Irregular Verbs of the Third Conjugation

Apparire, to appear

Ind. Pres.: Apparisco *or* appaio, apparisci *or* appari, apparisce *or* appare,
appariamo, apparite, appariscono *or* appaiono
Pass. Pross.: Sono apparito *or* apparso
Pass. Rem.: Apparii *or* apparvi, apparisti, apparì *or* apparve, apparimmo,
appariste, apparirono *or* apparvero
Imperat.: Apparisci, apparisca *or* appaia, apparisca *or* appaia, appariamo,
appariate, appariscano *or* appaiano
Sogg. Pres.: Apparisca *or* appaia, apparisca *or* appaia, apparisca *or* appaia,
appariamo, appariate, appariscano *or* appaiano
Part. Pres.: Appariscente *or* apparente[2]

---

[1] NOTE.—The Irregular Verbs of the Second and Third Conjugations may take
in the second person singular of the Subjunctive Mood, either *i* or *a*, as: *abbi*,
or *abbia; sappi*, or *sappia;* except in the case the termination *i* should be disagreeable, as: *dichi, finischi.* Regular Verbs have only one termination in *a.*

[2] NOTE.—The learner must take care not to mistake certain forms of this Verb
for those of *apparare*, to apparel, and *appaiare*, to couple.

Aprire, to open

Pass. Pross.: Ho aperto
Pass. Rem.: Io aprii *or* apersi, tu apristi, egli aprì *or* aperse, noi aprimmo, voi apriste, essi aprirono *or* apersero

Dire, to say

Ind. Pres.: Dico, dici, dice, diciamo, dite, dicono
Imperfetto: Dicevo, etc.
Pass. Pross.: Ho detto
Pass. Rem.: Dissi, dicesti, disse, dicemmo, diceste, dissero
Futuro: Dirò, etc.
Imperat.: Dì, dica, diciamo, dite, dicano
Sogg. Pres.: Dica, dica, dica, diciamo, diciate, dicano
Condiz. Pres.: Direi, etc.

Morire, to die

Ind. Pres.: Muoio, muori, muore, moriamo, morite, muoiono
Pass. Pross.: È morto, he is dead, he has died
Pass. Rem.: Morii, moristi, morì, morimmo, moriste, morirono
Futuro: Morrò *or* morirò, etc.
Sogg. Pres.: Muoia, muoia, muoia, moriamo, moriate, muoiano
Condiz. Pres.: Morrei *or* morirei, etc.
Part. Pres.: Morente
Gerundio: Morendo

Salire, to mount, to ascend

Ind. Pres.: Salgo, sali, sale, saliamo, salite, salgono
Imperfetto: Salivo, etc.
Pass. Pross.: Ho salito *or* sono salito
Pass. Rem.: Salii, salisti, salì, salimmo, saliste, salirono
Imperat.: Sali, salga, saliamo, saliate, salgano
Condiz. Pres.: Salirei, etc.
Part. Pres.: Saliente
Gerundio: Salendo

Udire, to hear

Ind. Pres.: Odo, odi, ode, udiamo, udite, odono
Imperfetto: Udivo, etc.
Pass. Rem.: Udii, udisti, udì, udimmo, udiste, udirono
Futuro: Udirò, etc.
Imperat.: Odi, oda, udiamo, udite, odano
Sogg. Pres.: Oda, oda, oda, udiamo, udiate, odano

Condiz. Pres.: Udirei, etc.
Part. Pres.: Udente
Gerundio: Udendo[1]

Uscire, to go out

Ind. Pres.: Esco, esci, esce, usciamo, uscite, escono
Imperfetto: Uscivo, etc.
Pass. Rem.: Uscii, uscisti, uscì, uscimmo, usciste, uscirono
Futuro: Uscirò, etc.[2]
Imperat.: Esci, esca, usciamo, uscite, escano
Condiz. Pres.: Uscirei, etc.
Part. Pres.: Uscente
Gerundio: Uscendo

Venire, to come

Ind. Pres.: Vengo, vieni, viene, veniamo, venite, vengono
Imperfetto: Venivo, etc.
Pass. Rem.: Venni, venisti, venne, venimmo, veniste, vennero
Futuro: Verrò, etc.
Imperat.: Vieni, venga, veniamo, venite, vengano
Sogg. Pres.: Venga, venga, venga, veniamo, veniate, vengano
Condiz. Pres.: Verrei, etc.
Part. Pres.: Veniente or vegnente
Gerundio: Venendo

Verbs in "isco"

108. Most Verbs of the Third Conjugation are conjugated like **abbellire** in the Present Tense of the Indicative, the Imperative and the Subjunctive Moods, and are Regular in the other Tenses.

Abbellire, to beautify

Ind. Pres.: Abbellisco, abbellisci, abbellisce, abbelliamo, abbellite, abbelliscono
Imperat.: Abbellisci, abbellisca, abbelliamo, abbellite, abbelliscano
Sogg. Pres.: Abbellisca, abbellisca, abbellisca, abbelliamo, abbelliate, abbelliscano

---

[1] NOTE.—*Udire* changes *u* into *o* when the stress of the voice is on the first syllable.

[2] NOTE.—This Verb changes *u* into *e* whenever the stress of the voice is on the first syllable.

Istruire, to instruct, to teach

Ind. Pres.: Istruisco, istruisci, istruisce, istruiamo, istruite, istruiscono
Pass. Pross.: Ho istruito *or* istrutto
Pass. Rem.: Istruii *or* istrussi, istruisti, istruì *or* istrusse, istruimmo, istruiste, istruirono *or* istrussero
Sogg. Pres.: Istruisca, istruisca, istruisca, istruiamo, istruiate, istruiscano[1]

Verbs in "ire" Conjugated Like "Abbellire"

abbonire, to improve, fertilize land
abbrividire, to shiver with cold
abbronzire, to scorch, to tan
abbrustolire, to crisp, to toast
abbrutire, to brutify
abolire, to abolish
accudire, to apply one's self to
addolcire, to sweeten
aderire, to adhere to
affievolire, to weaken
aggrandire, to enlarge
agguerrire, to train up to war
alleggerire, to lighten
allenire, to soften, to appease
allestire, to get ready, to prepare
ambire, to aspire to
ammannire, to prepare
ammansire, to tame
ammattire, to madden
ammollire, to soften
ammonire, to admonish
ammorbidire, to soften
ammortire, to faint away
ammuffire, to become musty
ammutire, to become dumb
ammutolire, to become dumb
anneghittire, to grow idle
annerire, to blacken
annichilire, to annihilate
appassire, to wither

appetire, to covet, to long for
appiccinire, to diminish
appiccolire, to grow short
arricchire, to enrich, to grow rich
arrossire, to blush
arrostire, to roast
arrozzire, to become rough
arruvidire, to grow coarse
asserire, to assert
assopire, to make drowsy
assordire, to deafen
assortire, to sort, to match
atterrire, to frighten
attribuire, to attribute
attristire, to afflict
attutire, to still, to silence
avvilire, to vilify
avvincidire, to soften (said especially of bread)
avvizzire, to wither, to fade away
bandire, to banish
blandire, to blandish
brandire, to brandish
brunire, to burnish
candire, to candy (fruit)
capire, to understand
chiarire, to clarify
circuire, to surround
colorire, to color
colpire, to strike

[1] Note.—Whenever any form of the following Verbs would sound disagreeably, as *gioiamo, fruiamo, ammattiamo,* etc., or in case it might be mistaken for some other verb, as *imbottiamo, ardiamo,* it will be well to resort to other Verbs of similar meaning or to change the form of the expression.

concepire, to conceive

condire, to season

conferire, to confer

contribuire, to contribute

costituire, to constitute

custodire, to keep in custody

deferire, to defer

definire, to define

demolire, to demolish

differire, to differ

digerire, to digest

diminuire, to diminish

distribuire, to distribute

erudire, to teach, to instruct

esaurire, to exhaust

esibire, to exhibit

fallire, to fail

favorite, to favor

finire, to finish

fiorire, to flourish, to bloom

fluire, to flow

fornire, to furnish

garantire, to guarantee

gestire, to gesticulate, to manage

ghermire, to seize, to snatch

gioire, to rejoice

granire, to seed, to become or yield seed

gremire, to fill, to become crowded

grugnire, to grunt

guaire, to howl, to wail

gualcire, to rumple

guarire, to heal

guarnire, to trim

illaidire, to make ugly

illanguidire, to grow faint, languid

illiquidire, to become liquid, to melt

imbaldanzire, imbaldire, to become proud, bold

imbandire, to set (the table)

imbarberire, to become barbarous

imbarbogire, to become senile

imbastardire, to degenerate

imbastire, to baste

imbestialire, to become brutal, irritated

imbianchire, to whiten, to turn pale

imbiondire, to make fair

imbizzarire, to make, or to become, excited

imbizzire, to fly into a rage

imbolsire, to become shortbreathed

imbottire, to stuff, pad

imbozzacchire, to be stunted in growth

imbricconire, to become a cheat

imbrunire, to become brown

imbruschire, to grow sour

immagrire, to become lean

immalinconire, to be afflicted

immalizzire, to grow malicious

immalvagire, to corrupt

impadronire, to make one master of

impallidire, to turn pale

impaurire, to frighten

impazientire, to grow impatient

impedire, to prevent

impermalire, to irritate, to provoke

impidocchire, to breed lice

impietrire, to petrify

impigrire, to become lazy

impoltronire, to become lazy

imporrire, to grow moldy

impostemire, to form an abscess

impoverire, to impoverish

imputridire, to putrefy

impuzzolire, to become stinking, to stink

inacerbire, to exasperate, to provoke

inacetire, to grow sour or acid

inacutire, to make sharper

inalidire, to grow dry

inagrestire, to grow sour

inanimire, to animate

inaridire, to dry up

inasinire, to become an ass

inasprire, to exasperate
inavarire, to grow avaricious
incallire, to grow callous
incalorire, to warm
incalvire, to grow bald
incancherire, to fester, to gangrene
incanutire, to become gray, white
incaparbire, to be obstinate
incaponire, to be obstinate
incattivire, to become naughty
incenerire, to burn to ashes
incimurrire, to have the glanders
inciprignire, to exasperate
incitrullire, to become a blockhead
incivettire, to become a coquette
incivilire, to become civil
incollerire, to throw into a passion
incrudelire, to grow cruel
incrudire, to irritate, to make harsh
indebolire, to weaken
indocilire, to render docile
indolenzire, to benumb
infarcire, to stuff
infastidire, to annoy
infellonire, to grow cruel
infeltrire, to reduce to felt
infemminire, to become effeminate
inferire, to infer
inferocire, to become ferocious
infertilire, to make fertile
inferire, to infer
infievolire, to debilitate
infingardire, to cause to grow lazy
influire, to influence
infoltire, to become crowded
infortire, to strengthen
infralire, to grow faint, weak
infrigidire, to make cold
infrollire, to become tender
ingagliardire, to grow strong
ingelosire, to make jealous
ingentilire, to ennoble, to tame
ingerirsi, to meddle

ingiallire, to make yellow, to grow
  yellow
ingigantire, to become a giant
ingrandire, to enlarge
inibire, to forbid
inorgoglire, to become proud
inorridire, to horrify
inquisire, to prosecute criminally
insalvatichire, to become wild
insanire, to grow mad
inserire, to insert
insignire, to confer a title
insignorire, to become master of
insolentire, to grow insolent
insollire, to be, or make, soft
insordire, to grow deaf
insospettire, to feel, or inspire,
  suspicion
insuperbire, to be, or make, proud
intenerire, to soften
intiepidire, to make tepid
intimidire, to intimidate
intimorire, to intimidate
intirizzire, to benumb with cold
intisichire, to grow consumptive
intormentire, to grow benumbed
intorpidire, to grow heavy, sleepy
intristire, to grow sickly, melancholy
invaghire, to inflame with love
invanire, to become vain
inveire, to inveigh against
invelenire, to become irritated
inverdire, to grow green
inverminire, to breed worms
invigorire, to invigorate
invilire, to dishearten
inviperire, to rage
involpire, to become as cunning as a
  fox
inumidire, to moisten
inuzzolire, to excite envy
inzotichire, to grow clumsy
irretire, to ensnare, to allure

to stiffen
..ire, to rust
..ire, to make sterile
..cuire, to institute
.stupidire, to make or grow stupid
largire, to give liberally
lenire, to mitigate
marcire, to become rotten
munire, to supply
nitrire, to neigh
ostruire, to obstruct
partorire, to bring forth children
patire, to suffer
pattuire, to make a covenant
pervertire, to pervert
piatire, to contend
poltrire, to lie in bed, to loiter
preferire, to prefer
presagire, to presage, to divine
preterire, to fail to effect
proferire, to offer
progredire, to progress
proibire, to prohibit
pulire, to polish, to clean
rapire, to ravish, to kidnap
rattiepidire, to make tepid
redarguire, to find fault with, to disprove
restituire, to restore, to return
retribuire, to retribute
reagire, to react
ribadire, to rivet
riferire, to refer
rifiorire, to blossom again
ringiovanire, to make, or grow, young again
rinsanire, to recover health
rinsavire, to grow wise again
rinverzire, to make, or become green again

ripulire, to cleanse
risarcire, to compensate
ritrosire, to grow shy
riunire, to reunite
riverire, to revere
sbalordire, to astound
sbigottire, to terrify
scalfire, to scarify, to scratch
scarnire, to thin, to scrape off flesh
scaturire, to spring, to issue
schermire, to fence, to ward off
schernire, to laugh at, to mock
schiattire, to squeak
scipidire, to grow, or make, insipid
seppellire, to bury
sgarire, to have the upper hand
smaltire, to digest
smarrire, to miss, to lose
sostituire, to substitute
spaurire, to frighten, be frightened
spedire, to dispatch
spessire, to thicken
squittire, to squeak
stabilire, to establish
starnutire, to sneeze
statuire, to resolve
stecchire, to become dry
stizzire, to irritate, to anger
stordire, to stun
stormire, to rustle
stramortire, to faint away
supplire, to supply
svanire, to vanish
tradire, to betray
trasferire, to transfer
trasgredire, to transgress
ubbidire, to obey
vagire, to cry (as a baby)

109. Verbs that may either end in **o** or in **isco** in the Present Tense of the Indicative Mood, and hence also in the Imperative and Subjunctive Moods (more usual form indicated in parentheses):

aborrire, to abhor
applaudire, to applaud
assorbire, to absorb
avvertire, to warn (o)
divertire, to divert (o)
pervertire, to pervert
sovvertire, to subvert
bollire, to boil
ribollire, to boil again
sobbollire, to boil slowly
compire, to complete (io)
adempire, to accomplish

empire, to fill
inghiottire, to swallow
lambire, to lap, to lick
languire, to languish
maledire, to curse[1]
benedire, to bless[1]
mentire, to lie
nutrire, to feed
offerire, to offer (o)
partire, to leave, to part (o)
compartire, to divide (o)
ruggire, to roar (isco)

Applaudire, to applaud

INDICATIVO

Presente

applaudisco or applaudo
applaudisci or applaudi
applaudisce or applaude

applaudiamo
applaudite
applaudiscono, or applaudono

Benedire, to bless

INDICATIVO

Presente

benedico or benedisco
benedici or benedisci
benedice or benedisce

benediamo
benedite
benedicono, benediscono

ALPHABETICAL LIST OF THE IRREGULAR VERBS

(All Compounds and Derivatives are excluded, except those that deviate in some forms from the simple Verb.)

	IND. PRES.	PASS. REM.	FUT.	PART. PASS.
accedere, to draw near	Reg.	accedei accedetti accessi	Reg.	Reg.
accendere, to light	Reg.	accesi	Reg.	acceso

[1] Conjugate as –isco verb or as compound of **dico.**

	IND. PRES.	PASS. REM.	FUT.	PART. PASS.
..., to perceive	Reg.	m' accorsi	Reg.	accorto
..e, to bring	adduco	addussi	addurrò	addotto
..ggere, to afflict	Reg.	afflissi	Reg.	afflitto
..ludere, to allude	Reg.	allusi	Reg.	alluso
andare, to go	vado or vo	Reg.	andrò	Reg.
annettere, to annex	Reg.	annessi	Reg.	annesso
apparire, to appear	apparisco	apparvi	Reg.	apparso
		apparii		apparito
appendere, to suspend	Reg.	appesi	Reg.	appeso
applaudire, to applaud	applaudisco	applaudii	Reg.	Reg.
	applaudo			
aprire, to open	Reg.	aprii	Reg.	aperto
		apersi		
ardere, to burn	Reg.	arsi	Reg.	arso
assidersi, to sit down	m' assiedo	m' assisi	m' assiederò	assiso
assistere, to assist	Reg.	Reg.	Reg.	assistito
assolvere, to absolve	Reg.	Reg.	Reg.	assolto
				assoluto
assorbire, to absorb	Reg.	Reg.	Reg.	assorto
				assorbito
assumere, to assume	Reg.	assunsi	Reg.	assunto
avere, to have	ho	ebbi	avrò	avuto
benedire, to bless	benedico	benedìi	Reg.	benedetto
	benedisco	benedissi		
bevere, to drink	bevo	bevvi	beverò	bevuto
bere		bevei,	berrò	
		bevetti		
cadere, to fall	cado	caddi	cadrò	Reg.
		cadei		
		cadetti		
calere, to matter (see "Defective Verbs")				
capere, to hold (see "Defective Verbs")				
cedere, to yield	Reg.	cedei	Reg.	ceduto
		cedetti		cesso
		cessi		
chiedere, to ask	chiedo	chiesi	Reg.	chiesto
	chieggo	chiedei		
chiudere, to shut	Reg.	chiusi	Reg.	chiuso
cingere, to gird	cingo	cinsi	cingerò	cinto
cignere	cigno		cignerò	
circoncidere, to circumcise (see incidere)				
circonflettere, to bend, has only	——	——		circonflesso

	IND. PRES.	PASS. REM.	FUT.	PART. PASS.
cogliere or corre, to gather (see sciogliere)				
collidere, to strike against (see elidere)				
colludere, to conspire (in a fraud) (see ludere)				
comparire, to appear (see apparire)				
comprimere, to com-press	Reg.	compressi	Reg.	compresso
concepire, to conceive		concepii		concepito
				concetto
			rarely	conceputo
connettere, to connect	Reg.	connessi	Reg.	connesso
conoscere, to know	Reg.	conobbi	Reg.	conosciuto
		conoscei		
		conoscetti		
consumere (not used) to consume	not used	consunsi	not used	consunto
contessere, to weave together	Reg.	Reg.	Reg.	contessuto
				contesto
coprire, to cover (see aprire)				
correre, to run	corro	corsi	correrò	corso
costruire, to construct	costruisco	costrussi	Reg.	costrutto
		costruii		costruito
crescere, to grow	cresco	crebbi	Reg.	cresciuto
cuocere, to cook	cuocio	cossi	cocerò	cotto
dare, to give	do	diedi	darò	dato
decidere, to decide	Reg.	decisi	Reg.	deciso
dedurre, to deduct (see addurre)				
deludere, to delude (see alludere)				
deprimere, to depress (see comprimere)				
difendere, to defend	Reg.	difesi	Reg.	difeso
dire, to say	dico	dissi	dirò	detto
dirigere, to direct	Reg.	diressi	Reg.	diretto
discutere, to discuss	Reg.	discussi	Reg.	discusso
distinguere, to distin-guish	Reg.	distinsi	Reg.	distinto
dividere, to divide	Reg.	divisi	Reg.	diviso
dolere, to ache, to be sorry	dolgo	dolsi	dorrò	doluto
	doglio			
dovere, to be obliged, to owe	devo	dovei	dovrò	Reg.
	debbo			
	deggio (arch.)	dovetti		
elidere, to elide	Reg.	elisi	Reg.	eliso
eludere, to elude (see alludere)				

	IND. PRES.	PASS. REM.	FUT.	PART. PASS.
ꙍ emerge	Reg.	emersi	Reg.	emerso
ꙍ erect	Reg.	eressi	Reg.	eretto
ꙍe, to exhaust	Reg.	Reg.	Reg.	esaurito
				esausto
escludere, to exclude	Reg.	esclusi	Reg.	escluso
esigere, to want	Reg.	esigei	Reg.	esatto
		esigetti		
esistere, to exist	Reg.	esistei	Reg.	esistito
		esistetti		
espellere, to expel	Reg.	espulsi	Reg.	espulso
esprimere, to express	Reg.	espressi	Reg.	espresso
essere, to be	sono	fui	sarò	stato
estinguere, to extin-	Reg.	estinsi	Reg.	estinto
guish				
evadere, to evade	Reg.	evasi	Reg.	evaso
fare, to do	faccio or fo	feci	farò	fatto
fendere, to split	Reg.	fendei	Reg.	fenduto
		fessi		fesso
figgere, to fix	Reg.	fissi	Reg.	fitto
				fisso
fingere, to feign	Reg.	finsi	Reg.	finto
friggere, to fry	Reg.	frissi	Reg.	fritto
genuflettere, to kneel	genufletto	genuflessi	genufletterò	genuflesso
giacere, to lie	giaccio	giacqui	Reg.	giaciuto
	giacio			
gire, to go (see "Defective Verbs")				
giungere, to join, to	giungo	giunsi	giungerò	giunto
arrive				
immergere, to immerge (see emergere)				
impellere, to excite (see espellere)				
imprendere, to undertake (see apprendere)				
imprimere, to imprint	Reg.	impressi	Reg.	impresso
incendere, to set on fire (see accendere)				
incidere, to engrave	Reg.	incisi	Reg.	inciso
indurre, to induce (see addurre)				
infliggere, to inflict (see affliggere)				
inflettere, to bend	Reg.	Reg.	Reg.	inflesso
infringere, to infringe (see cingere)				
insistere, to insist (see assistere)				
intridere, to knead	Reg.	intrisi	Reg.	intriso
intrudere, to intrude	Reg.	intrusi	Reg.	intruso
invadere, to invade	Reg.	invasi	Reg.	invaso

	Ind. Pres.	Pass. Rem.	Fut.	Part. Pass
ire, to go (see "Defective Verbs")				
istruire, to instruct (see costruire)				
ledere, to hurt	Reg.	lesi	Reg.	leso
leggere, to read	Reg.	lessi	Reg.	letto
licere, to be permitted (see "Defective Verbs")				
maledire, to curse	maledico	maledii	maledirò	maledetto
	maledisco	maledissi		
(Imperf.) malediva and malediceva				
mescere, to pour, to mix	Reg.	Reg.	(poured) (mixed)	mesciuto misto
mettere, to put	metto	misi	metterò	messo
mordere, to bite	Reg.	morsi (mordei, mordetti)	Reg.	morso
morire, to die	muoio	morii	morrò morirò	morto
mungere, to milk mugnere	mungo mugno	munsi	mungerò mugnerò	munto
muovere, to move	muovo	mossi	moverò	mosso
nascere, to be born	nasco	nacqui	nascerò	nato
nascondere, to hide	Reg.	nascosi	Reg.	nascosto
negligere, to neglect	———	———	———	negletto
nuocere, to prejudice	nuoco noccio	nocqui	nocerò	nociuto
offrire, to offer	offro	offrii offersi	offrirò	offerto
opprimere, to oppress (see comprimere)				
parere, to seem	paio	parvi	parrò	parso
partire, to depart (like sentire)				
partire, to divide	partisco, etc.	Reg.	Reg.	Reg.
pascere, to feed, to graze	Reg.	Reg.	Reg. (poet.)	pasciuto pasto
percuotere, to strike	percuoto	percossi	Reg.	percosso
perdere, to lose	Reg.	perdei (persi)	Reg.	perduto (perso)
persistere, to persist (see assistere)				
persuadere, to persuade	Reg.	persuasi	Reg.	persuaso
piacere, to please	piaccio piacio	piacqui	Reg.	piaciuto
piangere, to weep	Reg.	piansi	Reg.	pianto
pingere, to paint	Reg.	pinsi	Reg.	pinto

	IND. PRES.	PASS. REM.	FUT.	PART. PASS.
...ain	piovo	piovvi piovei	pioverà	piovuto
..., to offer	Reg.	porsi	Reg.	porto
...e, to put	pongo	posi	porrò	posto
...otere, to be able	posso	potei potetti	potrò	potuto
precludere, to preclude (see chiudere)				
premere, to press, to be important	Reg.	Reg.	Reg.	premuto presso
prendere, to take	Reg.	presi	Reg.	preso
presumere, to presume (see assumere)				
propendere, to incline	Reg.	Reg.	Reg.	propenso
proteggere, to protect	Reg.	protessi proteggei	Reg.	protetto
pungere, to prick	pungo	punsi	pungerò	punto
radere, to shave, to erase	rado	rasi radei	Reg.	raso
recidere, to cut off (see circoncidere)				
redimere, to redeem	Reg.	redensi redimei	Reg.	redento
reggere, to govern	Reg.	ressi	Reg.	retto
rendere, to render	Reg.	resi rendei rendetti	Reg.	reso renduto
reprimere, to repress	Reg.	repressi reprimei	Reg.	represso
rescindere, to cut off	Reg.	rescissi rescindei	Reg.	rescisso
resistere, to resist (see assistere)				
retundere, to blunt	Reg.	Reg.	Reg.	retuso
ridere, to laugh	Reg.	risi	Reg.	riso
ridurre, to reduce (see addurre)				
redire, riedere, to return (see "Defective Verbs")				
riflettere, to reflect	Reg.	riflettei riflessi	Reg.	riflettuto riflesso (reverberated)
rimanere, to remain	rimango	rimasi	rimarrò	rimasto
rincrescere (Impersonal), to regret	(mi) rincresce	rincrebbe	rincrescerà	rincresciuto
ripellere, to repel (see espellere)				

	IND. PRES.	PASS. REM.	FUT.	PART. PASS.
risolvere, to resolve	Reg.	risolvei risolvetti risolsi	Reg.	risolto risoluto
risorgere, to rise again	Reg.	risorsi	Reg.	risorto
rispondere, to answer	Reg.	risposi	Reg.	risposto
ritorcere, to twist again (see torcere)				
rodere, to gnaw	Reg.	rosi	Reg.	roso
rompere, to break	Reg.	ruppi	Reg.	rotto
salire, to ascend	salgo	salii	Reg.	Reg.
sapere, to know	so	seppi	saprò	Reg.
scegliere, to choose	scelgo	scelsi	sceglierò	scelto
scendere, to descend	Reg.	scesi scendei scendetti	Reg.	sceso
scindere, to separate	scindo	scissi	scinderò	scisso
sciogliere, to untie	sciolgo	sciolsi	scioglierò	sciolto
scorgere, to perceive	Reg.	scorsi	Reg.	scorto
scrivere, to write	Reg.	scrissi	Reg.	scritto
scuotere, to shake	Reg.	scossi	Reg.	scosso
sedere, to sit	siedo seggo	sedei sedetti	Reg.	Reg.
sedurre, to seduce (see addurre)				
seguire, to follow	seguo	Reg.	Reg.	Reg.
seppellire, to bury	seppellisco	Reg.	Reg.	seppellito sepolto
serpere, to wind (see "Defective Verbs")				
soffrire, to suffer (see offrire)				
solere, to use (see "Defective Verbs")				
solvere, to solve	solvo	solsi	solverò	soluto
sopprimere, to suppress (see opprimere)				
sorgere, to rise (see porgere)				
sospendere, to suspend (see appendere)				
spandere, to spill, to pour out	Reg.	spandei spandetti spansi	Reg.	spanduto spanso
spargere, to scatter	Reg.	sparsi spargei	Reg.	sparso
sparire, to disappear	sparisco	sparii (sparvi)	Reg.	sparito (sparuto, adj., spare, thin)

	IND. PRES.	PASS. REM.	FUT.	PART. PASS.
spegnere, spengere, to extinguish	spengo spegno	spensi	Reg.	spento
spendere, to spend (see appendere)				
sperdere, to waste (see perdere)				
spergere, to disperse	Reg.	spersi	Reg.	sperso
spingere, to push (see pingere)				
stare, to stand, to be	sto	stetti	starò	stato
stringere, to press	stringo	strinsi	stringerò	stretto
struggere, to destroy	struggo	strussi	Reg.	strutto
svellere, to root up	svelgo	svelsi	svellerò	svelto
tacere, to be silent	taccio tacio	tacqui	Reg.	taciuto
tendere, to extend (see attendere)				
tenere, to hold	tengo	tenni	terrò	tenuto
tergere, to wipe	Reg.	tersi	Reg.	terso
tingere, to dye	tingo	tinsi	tingerò	tinto
togliere, to take torre	tolgo	tolsi	toglierò torrò	tolto
torcere, to twist	torco	torsi torcei torcetti	Reg.	torto
tradurre, to translate (see addurre)				
traere, trarre, to draw	traggo	trassi	trarrò	tratto
uccidere, to kill	Reg.	uccisi	Reg.	ucciso
udire, to hear	odo	udii	udirò udrò	Reg.
ungere, to anoint	ungo	unsi	ungerò	unto
uscire, to go out	esco	uscii	uscirò	uscito
valere, to be worth	valgo	valsi	varrò	valuto valso
vedere, to see	vedo, veggio, veggo	vidi	vedrò	veduto visto
venire, to come	vengo	venni	verrò	venuto
vilipendere, to vilify	Reg.	vilipesi	Reg.	vilipeso
vincere, to win, to conquer	vinco	vinsi	Reg.	vinto
vivere, to live	Reg.	vissi	vivrò	vissuto
volere, to be willing	voglio	volli	vorrò	voluto
volgere, to turn	volgo	volsi	volgerò	volto

Rules on the Use of Moods and Tenses

Use of the Tenses of the Indicative Mood

110. The **Presente** is used instead of the **Passato** in animated language. Example:

Çristo levatosi da cena andò nell' orto; e quivi ASPETTA *chi il dcve tradire.*

Christ having arisen from his supper, went to the garden, and there awaited (awaits) the man who is to betray him.

111. The **Presente** instead of the **Futuro,** to express something as **positive.** Example:

Chi non lavora in gioventù, STENTA *in vecchiaia.*

He who does not work while young, will be in want in his old age.

112. The **Futuro** instead of the **Presente,** to express uncertainty. Example:

Grazie al cielo io sto bene, come io spero che SARÀ *di voi.*

Thank Heaven I am well, as I hope you are.

113. In animated descriptions the **Infinitivo** may sometimes be used instead of the **Presente.** Example:

Mezz' ora dappoi, ecco STRIDERE *le chiavi, la porta s' apre.*

Half an hour afterwards, I hear the keys rattle, the door opens.

Use of the Past Tenses

114. The **Imperfetto** is used in descriptions of character, manners, landscape, etc., and to represent the repetition of an action. Example:

La moglie del carceriere SOLEVA *portarmi il caffè mattina e dopo-pranzo; la* SEGUIVANO *ordinariamente sua figlia ed i due figliuoli; si* RITIRAVANO *poi colla madre e si* RIVOLTAVANO *a guardarmi dolcemente; gli uni* GIUOCAVANO, *mentre gli altri* BALLAVANO.

115. The **Imperfetto** points out the action that was going on when another began.

AVEVAMO *l' intenzione di partire domani, ma* RICEVEMMO *una lettera da Vienna che ci obbliga a restare quì ancora alcuni giorni.*

We intended leaving to-morrow, but we have received a letter from Vienna which obliges us to stay here a few days longer.

Noi SCRIVEVAMO, *quando il medico* ENTRÒ.

We were writing, when the physician entered.

NOTE.—In this case the *imperfetto* can always be rendered into English by using the *Present Participle* in connection with the Auxiliary *to be.*

Lo sorpresi mentre SCRIVEVA.

I surprised him while he *was writing.*

116. The **Imperfetto,** again, expresses accessory and explanatory circumstances while the **Passato Remoto** states principal facts, as:

La ricordanza m' AFFLIGGEVA *e m'* INTENERIVA. *Ma* PENSAI *anche alla sorte di tanti amici miei e non* SEPPI *più giudicare con indulgenza i miei avversari. Iddio* MI METTEVA *in una gran prova! Mio debito sarebbe stato di sostenerla con virtù. Non* POTEI, *non* VOLLI. *La voluttà dell' odio mi* PIACQUE *più del perdono:* PASSAI *una notte d' inferno.*

117. In English **could** or **should** is often used instead of the Italian **Imperfetto:**

DOVEVATE *dirmelo subito.*

You should have told me so at once.

POTEVI *bene avermelo detto prima.*

You could have told me so before.

118. The **Passato Remoto** is also called the Historical Tense, because it is used in narratives ro relate, to enumerate facts or actions following one another in a time entirely elapsed, as:

IERI EBBI *il piacere di vedere tuo cugino.*

Yesterday I had the pleasure of seeing your cousin.

FUI *molto lieto di vederlo.*

I was very glad to see him.

AVESTE *la bontà di consegnare la lettera al mio amico?*

Did you have the kindness to give the letter to my friend?

PARLASTI *al maestro?*

Did you speak to the teacher?

Sì, e LO PREGAI *di non venire domani.*

Yes, and I requested him not to come to-morrow.

CERCASTI *il mio schioppo?*

Did you look for my gun?

REMARK.—The *Passato Remoto* in these cases expresses actions entirely unconnected with other actions. The use of the *Imperfetto* in the last example, for instance, would make the sentence incomplete.

Cercavi il mio schioppo (quando entrai nella stanza)?

Were you looking for my gun (when I entered the room)?

119. The **Passato Remoto** is further required with Adverbs or Adverbial Expressions that point out either the beginning or the

end of an action, as: **allorchè, appena, subito che, dacchè, quando, allora,** etc. Examples:

ALLORCHÈ *Mentore* UDÌ *la voce della dea, che chiamava le sue ninfe,* DESTÒ *Telemaco.*

When Mentor heard the voice of the goddess calling her nymphs, he woke up Telemachus.

DACCHÈ PERDETTE *quanto aveva, non* EBBE *più amici.*

Since he lost all he owned, he had no more friends.

Io non avevo che tredici anni, QUANDO MI SEPARAI *dai miei cari genitori, ch' io non dovevo più rivedere.*

I was only thirteen years old, when I left my beloved parents whom I was to see no more.

Il generale SI TROVÒ *improvvisamente circondato dai nemici.*

The general was unexpectedly surrounded by the enemy.

120. The **Passato Remoto,** then, as was pointed out, generally denotes, either a fact that took place in a period of time wholly elapsed, or having no direct relation with any preceding or following action. The **Passato Prossimo,** on the contrary, is used to express an action at a period of time not entirely elapsed or expired: **Oggi, questa mattina, questa settimana, questo mese, quest' anno, questo secolo,** etc. Example:

Ieri incontrai tuo padre; oggi ho visto tua madre.

Yesterday I met your father, to-day I have seen (I saw) your mother.

SIETE STATO *in chiesa* QUESTA MATTINA?

Have you been at church this morning?

NOTE.—It is to be remarked, however that this distinction is not always strictly observed and that the *Passato Remoto* is often substituted for the *Passato Prossimo* with absolute propriety.

121. The **Passato Prossimo** expresses also events entirely past, but the consequences of which are still to be seen or felt at the present time. Example:

Ho perduto tutto il mio denaro.

I have lost all my money (and I am now poor, penniless).

122. There is between the **Trapassato Prossimo** and the **Trapassato Remoto** the same difference as between the **Imperfetto** and the **Passato Remoto;** but they express actions previous to those denoted by the latter Tenses. The **Trapassato Remoto** is an Historical Tense

278

and points out positive facts, while the **Trapassato Prossimo,** like the **Imperfetto,** is a descriptive Tense. Example:

Appena ebbi *terminato i miei affari, ripartii.*
As soon as I had finished my business, I set out again.
Appena ebbe *pronunciato queste parole, ch' egli se ne pentì.*
Scarcely had he uttered these words, when he repented.

But:

Avevo *già* terminato *i miei affari, quando ricevetti la vostra lettera.*
I had already finished my business, when I received your letter.
In campagna, quando avevo pranzato, *facevo un giro d' un' ora.*
In the country, after having dined, I used to take an hour's walk.

However, to express, not a habit, as in the last sentence, but a single isolated fact, it would be necessary to say:

Un giorno che ebbi ben pranzato, *feci un giro.*

123. The **Futuro** denotes generally future events, as:

Mio fratello andrà *a Pisa doman l' altro.*
My brother will go to Pisa the day after to-morrow.
Si dice che quel paese avrà *presto una rivoluzione.*
It is said that soon that country will have a revolution.

124. The **Futuro** is sometimes used instead of the **Imperative,** as:

Non ruberai, thou shalt not steal.
Ne beveremo *un bicchiere insieme per finirla.*
Come, let us have a glass together, to settle it.

125. **Avere da (a)** expresses a **Futuro** with the idea of compulsion or prohibition, as:

Questo matrimonio non s' ha a *fare.*—Manzoni.
This marriage must not (shall not) be performed.
In quanto al mio onore ha da *sapere che il custode ne son io.*
As to my honor, you have to know that I am its guardian.

126. The English expression **to be about to . . .** or any one of the Adverbs **soon, presently, directly,** and others, is to be rendered by **essere per** or **stare per** followed by the Infinitive, or else by **essere sul punto di . . ., essere in procinto di . . .** Example:

Ella sta or *è per partire.*
She is about to leave.
Sono sul punto (in procinto) di scrivergli.
I am going to write him presently.

127. The **Futuro Anteriore** refers to an action that is to take place before some other future action. Example:

Quando l' avrò visto, lo crederò.
When I (shall) have seen it, (then) I will believe it.
Appena avrò finito di pranzare, partirò.
As soon as I (shall) have dined, I will start.

Use of the Conditional

128. The **Imperfetto dell' Indicativo** may be sometimes used instead of the **Trapassato del Soggiuntivo** in the subordinate clause, and instead of the **Condizionale Presente** in the principal sentence. Thus: *Se l'* AVESSI VISTO, *glielo* AVREI DETTO, if I had seen him, I should have told him. so, may be replaced by: *Se* LO VEDEVO, *glielo* DICEVO; and less frequently: *Se lo* VEDEVO, *glielo* AVREI DETTO.

Still less frequently the **Imperfetto dell' Indicativo** in the principal sentence is used instead of the **Condizionale**:

E glielo DICEVA, *ma venne impedito di farlo.*
And he would have told it to him, but was prevented from doing so.

129. Very often the **Futuro Anteriore,** as well as the **Condizionale Passato,** has the meaning of the simple Tense:

Continua a spendere, e mi AVRAI ROVINATO.
If you go on spending, you will ruin me.

On the Imperative

130. The **Imperativo Negativo** in the second person singular is represented by **non** and the Infinitive. Thus: **Parla,** speak (thou); but: **Non parlar troppo,** do not speak too much.

131. The four Verbs **avere, essere, sapere,** and **volere,** form not only their third person singular and plural, as other Verbs do, from the **Soggiuntivo,** but also their second person singular and plural, but then the singular of the three first Verbs end in **i** only, while the singular of **volere** is wanting in the **Imperativo:**

Abbi pazienza, amico mio!
Be patient, my friend!
Siate buoni e sarete felici.
Be good, and you will be happy.

Sequence of Tenses

132. If the Verb of the principal sentence is in the **Presente** or **Futuro,** the Verb of the subordinate clause ought to be in the **Presente** or the **Passato Prossimo** of the **Indicativo,** or else in the **Presente** or the **Passato** of the Soggiuntivo:

Assicura che viene *domani.*
He says he will come to-morrow.
Mi potete indicare qualcuno che me lo voglia *dire?*
Can you point out anybody to me who will be willing to tell it to me?
Gli dirai che desideri *partire.*
You will tell him you wish to set out.
Farò in modo che egli me lo dia.
I shall see to it that he gives it to me.

133. If the Verb of the principal sentence is in the **Imperfetto, Condizionale, Passato Remoto, Trapassato Prossimo** or **Trapassato,** the Verb of the dependent clause should be in the **Imperfetto** or the **Passato** of the **Indicativo** or **Soggiuntivo** accordingly, as:

Quando Iddio creò la terra, le fece precetto che producesse erbe e frutti.
When God created the earth, He ordered her to bring forth herbs and fruits.
L' ape non potrebbe difendersi, se non avesse il pungiglione.
The bee could not defend herself, if she did not have a sting.
Gli ho detto che il padre era morto.
I told him that his father was dead.

134. The **Passato Prossimo** may be followed by either the **Presente** or by some past tense. If the Verb of the accessory sentence expresses a present action, it will be in the Present; if a past action, the Verb will be in some past Tense accordingly, as:

Iddio ci ha dato la coscienza, affinchè la ascoltiamo.
God has given us conscience that we may listen to it.
Egli ci ha scritto, che il generale aveva capitolato.
He wrote us that the general had capitulated.

Remark.—The actual meaning of the sentences may, however, make it necessary to deviate from these rules and to employ other Tenses in the subordinate clause. Example: *Si direbbe che non si son mai conosciuti,* one would say that they have nevèr known each other.

The Subjunctive Mood

135. The use of the Subjunctive Mood is much more frequent in Italian than in English.

The Verb of the dependent clause will be in the Subjunctive Mood:

a. When the verb of the principal sentence expresses doubt, fear, surprise: **dubitare, temere, meravigliarsi.** Example:

MI MERAVIGLIO *che* TU ABBIA tanto coraggio.

I am astonished at your being so courageous.

DA CHI SIA STATA *trovata la bussola*, è INCERTO *ancora.*—Redi.

It is still uncertain who invented the mariner's compass.

b. When the Verb of the principal sentence expresses an act of the will, as: **volere, comandare, pregare, desiderare, permettere, proibire, consigliare.** Example:

È VOLER DI *Dio che* VI AMIATE *l'un l' altro come fratelli.*—Segneri.

It is God's will that you should love each other like brothers.

c. When the Verb of the main sentence denotes necessity, convenience, probability, difficulty, as: **bisognare, bastare, occorrere, convenire, esser** or **far d' uopo.** Example:

Nelle amicizie è NECESSARIO *che si* APRANO *gli occhi.*

When it is a question of friendship, it is necessary to open one's eyes.

RARO È *che l'uomo* GIUNGA *coll' ingegno a correggere il cuore.*—Tommaseo.

Very seldom does man succeed in correcting his heart through his talent.

d. When the principal sentence expresses someone else's ignorance or uncertainty. Example:

Il ricco NON SA *che cosa* SIA *bisogno.*

The rich do not know what want is.[1]

---

[1] NOTE.—After the Verbs *temere, dubitare, sperare, sospettare, pretendere, volere,* etc., *conviene, bisogna,* etc., the Conjunction *che,* that, may be omitted before the dependent clause. Example: *L'uomo che pretende* SIANO REGOLATI *a sua voglia gli affari del mondo, è uno stolto,* the man who pretends that the affairs of the world be regulated according to his desire is a fool. *Non fare mai ad altri quello che non vorresti* FOSSE FATTO *a te.*

136. The **soggiuntivo** is also required after a **comparative** or a **superlative** followed by **che.** Example:

La maggior *difficoltà che* sia *nel parlare, nasce dalla scarsezza delle parole.*—Buonmattei.

The greatest difficulty one experiences in talking arises from the scarcity of words.

137. The **Soggiuntivo** is also used after **il primo, l' ultimo, unico, solo, nessuno, niente,** and a few other similar expressions, because they are to be considered as superlatives:

Era l'unico *figlio che io* avessi, *e m' è morto.*

He was the only son that I had, and he died.

Tu sei il solo *essere vivente su cui io* possa *contare.*

You are the only living being on whom I can rely.

138. These rules are not always obeyed, and the Indicative is freely used whenever the meaning admits of its use. Example:

Credimi che ti amo.

Believe me that I love you.

L'assicuro che sto perfettamente bene.

I assure you that I am quite well.

Non credo che verrà or che venga.

I do not think that he will come.

139. The **Soggiuntivo** is further used after certain Adverbs and Pronouns that express something vague or indistinct:

Chiunque sia *non voglio vederlo.*

Whoever it be, I don't want to see him.

Qualunque sia *la tua sorte.*

Whatever be your fate.

140. In sentences denoting desire, permission, invitation, anger, etc., an **Absolute Subjunctive** is employed, as: **Piacesse a Dio! Dio lo volesse!** Heaven grant! **Venga pure!** do but come! **Favorisca sedersi,** Please be seated.

141. Lastly the **Soggiuntivo** is required after many Conjunctions or Conjunctive Phrases:

abbenchè		quand' anche, even if, even though	
benchè		dato che	
sebbene		posto che	suppose that
quantunque		supposto che	
tutto che	though	(Supposto che i Romani vincano.	
non ostante che	although	Suppose the Romans win.[1])	
con tutto che		anzi che, rather than	
malgrado che		finchè	
avvegna che		sinchè	till
ancorchè		fintanto che	
acciocchè	so that	in caso che	
affinchè		caso che	in case that
purchè		posto il caso che	
solo che	provided	senza che, without	
solamente che		non che, not only, much less	
		a meno che, unless	

NOTE 1.—Even in this case the Indicative is sometimes admissible: *Combattemmo finchè potemmo*, we fought as long as we could.

Chè, which forms the last part of many compound Conjunctions, loses the accent when written separately, thus: *fin tanto che*, till. But *chè*, meaning *perchè*, never loses its accent: *inutile venire, chè arriveresti troppo tardi*.

Instead of repeating a Conjunction in subordinate clauses, the simple Conjunction *che* replaces its compound, for euphony's sake: BENCHÈ *egli mi abbia detto la verità, e* CHE *io gli creda perfettamente*.

Quantunque non fosse ricco, era generoso e felice.

Although he was not rich, he was generous and happy.

Purchè la cosa sia vera.

Provided it be true.

ON THE USE OF THE INFINITIVE MOOD

142. The **Infinito** is frequently used as a Substantive, and it then corresponds to the English Present Participle.

Lo scrivere è un' arte.

Writing is an art.

Promettere e dare son cose differenti.

To promise and to give are different things.

Il leggere libri utili giova a tutti.

Reading useful books helps everybody.

Il tramontar del sole.

The setting of the sun.

Il far del giorno.

Daybreak.

143. Some Verbs are followed by the **Infinito** of another Verb **without** connecting Prepositions. Such are:

ardire, osare, to dare
bramare, desiderare, to wish, to long for
dovere, to be obliged
dubitare, to doubt
fare, lasciare, to let, to allow
parere, sembrare, to seem

potere, sapere, to be able
volere, to be willing
solere, usare, to use, to be wont
conviene, it is convenient
bisogna, occorre, è d' uopo, fa d' uopo, è mestiere, fa di mestieri, it is necessary.

Example:

Desidero vederlo, I wish to see him.
Vuol venire, he will come.
Chi vuol vivere deve mangiare.

144. The Verbs **intendere, sentire, udire,** and **vedere** are followed by the **Infinito** without an intervening Preposition:

Lo vidi morire. I saw him die.
Lo sentii parlare. I heard him talking.

145. The Infinitive is often used elliptically, without a Preposition, after the words **che,** what; **chi,** who; **dove, ove,** where; **onde, donde,** whence:

Non so di che parlare.
I don't know what to talk about.
Non sapeva ove nascondersi.
He did not know where he could hide himself.

146. Again the Infinitive is used after **è meglio, è peggio, è più difficile, è facile, è pericoloso,** etc.:

È pericoloso sdrucciolare sulla neve.
It is dangerous to slide on the snow.
È facile cadere sul ghiaccio.
It is easy to fall on the ice.

147. After Verbs denoting belief, opinion, hope, desire, pleasure, etc., the **Infinito** may take or drop the Preposition **di,** as:

Desidero di trovarmi con te, or desidero trovarmi con te.
I wish to be with you.
Gli spiacque di dover partire or gli spiacque dover partire.
He was sorry to have to leave.

148. It is used with **di** as a complement of Substantives answering the questions **what? what kind of?**

L' arte di dipingere.
The art of painting.
La brama di parlargli.
The longing to speak to him.[1]

149. The **Infinito** must be employed after Adjectives requiring the Preposition **di**, as: **desideroso di, avido di,** desirous of; **contento,** contented; **malcontento,** dissatisfied; **geloso,** jealous; **impaziente,** impatient; **certo, sicuro,** sure, certain:

Sono desideroso di partire.
I am desirous to start.

150. After special Verbs: **godere di, rallegrarsi di,** to rejoice at; **meravigliarsi di,** to marvel at; **pregare,** to pray; **supplicare,** to beseech; and after some Impersonal Verbs like **importa,** it is of importance; **mi tarda, non vedo l' ora di . . .** I am eager; **conviene,** it is convenient, etc.

Mi son meravigliato di non trovarla a casa.
I was surprised not to find you at home.

151. After some Prepositions, Adverbs or Conjunctions requiring **di,** as:

Prima di partire, before starting.
Invece di dormire, instead of sleeping.
Per paura di offenderlo, fearing to offend him.

With the Preposition "da"

152. The Preposition **da** after **essere** and **avere** denotes aptness or fitness. In English the Passive Voice is often used instead, **as:**

Che c' è da fare? what is there to be done?
Non è da biasimare, he is not to be blamed.
Non hai niente da dirgli? have you nothing to tell him?

153. Da is also often used with an **Infinito** after **dare:**
Gli ho dato da mangiare, I gave him to eat.

---

[1] REMARK.—When the Infinitive expresses a future action it requires *da*: *Ho molto da fare,* I have much to do.

154. There are likewise Substantives that sometimes require **da** with an **Infinito.**

Una cosa da ridere, a ridiculous thing.
Una casa da vendere, a house for sale.

155. Adjectives, too, may be followed in many cases by **da** and the **Infinito:**

Una regola facile da comprendere, a rule easy to be understood.
Un pezzo difficile da sonare, a piece difficult to play.

156. The Preposition **da** is often replaced by **a** if the action is performed by the speaker himself:

Ho da fare una cosa, ho una cosa da fare, ho a fare una cosa.

Infinito with "a"

157. There are Adjectives that require the Preposition **a** answering the question **to what?** as:

risoluto a, resolved to	difficile a, difficult to
buono a, able to	sensibile a, ready to
disposto a, disposed to	pronto a, ready to
facile a, easy to	lento a, slow to

Pronto ad eseguir le imposte cose (Tasso), ready to execute the things ordered.

158. The following Verbs require **a** and an Infinito after them:

acconsentire, to consent	disporsi, to prepare
accostumarsi, to accustom one's self	adattarsi, to accommodate one's self
avvezzarsi, to accustom one's self	incoraggiare, to encourage
costringere, to oblige, to compel	esortare, to exhort
forzare, to oblige, to compel	impiegare, to employ
attendersi, to expect	esporsi, to expose one's self
affaticarsi, to endeavor	continuare, to continue
applicarsi, to endeavor	pervenire, to come, to get to
autorizzare, to authorize	incitare, to incite
condannare, to condemn	indurre, to induce
contribuire, to contribute	invitare, to invite
destinare, to destine	inclinare, to incline
risolversi, to determine, to resolve	determinarsi, to determine, to resolve
riuscire, to succeed in	offrirsi, to offer one's self
imparare, to learn	reggere, to endure, to last
tardare, to delay, to be late	passare, to pass

stimolare, to stimulate
aiutare, to help
insegnare, to teach
dare, to give
mettersi, to begin
insistere, to insist
persistere, to persist

spronare, to spur
sedurre, to seduce
bastare, to be enough, to suffice
tornare, to return
muovere, to move
esitare, to hesitate
rinunciare, to renounce

159. Mark the following expressions:

Stare a, essere a, to be just now doing something.

Dare a vedere a qualcheduno, to make anybody understand.

Dare a fare, to give to do, to occupy.

Dare a pensare, to make one think, to give him material for reflection.

Dare ad intendere, to make anybody believe.

Andare a trovare qualcheduno, to call on somebody.

Mandare a prendere, to send for.

Tornare a scrivere, to write once more.

Ad intenderlo sa tutto, if you listen to him, he knows everything.

Fu l' ultimo a parlare, il primo ad agire, he was the last to speak, the first to act.

Che fare? what are we to do? what am I to do?

Dove ricoverarsi? where can we get a shelter?

Io! spargere il sangue de' miei figli! how could I shed my children's blood.

160. In the following sentences the **Infinito** is used instead of a subordinate clause beginning with **che** :

Crede ESSERE *capace di farlo.*

He thinks he is able to do it.

Spera (di) TROVARE *sua madre.*

He hopes to find his mother.

PRIMA DI SCRIVERE, *dimmi quel che pensi.*

Before you write, tell me what you think.

DOPO AVERMI *ascoltato si pentì d' averlo fatto.*

After having heard me, he regretted having done it.

Gli dissi di TACERE.

I told him to be silent.

Anzichè venderlo, *lo distrusse.*

Rather than sell it, he destroyed it.

Oltre all' esser *grande, la vostra bontà è anche costante.*

Your goodness is not only great, but it is also constant.

161. But a Conjunction must be used whenever the principal and subordinate sentences have two different Subjects:

Prima ch' *io partissi per la guerra, egli mi diede la sua benedizone.*

Before I started for the war, he gave me his benediction.

Participio E Gerundio

162. The Italian **Participio Presente** is not frequently used:

Una città fiorente, a flourishing city.

Colli ridenti, charming hills.

Un quadro rappresentante i' presidente, a picture representing the president.

163. The English Present Participle is generally rendered by the **Gerundio,** which also corresponds to accessory sentences beginning with one of the Conjunctions **because, as, while, if,** etc. It always refers to the Subject of the sentence.

Ella mi raccontò il fatto ridendo.

She told me the occurrence laughing.

Essendo *sempre molto occupato non riceve nessuno.*

As he is always very busy, he receives nobody.

164. The **Infinito** used substantively frequently replaces the **Gerundio,** as:

Nel parlare = **parlando.**

Nello scrivere = **scrivendo.**

Nel vederlo = **vedendolo.**

Partendo (nel partire) mi raccomandò suo figlio.

165. The **Gerundio** accompanied by **andare, venire, stare,** denotes actuality and continuation of action. Example:

Io vo pensando *ai miei passati tempi.*—Petrarch.

I am thinking about my past times.

Convien fare in modo che le cose si vengano sbrogliando *da se.*

It is better to arrange matters so that they will go on unraveling by themselves.

Fatto il beneficio, non STATE PENSANDO *alla mercede che ve ne debba toccare.*

After having done the favor do not stop to think about the reward which is due you.

166. When the principal and the accessory sentences have two different Subjects, the use of the Pronouns is necessary:

Andando IO *a spasso,* EGLI *mi si avvicinò.*[1]

While I was walking, he came up to me.

Participio Passato

167. The **Participio Passato** used adjectively agrees in Gender and Number with the Substantive it refers to.
Example:

Legni TAGLIATI *a luna piena intarlano.*—Davanzati.

Wood which is cut when the moon is full will breed worms.

Risplendenti stelle vediamo nel cielo.

We see shining stars in the sky.

168. The **Participio Passato** agrees with the Subject of the sentence when it is coupled with **essere** or with other Verbs that are used instead of **essere,** as: **andare, restare, rimanere, venire, stare,** etc.

Mio fratello è ARRIVATO.

My brother has arrived.

Mia madre è MORTA.

My mother is dead.

I Cartaginesi vennero BATTUTI.

The Carthaginians were beaten.

I Romani rimasero VITTORIOSI.

The Romans were victorious.

169. The **Participio Passato** coupled with **avere** remains unaltered if the Verb is Transitive or followed by the Infinitive.

La colomba come ebbe VOLATO *tutto il giorno, ritornò all' arca.*

The dove having flown the whole day, returned to the ark.

Le famiglie che hanno SAPUTO *regolare le cose loro, tengono dovizia di tutto.*

Those families that have been able to manage their affairs, have everything plentifully.

---

[1] In such cases it is preferable to use the Conjunction, as: *Mentre io andavo a spasso, egli mi si accostò.*

170. The **Participio Passato** of a Transitive Verb coupled with **avere** may either remain unaltered or agree in Gender and Number with the complement. Example:

Cristo poichè ebbe LAVATI *i piedi agli apostoli, disse loro: Come ho io* LAVATO *i piedi a voi, così voi dovete lavarli l' uno l' altro.*— Cavalca.

Christ having washed the Apostle's feet, said to them: As I have washed your feet, so you have to wash one another's.

171. When the complement of the Transitive Verb is one of the Pronouns **mi, ti, si, vi, gli,** or **li, la, le,** the Past Participle takes generally the Gender and Number of these Pronouns. Example:

Dio CI *ha* FATTI *liberi.*

God has made us free.

172. The **Participio Passato** coupled with either the Noun or the Pronoun to which it refers is sometimes used in an absolute way:

Gli angeli, NATO CRISTO. *l' annunciarono con allegrezza ai pastori.*
—Cavalca.

Christ having been born, the angels announced Him with joy to the shepherds.

ADJECTIVES

173. All Adjectives agree in Gender and Number with the Substantive or Pronoun they relate to, as: **Il buon fanciullo,** the good child: **la buona donna,** the good woman; **ella è felice,** she is happy.

174. Adjectives are divided into two classes, viz: Qualifying and Determining Adjectives.

Qualifying Adjectives

175. There are three different endings for Adjectives, one in **o** for the masculine gender, one in **a** for the feminine gender, and one in **e** for both genders.

176. Adjectives form their plural in accordance with the rules laid down for Nouns.

Singular		Plural	
MASC.	FEM.	MASC	FEM.
vero	vera, true	veri	vere
bello	bella, beautiful	belli	belle
onesto	onesta, honest	onesti	oneste
bianco	bianca, white	bianchi	bianche

For Both Genders	For Both Genders
fedele, faithful	fedeli
amabile, amiable	amabili
crudele, cruel	crudeli
tale, such	tali
felice, happy	felici

Comparative Degree

177. To express quality **tanto, quanto; così, come; altrettanto, quanto; tale, quale; come, così; non meno, che** are used, as:

Tanto bella quanto buona; così bella come buona; non meno bella che buona.

178. To express superiority, the comparison is formed by **più** with **di, del, dello, della . . ., che, che non, di quello che,** as:

La virtù è più pregevole delle ricchezze, di quello che siano le ricchezze.

179. To express inferiority, the word **meno** with **di, del, dello, della . . ., che, che non, di quello che,** as:

L' avaro è meno *felice del povero. Il prodigo è* meno *reo dell' avaro.*

The Superlative Degree

180. There is a **Superlativo Assoluto** and a **Superlativo Relativo.**
The former expresses the quality in a very high degree without comparison and is formed by changing the terminations **e, o, a** into

Note.—*Più* and *meno* prefer to take the correlative *di:* (a) Before the pronouns *me, te, noi, voi, lui, lei, loro, colui, colei, coloro, costui, costei, costoro,* etc., as: *Giovanni è* più *studioso di me, di te, di loro,* etc., John is more studious than I, than thou, than they, etc.; (b) Before Nouns that reject the Article, as: *più valoroso di Pompeo,* more courageous than Pompey; *meno prudente di Fabio,* less prudent than Fabius. *Più* and *meno* prefer to take *che:* (a) When the comparison takes place between two qualities of the same thing, as:*Frutto più bello che buono, pane meno buono che bello;* (b) If the comparison refers to the same quality existing in two different things, then the correlation may be either *che* or *di,* as: *La primavera è più piacevole che l'autunno* or *dell' autunno,* spring is more pleasing than autumn. (c) Before an Infinito *che* is preferable; Example: *Niuna letizia può essere ai vecchi più grande che vedere la gioventù costumata, riverente, virtuosa* (Pandolfini), there can be no greater joy for old people than the sight of well-behaved, reverent and virtuous young people. (d) If the comparison is made between two Nouns, either *che* or *di* may be used as correlative; Example: *abbi più cara una povertà congiunta alla giustizia, che una ricchezza ingiusta* (Leopardi), poverty with justice conjoined must be dearer to you than riches unjustly acquired.

issimo, issima; or i, e into issimi, issime, as: grande, grandissimo; alto, altissimo; bella, bellissima; grandi, grandissimi; alte, altissime.

Example:

BELLISSIMA *cosa è amor di patria.*

Sono stolti, o per dir meglio, stoltissimi quei che non prezzano il tempo, vivendo oziosi.—Pandolfini.

181. The following adjectives have a superlative ending in **errimo**:

acre, sour: **acerrimo,** very sour.
celebre, celebrated; **celeberrimo,** very celebrated.
integro, irreprehensible; **integerrimo,** very irreprehensible.
salubre, healthy; **saluberrimo,** very healthy.
misero, miserable, has **miserissimo** and **miserrimo.**

182. The repetition of the same Adjective in the positive degree has the force of a **Superlativo Assoluto,** as: **nero nero,** very black; **forte forte,** very strong. An Adjective with the affixes **arci, oltre, stra, tra,** is also a **Superlativo,** as: **arcibello,** very beautiful; **stragrande,** very large; **arcibravo,** very brave; **stralungo,** very long. The expressions: **sopra ogni altro, oltremisura, sopra ogni dire, oltremodo,** when used before an Adjective, form as many Superlatives.

Molti sono scarsi, delle cose terrene, ma RICCHI OLTREMODO *in virtù.*
Many are sparingly provided with earthly things, but are very rich in virtue.

Allorchè la luna è scema manda un lume DEBOLE DEBOLE.
When the moon is decreasing, it gives a very feeble light.

183. The **Superlativo Relativo** expresses the quality in the highest degree of one object as compared with the rest, and is formed by putting **il, lo, la, i gli, le** before the words **più** and **meno** of the **Comparativo,** as: **il più bello, il più delicato, il meno piacevole.** Example:

IL PIÙ DELICATO *piacere è quello di far piacere altrui.*
The most delicate pleasure is to procure pleasure for someone else.
La pulitezza è LA PIÙ GRATA *cosa che sia* (Firenzuola).
Cleanliness is the most agreeable thing there is.

184. The Article is generally not repeated to form a Superlative when the Adjective preceded by **più** or **meno** follows a Noun which is already accompanied by the Definite Article, as: **Le amicizie più costanti, gli atti più innocenti,** and not **le amicizie le più costanti, gli atti i più innocenti.** Example:

Le amicizie PIÙ COSTANTI *son quelle che si fondano nella virtù.*
The most constant friendships are those based on virtue.
Il maligno ascrive a reità gli atti più innocenti.—Segneri.
Malignity ascribes to malice the most innocent actions.

185. The following Adjectives have for the **Comparativo** and **the Superlativo,** besides the common form, a special form for themselves:

	COMPARATIVO		SUPERLATIVO	
	Common	*Special*	*Common*	*Special*
alto, high	più alto	superiore	altissimo	supremo or sommo
basso, low	più basso	inferiore	bassissimo	infimo
buono, good	più buono	migliore or meglio	buonissimo	ottimo
cattivo, bad	più cattivo	peggiore or peggio	cattivissimo	pessimo
grande, large	più grande	maggiore	grandissimo	massimo
piccolo, small	più piccolo	minore	piccolissimo	minimo

Example:
Da Dio abbiamo l' essere, il vivere, l' intendere. L' essere è BUONO, *ma è comune anche ai sassi; il vivere è* MEGLIO, *ma è comune anche agli animali; l' intendere è* OTTIMO, *e questo è proprio dell' uomo—I tribunali* INFERIORI *sono soggetti al* SUPREMO.

PLACE OF THE COMMON OR QUALIFYING ADJECTIVE

186. A Common Adjective may either precede or follow the Noun it qualifies; there is no other rule for this than good taste, euphony, and use, *figliuolo* SAVIO or SAVIO *figliuolo.* Example:

L' uomo SAVIO *fa le* SAVIE *cose.*—Fior di Virtù.

187. Some Adjectives have a different meaning according to their position before or after the Noun, as: BUONA *famiglia,* a well-to-do family; *famiglia* BUONA, a good (virtuous) family; *libro* NUOVO, new book; NUOVO *libro,* another book. Example:

Non tutte le BUONE *famiglie sono da credere famiglie* BUONE.
Not all well-to-do families must be thought to be good (virtuous) families.
Quando la donna esce troppo di casa la famiglia è distrutta: la BUONA *società abolisce la società* BUONA.

Aggettivi Indicativi
(Definitive Adjectives)

188. The **Aggettivo Indicativo** merely indicates of **which** or of **how many** things it is a question, as: **questo,** this; **mio,** my; **tutti,** all.

189. The **Aggettivi Indicativi** may be divided into several small classes, namely: **Dimostrativi** (Demonstrative), **Possessivi** (Possessive), **Ordinativi** and **Numerali** (Ordinal and Numeral), **Universali** (Universal), and **Indefiniti** (Indefinite).

Aggettivi Dimostrativi e Loro Uso
(Demonstrative Adjectives and Their Use)

190. The Adjectives **questo-a, codesto-a, quello-a;** plural, **questi-e, codesti-e, quelli-e** indicate things of which there is question. **Questo,** this, indicates something near the speaker, or just mentioned, or very near as regards time. Example:

È singolar beneficio di Dio QUEST' *aria che si respira,* QUESTA *terra che ci alimenta,* QUEST' *anima che ci regge.*—Segneri.—*Pensa che tu hai sempre un testimone delle tue azioni;* QUESTO *testimone è la tua coscienza.*

NOTE.—*Questa* before the Nouns *mane, mattina, sera, notte* may be contracted into *sta,* and form the words: *stamane, stamattina, stasera, stanotte.* Example: *A ciascuna cosa che ho da fare pongo il tempo suo: questa stamane, questa oggi, quest' altra stasera,* I fix a time for everything I have to do: this this morning, that to-day, the other one this evening.

191. **Codesto,** points out something near the person spoken to, or something just mentioned. Its use in present-day speech is limited, and it tends to be replaced by **quello.** Example:

Se tu seguiti a brancicare CODESTE *pesche, le ammaccherai tutte.* If you go on handling those peaches (you have there), you will bruise them all.

192. **Quello** denotes something far from the speaker. Example:

Aggancia QUELLA *finestra che non sbatta.*

193. The words **questo, questa; codesto, codesta,** may be elided before any vowel, as: **quest' anno, quest'ora, codest' albero** (near you), **codest' erba,** that grass (near you).

194. **Questi, queste, codesti, codeste,** as a rule, are elided only before **i** and **e,** as: **quest' insetti, quest' erbette, codest' innesti, codest' erbuccie.** Example:

I nostri antenati non conoscevano i bachi da seta: ma quest' insetti
preziosi erano assai ben coltivati nella China.—Cantù.

Our forefathers did not know the silkworms: but these precious
insects were very well cultivated in China.

195. The words **quello, quella, quegli, quelle** before a vowel are
elided in the same way as the Articles **lo, la, gli, le,** as: **quell' orologio,
quell' ora, quegl' indici, quelle ombre** or **quell' ombre.** Example:

Anche l' uomo giusto trova di che temere in quell' ultima *ora; in*
quegl' istanti *estremi della vita.*

196. The words **quello, quegli** before a consonant, except **s impura,**
are abridged into **quel, quei,** as: **quel libro, quei libri;** and **quei** may
become **que',** in literary usage as: **que' compagni, que' fiori.** Example:

Spegni quel *lume; ch' egli è quasi giorno.*

Stesso, same; **medesimo,** same; **altro,** other; **tale,** such; **quale,**
which.

197. These Adjectives also point out things of which there is a
question.

Stesso and **medesimo** are frequently added to a Pronoun to give
it emphasis: Example:

Conoscere se stesso *è il primo grado del sapere.*

To know one's self is the first degree of knowledge.

198. **Il medesimo, lo stesso** without a Noun mean **the same thing.**
Example:

Fare servizio con buon garbo è lo stesso *che farlo doppio.*

Doing a service with good manners is like doing it twice.

199. **Altro, altri, altra, altre,** mean **other.** Example:

La sanità è il fondamento d' ogni altro *bene.*

Health is the foundation of all other good things.

200. **Altro** without a Noun means **something else;** and **ben altro,
tutt' altro** signify **entirely something else.** Example:

Altro *è cordialità,* altro *è buon cuore.*

Cordiality is one thing, a good heart is another thing.

201. **Tale,** such; **quale,** which. Example:

Chi è noioso è tale *quasi sempre.*

He who is tedious is nearly always so.

Note.—The expression *un tale* is rendered as *a certain one.* Example: *Un tale
chiamava pane inferigno quei benefizi che vengono fatti di mala voglia.*—Tommaseo.

Aggettivi Possessivi E Loro Uso

(Possessive Adjectives And Their Use)

202. **Mio-a, tuo-a, suo-a, nostro-a, vostro-a, loro,** my, thy, his or
her, our, your, their, are the Italian Possessive Adjectives, and here
are their respective plurals: **miei, mie; tuoi, tue; suoi, sue; nostri,
nostre; vostri, vostre; loro is invariable.**

These Adjectives are usually preceded by the Definite Article
except before Nouns indicating relationship. In this latter case
the Article is normally dispensed with in the singular; as: **il mio
libro, la mia penna, il suo tavolo, la sua vita, il nostro amico, la
nostra carta, il vostro temperino, la vostra candela, il loro scrittoio,
la loro infanzia, i miei denari, mio padre, i tuoi fratelli, mia sorella,
le loro zie,** etc.

203. **Il mio, il tuo, il suo, il nostro, il vostro, il loro,** without a
Noun, mean: **my property** or **what is mine,** etc., while **i miei, i tuoi,
i suoi, i nostri, i vostri, i loro,** mean **my relatives, your relations,** etc.

Aggettivi Numerali E Ordinali

(Numeral and Ordinal Adjectives)

204. Numeral Adjectives:

Un, uno, una	1
due	2
tre	3
quattro	4
cinque	5
sei	6
sette	7
otto	8
nove	9
dieci	10
undici	11
dodici	12
tredici	13
quattordici	14
quindici	15
sedici	16
diciassette	17
diciotto	18
diciannove	19
venti	20

ventuno	21
ventidue	22
ventitre, etc.	23, etc.
trenta	30
trentuno	31
quaranta	40
quarantuno, etc.	41, etc.
cinquanta	50
sessanta	60
settanta	70
ottanta	80
novanta	90
cento	100
duecento ⎫	
ducento ⎬	200
dugento ⎭	
trecento	300
quattrocento, etc.	400, etc.
mille	1,000
duemila	2.000
quattromila	4,000
centomila	100,000
un milione	1,000,000
due milioni	2,000,000

205. Numeral Adjectives or Cardinal Numbers, are invariable, with the exception of those ending in **uno** which agree in Gender with the Substantive they determine. Said Substantive will be plural if it precedes the Adjectives, as: **anni ventuno** (21 years), **settimane trentuna** (31 weeks); and is occasionally employed in the singular if it stands after it, as: **ventun anno** (21 years), **trentuna settimana** (31 weeks). Example:

Torquato Tasso morì di CINQUANTUN ANNO.

206. **Mille,** a thousand, has **duemila, tremila** (2000, 3000), and so on, in the plural.

207. The words **cento, ducento, trecento,** etc., may drop the syllable **to** when followed by a Numeral or an Ordinal Adjective,

NOTE.—If the Noun modified by the Ordinal Numbers *ventuno, trentuno* and others ending in *uno* relates to a plural Verb, or if these Adjectives are preceded by some *definite plural word*, the Noun must also be in the plural, as: *Erano quarantuno cardinali*, there were 41 cardinals; *tocco i ventun anni*, I am 21 years old; *questi trentun uomini*, these 31 men.

298

thus: **cenquattordici** (114), **duecencinquanta** (250), **il cenquattordicesimo** (the 114th). This is a literary usage.

208. The first day of the month is indicated by the Ordinal Adjective **primo;** the remaining days by the Numeral Adjectives, as: **il primo di gennaio,** January 1st; **ai due** or **il due di febbraio,** February 2nd; and if the Noun **giorno = dì** is used, the date of the month may be given by either the Ordinal or the Cardinal Adjective, as: **il dì otto, il dì ottavo,** the 8th day. Examples:

La tua del PRIMO *corrente mi ha molto consolato.*
Yours of the 1st inst. has consoled me much.
Galileo nacque (was born) *il 18 di febbraio del 1564 e morì* (died)
il dì otto di gennaio del 1641.

209. The year is indicated by the Cardinal, and the series of the centuries and of sovereigns by the Ordinal numbers; as: **L' anno mille ottocento settantotto,** the year 1878; **il secolo ventesimo,** the twentieth century; **Pio nono,** Pius IX; **Enrico ottavo,** Henry VIII.

210. The Adjectives **ambo, ambi, ambe, ambidue, ambedue, amendue, entrambi, l' uno e l' altro,** mean **both** and belong to the Cardinal Numbers.

Ambi, ambidue, entrambi are masculine; **ambe** is feminine; **ambo, ambedue, amendue** are of both genders. Examples:

AMBI *gli occhi si muovono sempre insieme.*
Both eyes always move together.
AMBO *le mani per dolor si morse* (Dante).
He bit both hands out of pain.
Beniamino e Giuseppe erano cari a Giacobbe più che la vita AMBEDUE.
Benjamin and Joseph were both dearer than life to Jacob.
Elisabetta d'Inghilterra e Caterina di Russia furono AMDEDUE
sovrane famose.
Elizabeth of England and Catherine of Russia were both famous sovereigns.

211. The Adjective **uno** may be accompanied or not by the Substantive it refers to, and when used together with **altro,** it may take the Definite Article and be plural. Examples:

La doppiezza vi può salvare UNA *volta, nuocere più d'* UNA.
Duplicity may save you once and hurt you more than once.

NOTE.—The names of the months ought not to be written with a capital initial although they often are.

Se un cieco guida un altro cieco, l' uno e l' altro cadono nella fossa.
If a blind man guides another blind man, both will fall into the
ditch.

I libri nel tempo sono come i telescopi nello spazio: così GLI UNI *come*
GLI ALTRI *ci avvicinano gli oggetti lontani.*
Books in time are like telescopes in space: both approach to us
faraway objects.

212. **L'uno e l' altro,** referring to two objects of different gender,
may either take the gender of the Noun they refer to, or, more
seldom, remain invariable in the masculine gender. Example:

Zaccaria ed Elisabetta erano senza figliuoli, E L' UNO E L'ALTRA
(or *l' uno e l' altro) già innanzi negli anni, quando nacque San
Giovanni Battista.*

213. **Uno** is frequently used instead of **stesso, certo, ciascuno . . .**
Example:

Non s' annotta in tutto il mondo ad UN' ORA (Segneri).
It does not become night (grow dark) in the whole world at the
same time.

Aggettivi Universali E Loro Uso

(Universal Adjectives and Their Use)

214. The Adjectives **ciascuno** (each one), **ciascheduno** (everyone),
tutto (all), **ogni** (every), **niuno, nessuno** (nobody), **veruno** (no, not
any), express totality, and for that reason are called **Universali.**

215. **Ciascuno, ciascheduno** denote persons and things; as **ciascun
uomo, ciaschedun' arte** (each man, every art). They have no plural
and refer more frequently to some Noun which is understood.
Example:

CIASCHEDUNO *deve fare quel bene che può* (Cavalca).
Everyone has to do the good he can.

216. **Ogni** is invariable as to gender, and is used only in the
singular. Example:

Non OGNI *discorso s' addice ad* OGNI *bocca.*

NOTE.—Instead of *ciascuno il* is sometimes used. Example: *Sette volte il dì
cadrà il giusto, e rileverassi.*—San Gregorio.

217. Ogni, when followed by a Numeral Adjective, is used in union with a plural Noun. Examples:

Rinnovandosi ogni due, ogni tre mesi, anzi ogni mese, nuova semente, l' orto ha bisogno di nuovo cibo (Soderini).

As the seed is renewed every two, every three months, and even each month, so the kitchen-garden needs new food.

218. Ogni, forming one word with **Santi** (Saints), gives the masculine Noun: **Ognissanti** that means **All Saints' Day.** Example:

Benvenuto Cellini nacque (was born) *la notte* D'OGNISSANTI *dell' anno* 1500.

219. Niuno, nessuno, veruno are equally used in connection with Nouns of persons or of things, as: **niun compagno, nessuna allegria;** and are seldom employed in the plural. They may either follow the Indefinite Article **un, uno, una, un',** or remain invariable. Whenever these Adjectives follow the Verb, the same must be preceded by a negation. **Niuno** and **veruno** are literary and obsolescent. Examples:

NESSUNO *è contento del proprio stato, perchè* NESSUNO *stato è felice.*

Nobody is satisfied with one's condition, because no condition is happy.

Non v' è peggior mestiere che il non averne VERUNO.

There is no worse profession than that of having none.

Non farai ingiuria a VERUNO (Cavalca); *a* NESSUNO *farai ingiuria.*

Aggettivi Indefiniti
(Indefinite Adjectives)

220. Alcuno, taluno, some, someone; **qualcuno, qualcheduno,** someone, somebody; **qualche,** some, any; **certo,** anyone, certain; **qualunque, qualsivoglia,** whatever, whoever, whichsoever; **parecchi,** several; **troppo,** too much; **molto,** much; **poco,** little, are called Indefinite Adjectives, because they express a number or quantity which is not determined.

NOTE.—In similar expressions the Adjective *ogni* really relates to some Noun which is understood, as: *Ogni spazio* (space) *di due mesi, ogni intervallo di tre mesi, ogni periodo di sei settimane.*

NOTE—*Ogni,* before a vowel, may either drop, or keep the final *i,* thus: *ogn' uomo* or *ogni uomo; ogni anno* or *ogn'anno.*

NOTE.—*Nessuno* and *veruno* are sometimes used instead of *alcuno.* Example: *Bisogna che quando tu riprendi* (correct) **nessuno, tu lo faccia dolcemente.**

221. **Alcuno** is used with a Noun, expressed or understood. Its plural is **alcuni**.

Se ALCUNO *ti domanda* ALCUNA *cosa, rispondi sbrigatamente* (quickly).—Tommaseo.

222. **Taluno** generally refers to some Personal Noun, which is understood; plural **taluni**. Example:

TALUNO *intenderebbe correggere i nostri difetti dandoci i proprii* (his own).

223. **Qualcuno, qualcheduno** are generally related with some Noun which is also understood, and rarely admit the plural. Example:

Allorchè (when) *conversi con* QUALCHEDUNO *parla chiaro e con dolcezza* (affability).

224. **Qualche** must always be followed by a Noun, either masculine or feminine; but it is very seldom accompanied by a plural Substantive. Example:

Non lasciate passar giorno senza far QUALCHE *cosa di bene.*

Do not let pass one single day without doing something good.

225. **Qualunque** may either be accompanied or not by a Noun of either Gender and Number. Example:

Fa d' uopo (it is necessary) *adempiere il proprio dovere a* QUALUNQUE *costo* (at any cost) (Tommaseo); *tutti gli uomini,* QUALUNQUE *sieno, han da morire* (have to die).—Segneri.

226. **Qualsisia, qualsivoglia** have in the plural **qualsisia, qualisivoglia, qualsisiano, qualsivogliano,** but these forms are antiquated. Their Noun may either be expressed or understood. Example:

Impedito (obstructed) *il respiro per* QUALSIVOGLIA *cagione, si muore.*

227. **Certo** (plural **certi**), as an Indefinite Adjective, refers both to persons and things, and its Noun may be expressed or understood. Example:

Non tutti in tutte cose, ma CERTI *in* CERTE *cose si trovano migliori o peggiori.*—Fra Bartolomeo.

228. **Troppo, soverchio, molto, poco, parecchio, tanto, altrettanto, alquanto,** in the singular, indicate quantity or size; in the plural they mean number, and are either employed alone or with a Noun. Example:

I nutrimenti quando sono TROPPI *generano troppa quantità di umori.*

Tante in the expressions *dirne tante, farne tante, darne tante, toccarne tante,* refers to the Nouns *cose* (things), *villanie* (villainy), *busse* (blows).

229. **Assai,** much; **guari,** much, long; **più,** more; **meno,** fewer, are of both Genders and Numbers. Example:

ASSAI *fumo e poco arrosto.*

Much smoke and little roast (much smoke and little fire).—MENO *siamo a tavola, e* PIÙ *si mangia.*

Assai, molto, poco may take the superlative termination as *assaissimo, moltissimo, pochissimo.*

DEL PRONOME—ON THE PRONOUN

230. There are three kinds of Pronouns: **Pronomi di Persona** (Personal Pronouns), **Pronomi di Cosa** (Pronouns representing things), and **Pronomi Congiuntivi** (Conjunctive Pronouns). (Example: *Nè* IO, *nè* TU, *nè* ALTRI *è quaggiù pienamente felice.*—San Gregorio.

Personal Pronouns

231.

		Nominative	Dative	Accusative	Absolute and Prepositional Accusative
	1st per.,	*io*	*mi*	*mi*	*me*
	2d per.,	*tu*	*ti*	*ti*	*te*
Sing.	3d mas.,	*egli*	*gli*	*lo*	*lui*
	3d fem.,	*ella*	*le*	*la*	*lei*
	1st per.,	*noi*	*ci*	*ci*	*noi*
Plur.	2d per.,	*voi*	*vi*	*vi*	*voi*
	3d p. mas.,	*essi*	*loro*[1]	*li*	*loro*
	3d p. f.,	*esse*	*loro*	*le*	*loro*
Reflexive, common to both Genders and Numbers		*(none)*	*si*	*si*	*sè*

USE OF THE CASES

232. The Nominatives of the Personal Pronouns are usually omitted except when required for emphasis, contrast or clearness.

The pronouns **lui, lei, loro** are used as Nominatives instead of **egli, ella, essi, esse:**

---

[1] For euphony's sake *gli* (to him) may sometimes replace *loro* (to them).

a. In familiar conversation. Example:

A persona che arrivi gradita si dice: lei non scomoda mai, anzi accomoda sempre.

b. Sometimes after **come, siccome, quanto, ancora,** or after some form of the Verb **essere.** Example:

L' uomo rio (bad, guilty) *crede che ogni altro sia* COME LUI (Virtù e Vizi).—*Dio va preferito* (has to be preferred) *a tutti i beni che non* SONO LUI.—Segneri.

c. After an Adjective used as an exclamation. Example:

Il buon ladrone credette, BEATO LUI!

233. **Egli** is frequently shortened in literary usage into **ei** or **e'** in both Numbers. Example:

L' uomo prudente non s' ingerisce (does not meddle) *di ciò ch'* EI *non conosce.*

234. **Ella** is sometimes changed into **la.** Example:

La sincerità viene dal cuore; se il labbro tace, LA *traspare dagli occhi.* Sincerity comes from the heart; if the mouth is silent, it will transpire from the eyes.

235. The Dative and Accusative pronouns: **mi, ti, gli, lo, le, la; ci, vi, li, le, si** can be used only in connection with a Verb and are generally placed before it; but they follow the Affirmative Imperative, the Infinitive, the Gerund and the Past Participle and form one single word with them, as: *Iddio* MI *ha dato la vita.—Come* TI *comanda Iddio.—Chi* VI *loda e* VI *tace il vero* VI *sprezza.—Amami,* love me; *scrivimi,* write me; *perdonaci,* pardon us; *vedendolo,* on seeing him; *trovatolo,* having found him. Whenever the verbal form ends with an accented vowel or is a monosyllable the pronouns *mi, ti, vi,* etc., double the consonant, as in the preceding examples: *saravvi, statti, dacci.* **Loro** usually follows the verb and is never joined to it.

236. Occasionally, in literary usage, these Pronouns follow the Verb even in other cases and always form, then, but one word with it, as: **Saravvi,** there will be. Example:

Perdonate, e SARAVVI *perdonato.*

Pardon and you will be pardoned.

DIMMI *con chi pratichi e* TI *dirò chi sei.*

237. The Pronouns **mi, ti, ci, vi,** before **ne, lo, la, le, li, gli** change **i** into **e,** as: **me ne, te lo, ce la, ve le,** etc. Example:

Iddio MI *ha dato la vita, ed egli* ME LA *conserva.*—Cavalca.

See Note on next page.

238. Me lo, te lo, ve lo, glielo, before a consonant, except **s impura,** may in literary usage be contracted into one word, as: **mel, tel, cel, gliel.** Example:

Non indugierò a porgere aiuto a chi MEL *chiede.*
I shall not hesitate to give help to him who asks me for it.

239. Me, te, se form with **con** the words **meco, teco, seco,** with me, with thee, with one's self.

240. Di lui, di lei usually follow the Noun to which they refer: **Il volto di lui,** his face; **l' amicizia di lei,** her friendship.

241. Di, a are usually dropped before **loro.** Example:
Il LORO *figlio,* instead of *il di loro figlio,* their son.

242. Lo, la, le, li, se, si may be elided before any vowel. Example:
Chi S' *aiuta, il ciel* L' *aiuta.*

243. Egli, gli are optionally elided only before **i. Gl' Italiani sono numerosi in questa città.**

244. Loro may become **lor** before a vowel or before a consonant, except before an **s impura.** Example:
Date a tutti ciò che LOR *è dovuto.*
Give to all that which is due to them.

245. Sè before **stesso** or **medesimo,** usually drops the accent: **Se stesso, se medesimo,** one's self.

Questi, costui, costei, cotesti or **codesti, quegli, colui, colei, altri, altrui, chicchessia, certuni, il tale.**

246. These Pronouns indicate only person.

a. **Questi, costui,** mean this man; plural, **questi, costoro.**

b. **Cotesti,** that man (near the person spoken to); plural, **cotesti.**

c. **Quegli, colui,** that man (yonder); plural, **quegli, coloro.** Example: *Se mai fu uomo schernito* (if there has ever been a much derided man) *per la sua virtù,* QUESTI *fu Noè.*

247. Costei, this woman; plural, **costoro.**

248. Questi, codesti, quegli, in the singular take usually the

---

NOTE.—*Gli* adds an *e* instead before the same Pronouns, and forms only one word with them, as: *glielo, gliene, glieli,* and has the same form for both Genders. Example: *Il moto conserva all' acqua la sua chiarezza; la quiete gliela toglie* (takes it away from it).

place of a Subject, while **costui, costei, colui, colei,** are equally used as Subjects or as Complements. Example:

È temerario QUEGLI *che vuol sapere perchè dà Iddio un dono a* COSTUI *e non a* COLUI.

249. **Questi, costui** are also used to mean the latter, and **quegli, colui** the former. Example:

È peggiore un cattivo filosofo che un idiota; QUESTI *non ragionando lascia sussistere gli errori che ci sono;* QUEGLI *mal ragionando ne accresce il numero.*

250. **Altri,** in the singular, means **another person, some person, no one else,** and is used without the Article. Example:

Chi lascia ch' ALTRI *noccia ingiustamente al fratello, quegli tradisce il fratello.*

251. **Altrui** has the same meaning as the Pronoun **altri** used in the singular, but it is used generally only as a Complement, while the latter may be employed as a Subject, too. Example:

Ogni uomo deve vivere della sua fatica per non gravare ALTRUI.

252. **Di altrui,** as well as **di costui, di costei, di costoro,** and **ad altrui,** very frequently drop the Preposition. Example:

L' invidia si rode del bene ALTRUI; *l' astio cerca l'* ALTRUI *male.*— Tommaseo.

253. **Chicchessia,** anyone; plural, **chicchessiano** (obsolescent). Example:

Ai vecchi si deve da CHICCHESSIA *portar rispetto.*—Segneri.

254. **Certuni,** masculine, and **certune,** feminine, signify **certi uomini, certe donne, certe persone, alcuni,** etc., and have no singular. Example:

CERTUNI *si stimano liberi perchè vanno fuori di strada.*—Segneri.

255. **Il tale,** such, such a one. Example:

A chi dice: Il TALE *poteva far meglio, dovete rispondere poteva far peggio.*

To him who says, "such a one could have done better," you have to answer, he could have done worse.

NOTE.—The expression *l' altrui* means *l' avere, la roba d' altri,* someone else's fortune (property).

306

Pronouns Indicating Persons And Things

256. **Questo, questa, codesto, codesta, quello, quella, esso, essa, desso, dessa, ognuno, ognuna,** having in the plural **questi, queste, codesti, codeste, quelli, quelle, essi, esse, dessi, desse,** represent both persons and things.

257. **Questo, codesto, quello,** as Pronouns representing **persons,** are generally used as a Complement only; in the other case, they may be either Subject or Complement.

Questa, queste, codesta, codeste, quella, quelle, questi, codesti, quelli or **quegli, quei,** in the plural, may be either the Subject or the Complement of a proposition, whether they represent a person or a thing. Examples:

> *Mosè ed Aronne erano fratelli; a* QUESTO *fu commesso da Dio l' ufficio di sacerdote, a* QUELLO *l' incarico di condottiero.—Il contadino* (the peasant) *affida* (entrusts) *alla terra piante e semi;* QUESTI *moltiplicano,* QUELLE *crescono e fruttificano* (grow and fructify).

258. **Esso, essa, essi, esse** mean **egli, ella, eglino, elleno,** but the latter are said only of persons and as **subject;** the **former** represent both persons and things and are used in all the cases. Example:

> *Non offrirai a persona il tuo moccicchino, comechè* ESSO *sia di bucato.*

> Do not offer to anyone your pocket-handkerchief, no matter how clean it may be.

Eglino and **elleno** are considered obsolete and are not used. In their stead are used **essi** and **esse.**

259. **Desso** is stronger than **esso** and properly means **he himself, that very same man,** etc., and is used attributively with **essere, parere, sembrare** (to seem). Example:

> *La vite al vederla sfrondata* (stripped of leaves) *e nuda nel tardo autunno non sembra più* DESSA.

260. **Ognuno,** everybody, everything, has no plural. Example:

> *Ognuno nel grado suo può farsi onore.—Vi ha molte schiatte* (there are many kinds) *di fichi, ed ognuna è differente di sapore.—* Barbieri.

More Pronouns Representing Persons and Things

Ne, ci, vi, il, lo, la, li or **gli, le.**

261. **Ne,** representing a person, may replace **di lui, da lei, da loro, di esso, da esso.** Example:

*Molti osservano altrui per notar*NE *i difetti.*— *Hai tu provato il tuo compagno infido* (unfaithful)? *Sii sollecito a staccarte*NE.— Segneri.

262. **Ne** representing a thing may mean **di questo, di esso, di ciò, da questo luogo, da quel luogo, da esso, da ciò,** etc. Example:

L' avaro non è signore del denaro, ma NE *è servo.*

263. **Ci** representing a person means **noi** (Complement) and **a noi;** representing a thing it means **a tal cosa, a ciò, in questo, in quel luogo, ad esso, in esso.** Example:

Un nemico può tentare di recarmi molestie, e non CI *(a ciò) può riuscire.*

A foe may try to injure me and he many not succeed *in it.*

264. The Pronoun **vi** means **voi** (Complement) and **a voi,** and also **a ciò, a questo, ad esso, in esso, a questo, a quel luogo.** Example:

I ragazzi sono come la cera (wax), *quel che* VI *si imprime, resta.*

265. **Lo, la, li** or **gli, le,** refer both to persons and things.

266. **Ciò, checchè, checchessia, tutto, niente,** are Pronouns representing things.

Ciò means **questa cosa, quella cosa, quelle cose, la cosa,** and is masculine and always used in the singular. Example:

Al malato si dà CIÒ *che giova, non* CIÒ *che piace.*—Segneri.

267. **Checchè, checchessia,** anything, are masculine and singular. Example:

Gli occhi dimostran chiarissimo, CHECCHÈ *il cuore si voglia o non si voglia.*

NOTE.—*Ci* is sometimes used erroneously instead of *a lui, a lei.*

Ne, ei, vi, il or *lo, la, li* or *gli* are sometimes mere pleonasms. Example: *GLI è bel tempo.* The weather is fine.

NOTE.—*Questo, quello, codesto, il, lo,* etc., when they do not refer to any particular Noun, mean *ciò.* Example: *Chi ha sanità, è ricco, e non lo sa.*

The expressions *tutt' uno, tutt' una* mean *la stessa cosa.* Example: *Riposo ed ozio non son tutt' uno.*—Segneri.

Sometimes *niente* takes the place of *qualche cosa, alcuna cosa.* Example: *Se hai niente di bene, tutto ti è venuto dall' alto.*

308

268. **Tutto,** when not referring to a Noun, and **il tutto** mean **everything.** Example:

Ci son certi che in TUTTO *trovano la sua eccezione; in* TUTTO *la sua difficoltà.*

269. **Niente, nulla,** nothing, are masculine and have no plural. Example:

C' è della gente affaccendata (busy) *a non far nulla.*

These words require the negation before the Verb whenever they follow the same, and reject it when they precede it. Example:

Dio non è debitore di NULLA, *a nessuno; A chi* NULLA *tenta,* NULLA *riesce.*

Pronomi Relativi—Relative Pronouns

270. **Quale, che, cui, onde, donde, ove, dove** are so called because they relate to some preceding Noun. Some call them (perhaps more properly) Congiuntivi, because they join a sentence to the Noun or Pronoun to which they refer.

271. **Quale** must be accompanied by the Article: **il quale, la quale; i quali, le quali,** and is used either as a Subject or a Complement. Example:

Sventurato quel figliuolo il QUALE *contrista i suoi genitori!*

272. **Che** may mean **il quale, la quale, i quali, le quali,** and relates both to persons and things. Example:

Onora i suoi genitori quel fanciullo CHE *si astiene* (abstains) *da ogni atto* CHE *indichi noncuranza e disprezzo* (neglect and contempt).

273. The Pronoun **che,** referring to persons, is used as a Nominative and an Accusative; referring to things, it may be used in any case. Example:

Dio CHE *è sapienza infinita, permette le tribolazione per correzione di coloro* CHE *egli ama.*

NOTE.—*Che* may be elided for euphony's sake before a vowel. *Che* is not a Pronoun, but a Conjunction whenever it cannot be rendered by *il quale, la quale.*

NOTE.—The Pronoun *che,* when referring to Nouns indicating *time, manner, degree, cause* and the like, may drop the Prepositions *in, con, per, di, a, da.* Example: *La festa va fatta il giorno che viene.*

274. The Pronoun **cui** means **che,** but it appears in literary usage only as a Complement. Example:

L' uomo ha dei nemici CUI *deve curare di vincere.*

Man has foes whom he must try to vanquish.

275. Che, quale, without an Article and preceding a Noun, are Adjectives. Example:

CHE *libro vuoi?* QUAL *cuore hai?*

276. Che preceded by the Article **il,** refers to a whole sentence and means **la qual cosa,** that which, etc. Example:

Il miglior odore è non sapere odore: IL CHE *si ottiene colla nettezza.*

277. Che, interrogatively used, means **che cosa? qual cosa?** what? Example:

CHE *vale il denaro senza la sanità?*

278. The Adverbs **ove, dove, onde, donde,** are frequently employed as Relative Pronouns relating to things.

Ove, dove mean then **in cui, a cui, su cui.** Example:

Non urtar (push) *la tavola* DOVE (*su cui*) *altri scrive o legge.*

Onde signifies **di cui, da cui, per cui, con cui.** Example:

Il ramo per onde (*per cui*) *ha da passare l' innesto, sia fresco, sano e liscio e nuovo e senza magagne.*—Volgarizzamento di Palladio.

Donde replaces **da cui.** Example:

La città donde venne.

Chi, Chiunque

279. Chi refers to persons and is also a Relative Pronoun and may mean **colui il quale, colei la quale, alcuno il quale, persona la quale, quale persona,** and seldom also **coloro i quali,** etc. Example:

CHI *lavora è lieto, e* CHI *è lieto è sano.*

Chi cannot be used instead of the two Pronouns, if these be governed by different Prepositions. Thus do not say:

NOTE.—*Di cui* may precede or follow the Noun to which it refers. In the first case it loses *di*. *A cui* may drop the Preposition *a*. To avoid ambiguity it may become necessary or advisable either to replace *che, il quale, la quale,* etc., by *cui,* or *che* by *il quale, la quale,* etc., as the case may be.

NOTE.—*Cosa?* instead of *che cosa?* or *che?* may be used only in familiar conversation.

Sii grato A CHI *ricevesti beneficio;* but *sii grato* A COLUI DAL QUALE *ricevesti beneficio.*

280. Chi, interrogatively used, means **qual persona?** who? Example: *A* CHI *non è noto lo stile incantatore del Buffon?*—Monti.

281. Chi, repeated, means **l' uno, l' altro, alcuno, alcuni,** the one, the other, etc. Example:

CHI (the one) *ha naturalmente modi lieti* (gay manners) *e* CHI (the other) *tristi;* CHI *timorosi e* CHI *orgogliosi.*

282. Chiunque, whoever, means **qualunque persona, qualunque persona che, ognuno che.** Example:

Rendete a CHIUNQUE *ciò che gli spetta.*

DELLA PREPOSIZIONE—On The Preposition

283. There are very few simple Prepositions in the Italian language that govern the noun or pronoun directly, most of them requiring at least another Preposition after them. To make the matter easier for the student, a list of all, simple and compound, Prepositions is given below:

A, ad, at, to, in. With the Definite Article: **al, allo, alla, ai, alle, all', agli.**

Accanto a, near; **accanto al tavolo,** near the table.

Allato a, beside; **sedevo allato a lui,** I sat beside him.

Anzi, before, is very seldom used as a Preposition.

Appo, near, in the eyes of; **appo la casa,** near the house; **appo Dio e appo gli uomini,** in the eyes of God and men.

Appresso, see **presso.**

Avanti, before, occurs with **di** and **a; avanti di me,** before me; **avanti alla casa,** before the house.

Circa, towards, about, concerning; **circa la faccenda,** concerning the matter. Sometimes with **a: circa a quella storiella,** as to (concerning) that story.

Contro, contra, against; **contro la verità,** against truth. Before Personal Pronouns it may take **di,** as: **contro di me,** against me.

NOTE.—*Di chi* means *di colui il quale* or *del quale, di colei la quale* or *della quale.,* etc.; *a chi, a colui il quale* or *al quale, a colei la quale* or *alla quale; da chi, da colui il quale* or *dal quale, da colei la quale* or *dalla quale.* Example: *Da chi ti loda, guardati* (beware).

Instead of *chi* sometimes *cui* is used.

Less frequently **contro a,** as: **contro al destino,** against fate. N. B.—
Contra is seldom used.

Da, from, at, by, since; with the Definite Article: **dal, dallo,
dalla, dall', dai, dagli, dalle.**

Dattorno, near, in the neighborhood, takes **di** and **a,** as: **dattorno
al** (**del**) **mio paese,** in the neighborhood of my village.

Davanti, before: **davanti il, al,** (and seldom) **dal, del giudice,** before
the judge.

Dentro, in, within, more frequently governs the noun **directly,**
but is also used with **di** before Personal Pronouns; as:

> *dentro* IL *mio cuore, dentro* AL *mio cuore,* within my heart; *dentro
> di me,* within me.

Di, of; with the Definite Article: **del, dello, della, dell', dei, degli,
delle.**

Dietro, behind; usually with **a,** as: **dietro alla casa, dietro la casa,**
behind the house; **dietro di me,** behind me.

Dinanzi, before; usually with **a,** as: **dinanzi al re,** before the king;
and alone: **dinanzi il teatro,** before the theater.

Dopo, after, behind. More frequently with the noun, as: **dopo il
papa,** after (behind) the Pope. Before Personal Pronouns also with
di: **dopo di me, dopo me,** after me.

Entro, in, within; sometimes with **a,** as: **entro** (**a**) **due mesi,** within
two months.

Fino, sino, infino, insino, till, until, generally take **a,** seldom **the**
noun directly: **fino alla chiesa** (**fino la chiesa**), as far as the church.
With **per, persino,** even, as: **persino il re,** even the king. **Fino** is used
also as an Adverb: **l' ho fino accolto in casa mia,** I have even received
him in my house.

Fra, infra, tra, between, among. Usually with the noun, as: **fra la
casa ed il giardino,** between the house and the garden. Before Personal
Pronouns, also with **di,** as: **dissero fra** (**di**) **loro,** they said to each
other.

Fuori, fuora (seldom), out of, outside. Usually with **di,** as: **fuor
d' uso,** out of use.

Giusta, according to: **giusta la prescrizione,** according to (in
conformity with) the prescription.

In, in, with the noun. **In,** combined with the Article: **nel, nello,
nella, nell', nei, negli, nelle. In** is frequently coupled with **su,** as:
in sulla tavola, on the table; **in sulla sera,** towards the evening.

Incontro, incontra, against, contrary to, opposite, as: **incontro al suo volere,** against his will; **andare incontro a . . .,** to go to meet somebody. **Incontra** is rarely used.

Infra, see **fra.**

Innanzi, before (of time); with the noun, and with **a** also, as: **innanzi (a) quel tempo,** before that time. In other acceptations it always takes **a,** as:

L' amo innanzi AD *ogni altro.*

I love him more than any other.

Intra, see **tra.**

Lungo, along: **lungo la spiaggia,** along the shore.

Oltre, above, besides; usually with **a,** and also with the noun: **oltre a due mesi,** more (longer) than two months; **oltre le sue forze,** above his strength. Sometimes with **di, oltre di ciò,** besides that; **oltre a ciò** is usually contracted: **oltracciò.**

Per, for, through; with the Article only two contractions are customary: **pel** and **pei.**

Presso, near: **presso la chiesa,** near the church. Also with **a,** as: **presso alla città,** near the city. Sometimes with **di,** before Personal Pronouns, as: **presso di me,** near me. Meaning about, with **a** only, as: **presso a quattro milioni,** about four millions.—**Appresso,** Adverb, sometimes means **after,** as: **appresso la cena,** after supper.—**A un di presso,** is an idiom that means: thereabout, near, almost.

Secondo, conformably, according to: **secondo la stagione,** according to the season.

Senza, without: **senza denaro,** without money. Before Personal Pronouns, with **di : senza di me,** without me.

Sopra, sovra, on, upon, above, usually governs the noun directly, rarely with **di** and sometimes with **a,** especially with Personal Pronouns, as: **scagliarsi sopra il nemico,** to rush upon the enemy; **sopra del tetto,** upon the roof; **sopra di me,** above me; **sopra al monte,** on the mountain.

Sotto, under, beneath; usually with the noun: **sotto la tavola,** under the table. Before Personal Pronouns, also with **di : guardate sotto di voi,** look beneath you. Sometimes with **a,** as: **sotto al tavolo.**

NOTE.—Some Adjectives and Participles are used as Prepositions and these always govern the noun directly. *Durante il giorno,* during the day; *eccetto questa regola,* this rule excepted; *nonostante questa difficoltà,* notwithstanding this difficulty; *rasente il muro,* along the wall; *salvo errori,* errors excepted, etc.

Su, (sur), on, upon; usually with the noun. Before Personal
Pronouns, also with **di,** as: **su di me,** upon me. (**Su** with **in,** see **in.**)

284. In order to show how to translate into Italian the most
commonly used English Prepositions, the following list is given:

At: At dinner, **a pranzo;** at school, **a scuola;** at eleven o'clock, **alle
undici;** at Turin, **a Torino.** I was at your house, **io fui da voi** (or **a
casa vostra);** I was at home, **fui a casa mia** (here **da me** would be
incorrect).

By: By my father, **da mio padre;** by night, **di notte;** by God,
per Dio; word by word, **parola per parola;** by the bridge, **presso il
(vicino al) ponte;** by land or water, **per mare e per terra;** by force,
con (per) forza; by practice, **con esercizio.**

In: In Paris, **a Parigi;** in London, **a Londra;** in Spain, **in Ispagna.**
Into: Put it into your pocket, **mettetelo in tasca.**

On: On the table, **sulla tavola;** Frankfort on the Main, **Franco-
forte sul Meno;** on Monday, **lunedì;** on Tuesday, **martedì;** on which
day? **qual giorno?** go on! **avanti!** on my arrival, **al mio arrivo;** on
horseback, **a cavallo;** on foot, **a piedi;** on that condition, **con (a)
questa condizione.**

To: I am going to Paris, **vado a Parigi;** we are going to London,
andiamo a Londra; I am going to Spain, to America, **vado in Ispagna,
in America;** I am going to my aunt's, **vado da mia zia.**

With: He came with me, **egli venne con me;** satisfied with a little
bread, **contento d' un poco di pane;** filled with gold and silver, **pieno
d' oro e d'argento;** to begin with, **cominciare con;** with me, with thee,
with him, **con me** or **meco, con te** or **teco, con se** or **seco.**

ADVERBS

285. An Adverb is a word used to modify the meaning of a Verb,
an Adjective, or an Adverb. Sometimes an Adverb modifies a phrase
or an entire proposition. Example:

È AL CERTO *cosa* POCO *sana tenere il capo* TROPPO *caldo* (Cantù).
It is certainly unhealthy to keep one's head too warm.

286. The Adverb in **mente** is formed by adding this termination
to the qualifying Adjective ending in **a** or in **e,** as **timida-mente,
veloce-mente.** The masculine adjective in **o,** changes **o** to **a** before
adding the Adverbial termination. Example:

Il ragno tesse (the spider weaves) *con molto studio la sua tela; ma
da un* SUBITO *soffiar di vento,* SUBITAMENTE *è disfatta.*—Fra
Bartolomeo.

Forms of the Adverb

287. There are simple and compound Adverbs, as well as Adverbial Phrases.

Simple, if consisting of one single word; as: **quì,** here; **oggi,** to-day, etc.

Compound, if formed by two or more words, separately or con-tracted. Examples: **Rare volte,** rarely; **quaggiù,** here below; **appieno,** fully.

Adverbial Phrases are certain expressions used with the meaning and the force of an Adverb. Example: **Di proposito,** intentionally; **alla lunga,** diffusedly; **di buon cuore,** heartily.

Degrees of the Adverbs

288. Adverbs derived from qualifying Adjectives, and **mente,** have a comparative and a superlative degree. The former is formed, like that of the Adjectives, by **più** and **meno,** which may be strength-ened by **assai, molto, vie,** as: **temperatamente, più (meno) tem-peratamente, vieppiù temperatamente.**

The superlative is formed by changing the termination into **issimamente: facilmente, facilissimamente,** easily, very easily. Some-times the superlative is formed by repeating the word, as: **pian piano,** very slowly; **subito subito,** immediately.

Frequently the Adjective is used instead of the Adverb.

289. Some Adverbs have an irregular comparative and superlative degree:

Male, badly; **peggio,** worse; **pessimamente,** worst.

Bene, well; **meglio,** better; **ottimamente,** best.

Poco, little; **meno,** less; **minimamente,** least.

Sopra, above; **superiormente,** better; **supremamente,** supremely.

Sotto, under; **inferiormente,** in an inferior manner; **infimamente,** in the lowest way.

Grandemente, greatly; **maggiormente,** more; **massimamente,** most.

290. An Adverb modifies by expressing Affirmation, Negation, Manner, Degree, Place, Time.

Note.—Adjectives ending in *le* and *re* drop *e* before adding *mente,* thus: Example: *Mantieni fedelmente* (from *fedele*) *le promesse fatte,* keep faithfully your promises. *Il sale penetra celermente le carni su cui si sparge, e le conserva.*—Segneri.

a. Affirmation: **Sì,** yes; **bene,** well; **appunto, per l' appunto,** precisely; **certo, di certo, al certo, per certo, certamente,** certainly; **pure,** also; **senz' altro,** immediately; **senza dubbio,** undoubtedly; **senza fallo,** without fail; **in fatto, di fatto,** in fact; **invero, davvero, veramente,** truly; **sicuramente, per fermo,** surely.

b. Negation: **No,** no; **non,** not; **non mai, mai no,** never; **niente affatto, per nulla, per niente,** not at all; **nè** (neither . . . nor), **nè manco, neppure,** not even; **in nessun modo, per nessun modo, in nessuna guisa,** in no way.

Non and **lo** may in literary usage be contracted into **nol**: Vorrei partire e nol (non lo) posso.

291. **Non,** not, may be strengthened by adding **no, punto, mica,** at all; **già** (already), **nulla, per nulla** (at all), as:

No, non lo fare.—NON *si può* MICA *cantare e portar la croce.*— Proverbio toscano.

292. Adverbs expressing a doubt: **Se,** if; **se mai,** if ever; **forse, per avventura, per sorte,** perhaps; **probabilmente,** probably; **incirca, all' incirca, presso a, presso a poco, a un di presso,** about; **pressochè,** nearly.

Adverbs Denoting Place

293. The following Adverbs indicate a place near the speaker: **Quì,** here; **qua,** hereabout; **quaggiù,** down here; **quassù,** up here; **ci,** there; **quinci,** hence, from here, hereafter; **di quì, di qua,** from here; **per quì, per di quì,** through here. Examples:

Vieni quì.
Come here.
Quì tu hai sbagliato.
Here you have made a mistake.

294. Adverbs indicating a place near the person spoken to: **Costì,** there; **costà,** thereabout; **di costì, di costà,** from there; these are all obsolescent.

Non stare costì alla corrente, piglierai un raffreddore.
Do not stay there in the draught, you will catch a cold.

NOTE—*Se no* means *altrimenti, in caso diverso,* otherwise.
NOTE.—*Un* before a number means about: *Un trent' anni fa,* about thirty years ago.

295. Adverbs indicating a place distant both from the speaker and from the person spoken to: **Lì,** there; **là,** thereabout; **colà,** there, yonder; **quivi, ivi,** there; **indi, quindi,** from there, thence; **di lì, di là, di quivi, per là,** through there; **in là,** off, far; **ad di là,** on the other side, over there, beyond; **da quivi,** from there.

296. **Ove, dove,** where; **onde, donde,** whence, from where; **ovunque, dovunque, ovechè, dovechè, dovecchessia,** everywhere; **ondechè, ondecchessia, dondecchessia,** from everywhere; **altrove,** somewhere else; **altronde,** from somewhere else.

More Adverbs of Place

297. **Sopra, di sopra,** on, upon; **al di sopra,** above; **su, di su,** on, upon; **al di su,** above; **all' insù,** upwards; **sotto, al di sotto,** under, below; **giù, di giù, all' ingiù,** down, downwards.

298. **Entro, dentro, per entro, in dentro, per di dentro, addentro,** within, internally. **Fuori, di fuori, infuori, fuor fuori,** without, externally, outside.

299. Indicating distance: **Lontano, da lontano, lungi, di lungi, dalla lunga, discosto, da parte;** far, from afar, apart, etc. Indicating nearness: **Presso, dappresso, appresso, da vicino, allato, intorno,** near, besides, around.

300. Indicating a place opposite: **Contro, contra, di contro,** against; **all' incontro, a rincontro,** on the contrary; **appetto, a fronte, dirimpetto,** opposite.

Adverbs Expressing Time

301. Indicating present time: **ora, adesso, mo', al presente, presentemente,** now, immediately, presently; **oggi,** to-day; **oggidì, oggigiorno, al dì d' oggi,** nowadays.

Note.—*Ci* and *vi* are sometimes used one for the other indifferently. *Ci* ought to mean only here, and *vi,* there.

There is a spoken-language tendency to use *altronde* or *d' altronde* instead of *del resto, del restante, del rimanente, d' altra parte,* on the other hand, *per altro,* otherwise, or instead of *finalmente* (finally), *per finirla* (to cut it short), *in somma* (in short), or also instead of *laddove* (where), *per lo contrario* (on the contrary).

Note.—*Quì* is also occasionally used as an Adverb of Time, meaning this time, at present. Example: *Ti ringrazio della cordialità che mi hai usato fin quì,* I thank you for the cordiality you have shown me thus far.—In contemporary usage, *qui* is often written without an accent.

302. Indicating a period of time just elapsed: **dianzi, poc' anzi, poco, pur ora, pur mo', poco fa, or ora, di fresco, di corto, di poco.**

303. Indicating a future time very near the present: **di presente, subito, di subito,** presently; **tosto, immantinente, incontinente,** at once; **ad un tratto, di botto, d' improvviso, di repente,** suddenly; **in brevissimo andare, a breve andare, al più presto, al più tosto,** soon, at the earliest time possible.

304. Indicating a definite past time: **ieri,** yesterday; **ieri l' altro, avant' ieri, l' altro ieri,** the day before yesterday; **stamane, stamattina,** this morning.

305. Indicating a future definite time: **domani,** to-morrow; **posdomani, doman l' altro,** the day after to-morrow; **domani mattina, domattina,** to-morrow morning; **domani a sera, domani sera,** to-morrow evening (night); **stasera,** this evening; **stanotte,** to-night.

306. Indicating an indefinite past time: **avanti, innanzi,** before; **prima, in prima, da prima,** first, at first; **addietro, in addietro, per l' addietro,** formerly, heretofore.

307. Indicating an indefinite future time: **poi, di poi, dappoi, poscia,** then: **dopo, appresso, indi, quindi,** after, afterwards; **innanzi, per innanzi, in là,** after, hereafter.

308. Indicating **in ogni tempo** (always, yet, still, continuing action): **sempre, sempre mai, mai sempre, continuamente, tuttavia, tuttavolta, tutto dì, tutto il dì, tuttora, ognora.**

309. Meaning **in qualunque tempo, in qualunque tempo che,** whenever, at any time (that): **quando,** when; **quandochè, qualora, qual volta, qualunque ora, ogni volta che, ogni qual volta, quante volte, sempre che, sempre quando.**

310. Meaning **quasi sempre** (almost always): **il più, per lo più, il più delle volte, le più volte, il più del tempo, più.**

311. Meaning **in qualche tempo, in alcun tempo** (sometimes): **qualche volta, talora, tal fiata, talvolta, alle volte, delle volte, alcuna volta, un tempo, una volta, quando che sia.**

312. Meaning **in nessun tempo** (never): **non mai, non giammai;** and **in alcun tempo** (ever): **mai, giammai.**

NOTE.—*Mai* and *giammai,* before the Verb, may mean *never.* Whenever they are accompanied by the Preposition *non* they have a negative value.

313. Indicating in molti tempi (repetition): **spesse volte, spesso, soventi volte, sovente, assai volte, frequentemente, ogni poco, ad ogni tanto,** often; **di tanto in tanto, a quando a quando, a tempo a tempo, di tempo in tempo, ad ora ad ora, d' ora in ora, tratto tratto, ad ogni tratto, a mano a mano, volta per volta,** from time to time, now and then.

314. Meaning **still, yet; ancora, anco, anche, per ancora, per anco, per anche, tuttora, tuttavia, pure,** etc.

315. **Già, di già,** already; **oramai,** now; **lungamente, a lungo,** a long while; **per tempo, assai per tempo, di buon'ora, ad assai buon'ora, a buon' ora,** early; **al fine** or **alla fine, alla perfine, alla fin fine, alla fin dei fini,** finally, at last, ultimately, etc.

Adverbs of Quantity

316. **Molto, assai,** much; **moltissimo, assaissimo,** very much; **troppo, soverchio, soverchiamente,** too much; **più, di più,** more.

317. **Poco meno** or **manco,** a little less; **un pochino, un pocolino, un tantino, un pochettino, alquanto,** a little bit, somewhat.

318. **Solo, solamente, soltanto, pure, pur solamente, tanto,** only, no more.

319. **Parte, parte,** some, some; **sì, sì,** as well as; **così come, tanto quanto,** both, as well as, etc.

320. **Quasi, quasichè, pressochè, appressochè, presso, a un di presso, press' a poco,** about, nearly; **poco meno,** a little less; **circa,** about.

Al tutto, del tutto, in tutto e per tutto, entirely, wholly, through and through.

Adverbs Indicating Manner

321. **Bene,** well; **male,** badly; **volentieri, di buon grado, di buona voglia, di buon animo,** willingly; **di mala voglia,** unwillingly; **a bello studio, a posta,** intentionally, etc.

A vicenda, vicendevolmente, mutually; **gradatamente,** gradually; **primieramente, primamente,** first; **finalmente, ultimamente, da (per, in) ultimo,** finally, etc.

322. **Anzi, meglio, piuttosto, avanti, prima, più presto, anzichè,** rather.

CONJUNCTIONS

323. Conjunctions generally requiring the Subjunctive:

se, if
finchè, till
supposto che, suppose, provided that
acciocchè ⎫
affinchè ⎭ that, in order to
prima che, before, sooner
quand' anche, though
purchè, provided

benchè ⎫
sebbene ⎪
ancorchè ⎬ though, although
quantunque ⎭
senza che, without that
non ostante che, notwithstanding
per quanto, however

NOTE.—Some of these conjunctions, however, govern the Indicative whenever the action expressed by the Verb admits of no doubt.

324. Conjunctions most frequently used:

e, and
e . . . e, as well as, both . . . and
tanto . . . quanto, as well as
quando, when
come, as
dopo che, after
appena ⎫
a pena ⎭ scarcely
anche, also, too
allorchè, then, when
perchè ⎫
poichè ⎬ because
giacchè ⎭
sicchè, so that
quindi, therefore, consequently
dacchè, because, since
mentre, while
se, whether
o, or
o . . . o, either . . . or
ovvero ⎫
ossia ⎬ or
oppure ⎭
nè . . . nè, neither . . . nor

ora . . . ora, now . . . now
anzi, even, rather
neppure ⎫
nemmeno ⎭ not even
(im) perciocchè, since, whereas
se anche, even if
di maniera che ⎫
di modo che ⎭ so that
tosto che ⎫
subito che ⎭ as soon as
però, though, however, but
dunque, so, therefore
eziandio ⎫
ma anco ⎭ but also
perciò, therefore
nullameno ⎫
nientemeno ⎭ nevertheless
altresì, besides
per altro, however
ma, but
eppure, and yet
siccome ⎫
considerando che ⎬ whereas
stante che ⎭

325. Why? and Because are rendered by the same word **perchè**:[1] **Perchè non parla?** Why do you not speak?—**Perchè non ho voglia,** Because I do not feel inclined to do so.

326. **Poichè: Poichè non viene, andremo noi,** as (because) he does not come, we shall go.

327. **Dunque,** at the beginning of a sentence, means *thus, therefore, so,* as: Dunque *non lo farò,* therefore (so) I shall not do it. When *dunque* follows the Verb, it is rendered by *but, so,* etc.: *Scrivete* dunque, *mio caro!* so (but) write, my dear!

328. **Se** means both **if** and **whether**: Se *lo facciamo,* if we do it.— *Non sanno* se *lo potranno fare,* they don't know whether they will be able to do it.

329. **Quando,** like **se,** expresses sometimes a condition, but in an indefinite way, as: **Quando lo fa, lo fa male,** if (when) he does it (at all), he does it badly. Whenever it expresses time only, it translates the English when? as: Quando *lo farete?* when will you do it?

330. **Per . . . che,** separated by an Adjective or an Adverb, means However, as: Per *ricco* che *sia, morrà,* however rich he may be, he will die. This Conjunction always requires the Subjunctive Mood.

INTERJECTIONS—INTERIEZIONI

331. List of interjections:

a. Of **joy** and **exultation: Oh! viva! evviva! bene! buono!** O! eigh! eh! hey! aha! ah! hurrah! good!

b. Of **sorrow, grief** or **pity: ah! ahi! ahimè! ohimè! ahi lasso!** Oh! alas! ah! alack!

c. Of **surprise, wonder: O! oh! capperi! come! bello! sì!** etc., hah! what! h'm! heigh! strange! indeed!

d. Of **contempt** or **aversion: deh! oh! veh! guarda! ohibò! puh! va via!** etc., pshaw! but! tush! bah! off! begone!

e. Of **attention** or **calling: eh! olà! oh! o! ehi! eh là! ho! lo!** behold! look! see! hark! halt! etc.

f. Of **silence: zitto! zitto zitto! hush! hist! 'st!**

g. Of **interrogating: ebbene? che? come? sì?** eh? hem or h'm?

It is difficult to make a satisfactory classification of interjections. Most of them are used in various senses, and the learner should determine their meaning from the spirit of the sentence or discourse.

---

[1] Note.—*Perchè* means also *that, so that, in order to,* etc., as: *Ero troppo ammalato perchè potessi uscire,* I was too sick to go out.

VOCABULARY

abbastanza, enough, rather
abilità, *f.* ability
abitare, to live, dwell
abito, *m.* suit
abituare, to accustom
abusare, to abuse
accendere, to light
accento, accent
acciocchè, in order that
accogliere, to welcome
accordo, *m.* agreement
accorto, careful, prudent
acqua, *f.* water
acre, bitter
adagio, slowly
adesso, now
adirarsi, to become angry
adoperare, to use
affamato, famished, starved
affare, *m.* business
affatto, entirely
affinchè, so that, in order that
aggredire, to attack
agile, nimble
agnello, *m.* lamb
agricoltore, *m.* farmer
albergo, *m.* hotel
albero, *m.* tree
alcuni, some, a few
allegro, merry, cheerful
allevare, to raise, teach
allora, then, therefore
almeno, at least
alquanto, somewhat, quite
alto, high, tall
altrimenti, otherwise
altro, other, more
amare, to love

amaro, bitter
amicizia, *f.* friendship
amica, *f.*, amico, *m.* friend
anche, also, too
ancora, still, yet
andare, to go
animale, *m.* animal
anno, *m.* year
annunciare, to announce
ansioso, anxious
antenato, *m.* ancestor
antico, old, ancient
aperto, open
apparire, to appear
appetito, *m.* appetite
apposta, purposely
apprendere, to learn
aprire, to open
aquila, *f.* eagle
arancia, *f.* orange
ardire, to dare
aria, *f,* air
arrestare, to arrest
arrivare, to arrive
ascensore, *m.* elevator
ascoltare, to listen to
asino, *m.* donkey
aspettare, to wait, wait for
assai, much, many
assente, absent
assistere, to attend
astuto, sly, cunning
attenzione, *f.* attention
attività, *f.* activity
attrarre, to attract
attribuire, to attribute
augurare, to wish
avanti, ahead, forward

321

avere, to have
avvenire, to happen
avviarsi, to set out
avviso, *m.* sign, poster
avvocato, *m.* lawyer
azione, *f.* action, deed

baciare, to kiss
bagaglio, *m.* baggage
bagno, *m.* bath
baleno, *m.* lightning
ballare, to dance
banca, *f.* bank
banda, *f.* band
bandiera, *f.* flag
barba, *f.* beard
barbiere, *m.* barber
barca, *f.* boat
basso, low, short
battaglia, *f.* battle
battere, to beat, strike
beato, fortunate, blessed
beffa, joke, trick
bellezza, *f.* beauty
bello, beautiful
bene, well, quite
benevolo, kindly
benvenuto, welcome
bere, to drink
berretto, *m.* cap
bianco, white
biblioteca, *f.* library
bimbo, *m.* baby
biondo, blond
biscotto, *m.* biscuit
bisogno, *m.* need
bocca, *f.* mouth
bontà, *f.* goodness
bottega, *f.* shop
bottiglia, *f.* bottle

bove, *m.* ox
braccio, *m.* arm
bramare, to desire, wish
breve, brief, short
brodo, *m.* broth, soup
brutto, ugly
bugia, *f.* lie
buono, good, kind
burro, *m.* butter
bussare, to knock
buttare, to throw

cabina, *f.* cabin
cadere, to fall
caffè, *m.* coffee
calamaio, *m.* inkwell
caldo, warm, hot
calunnia, *f.* calumny
calzoni, *m.* trousers
cambiare, to change
camera, *f.* room
cameriere, *m.* waiter
camminare, to walk
campagna, *f.* country
campo, *m.* field
cane, *m.* dog
cantare, to sing
capire, to understand
capitale, *f.* capital
capo, *m.* head
carattere, *m.* character
carino, darling
carne, *f.* meat
carrozza, *f.* carriage
casa, *f.* house
castigo, *m.* punishment
cavallo, *m.* horse
celebrare, to celebrate
celeste, blue, sky-blue
cena, *f.* supper

cenere, *f.* ashes

centro, *m.* middle

cercare, to search

certo, certain

checchè, whatever

chiaro, clear, light

chiasso, *m.* noise, racket

chiedere, to ask, ask for

chiesa, *f.* church

chiudere, to close, shut

chiunque, whoever

cieco, blind

cielo, *m.* sky, heaven

cima, *f.* top, summit

cioccolata, *f.* chocolate

cioè, that is, namely

circolo, *m.* club, society

circondato, surrounded

cliente, *m.* client, customer

clima, *m.* climate

colazione, *f.* meal

collo, *m.* neck

colpa, *f.* blame, fault

colpire, to strike, hit

combattere, to fight

cominciare, to begin, start

commercio, *m.* commerce

comodo, comfortable

compagnia, *f.* company

compera, *f.* purchase

compleanno, *m.* birthday

completamente, completely

comporre, to compose

compare, to buy, purchase

comprendere, to understand

comune, common

conciare, to mend, fix

concludere, to conclude

condotta, *f.* conduct

conferenza, *f.* lecture

conoscenza, *f.* acquaintance

conoscere, to know

consacrare, to consecrate

conscio, aware

conservare, to save, conserve

contadino, *m.* peasant

contare, to count

contenere, to contain

contento, satisfied, happy

contesa, *f.* dispute

continuo, continuous

contrario, contrary

controllare, to control

conveniente, convenient

conversazione, *f.* conversation

convincere, to convince

coraggio, *m.* courage

corpo, *m.* body

correggere, to correct

correre, to run

corretto, correct

corrompere, to corrupt

corsa, *f.* race

cortese, courteous

corto, short, brief

cosa, *f.* thing

costa, *f.* coast

costare, to cost

costituire, to constitute

costringere, to oblige

costruire, to build

credere, to believe

crescere, to grow

crisi, *f.* crisis

criticare, to criticize

crudele, cruel

cucina, *f.* kitchen

cugino, *m.* cousin

cultura, *f.* cultivation, culture

cuocere, to cook

cuore, *m*. heart
cura, *f*. care, cure, treatment
curioso, curious

dare, to give
dattilografa, *f*. typist
davvero, truly, really
debito, *m*. debt
debole, weak
decidere, to decide
dedicare, to dedicate
defraudare, to defraud
denaro, *m*. money
dente, *m*. tooth
dentro, *m*. inside, within
derivare, to issue, come
descrivere, to describe
desiderare, to desire
dì, *m*. day
dichiarare, to declare
dietro (a), behind
difatti, in fact
difendere, to defend
difficoltà, *f*. difficulty
diletto, *m*. pleasure, delight
dimenticare, to forget
dimostrare, to show, prove
dinanzi (a), in front of
Dio, *m*. God
dire, to say, tell
direttamente, directly
dirigere, to direct
discutere, to discuss
disparte, apart, aside
disperare, to despair
disprezzare, to despise
dissuadere, to dissuade
dito, *m*. finger
divenire, to become
diverso, different

docile, docile, gentle
dolce, sweet
dolente, sorry, grieved
dolore, *m*. pain, grief
domandare, to ask, ask for
domani, tomorrow
domenica, *f*. Sunday
donare, to give, donate
dopo, after, afterwards
doppio, double
dormire, to sleep
dorso, *m*. back
dove, where
dovunque, wherever
dubbio, *m*. doubt
duro, hard, difficult

ebbene, very well
eccetto, except
eccezionale, exceptional
ecco, here is, here are
edificio, *m*. building
educazione, *f*. upbringing
effetto, *m*. effect, result
elemosina, *f*. charity
entrare, to enter
eppoi, and then
eppure, and yet
erba, *f*. grass
eroe, *m*. hero
errore, *m*. error, mistake
esagerare, to exaggerate
esaminare, to examine
esclamare, to exclaim
esempio, *m*. example
essere, to be
estasi, *f*. ecstasy
estate, *f*. summer
età, *f*. age

evento, *m.* event
evitare, to avoid

fabbricare, to build
faccenda, *f.* duty, task
facchino, *m.* porter
faccia, *f.* face
facilità, *f.* facility, ease
fama, *f.* fame
fame, *f.* hunger
fanciullo, *m.* child
fare, to do, make
farina, *f.* flour
farmacia, *f.* pharmacy
fatica, *f.* effort, toil, work
fatto, *m.* deed, fact
favore, *m.* favor
fedeltà, *f.* faithfulness
felice, happy, glad
femminile, feminine
ferire, to wound, injure
ferita, *f.* wound, injury
fermare, to stop
feroce, ferocious, wild
fiammifero, *m.* match
fiducia, *f.* faith
fiero, proud, haughty
figlia, *f.* daughter
figlio, *m.* son
fine, *f.* end
fine, *m.* goal, end
finestra, *f.* window
finire, to finish
fino, fine, thin
finta, *f.* feint, deceit
fiore, *m.* flower
fiume, *m.* river
folle, insane
fondare, to found
formare, to form

fornaio, *m.* baker
fornire, to furnish
foro, *m.* opening, hole
forse, perhaps, maybe
forte, strong
fortuna, *f.* fortune
forza, *f.* strength
fra, between, in, within
franco, frank, candid
frase, *f.* sentence
fratello, *m.* brother
frattempo, *m.* meanwhile
freddo, *m.* cold
frequentare, to frequent
fresco, fresh, cool
fretta, *f.* hurry, haste
fronte, *f.* forehead
frutta, *f.* fruit
fumare, to smoke
fuoco, *m.* fire
fuorchè, except
fuori, outside, out
furto, *m.* theft, robbery
futuro, future

galantuomo, *m.* gentleman,
    honest man
garbo, *m.* gracefulness
gatto, *m.* cat
gente, *f.* people
gentile, kind
già, already
giacchè, since
giallo, yellow
giardino, *m.* garden
giocare, to play
giornale, *m.* newspaper
giornata, *f.* day
giorno, *m.* day
giovedì, *m.* **Thursday**

gita, *f.* trip
giù, down, below
giudicare, to judge
giugno, *m.* June
giustizia, *f.* justice
godere, to enjoy
governare, to govern
gradire, to welcome
grande, big, large, famous
grasso, fat
grazie, thanks
grazioso, pretty
grosso, big
gruppo, *m.* group
guanto, *m.* glove
guardare, to look
guerra, *f.* war
guidare, to guide
gusto, *m.* taste

idea, *f.* idea
Iddio, *m.* God
ieri, yesterday
ignoranza, *f.* ignorance
imitare, to imitate
immaginarsi, to imagine
immediato, immediate
imparare, to learn
impegno, *m.* obligation
imperatore, *m.* emperor
impiegare, to use, employ
importanza, *f.* importance
impossibile, impossible
impressione, *f.* impression
imprevisto, unforeseen
incontrare, to meet
indicare, to indicate
indirizzare, to address
indomani, *m.* next day
indovinare, to guess

infatti, in fact
inferiore, lower
infermiere, *m.* nurse
infimo, lowest, basest
infine, finally, at last
informarsi, to inquire
infortunio, *m.* accident
ingrato, ungrateful
ingresso, *m.* entrance
inoltre, beside, moreover
insegnare, to teach
inseparabile, inseparable
insieme, together
insistere, to insist
intendere, to understand, mean
interessare, to interest
interno, internal
intero, entire, whole
interrompere, to interrupt
intorno (a), around, about
inutile, useless
invano, in vain
invece, instead
inverno, *m.* winter
invitare, to invite
io, I
irregolare, irregular
irrequieto, restless

labbro, *m.* lip
ladro, *m.* thief
lago, *m.* lake
lapis, *m.* pencil
largo, wide, broad
lasciare, to let, allow
latte, *m.* milk
lavare, to wash
leggere, to read
leggiero, light
lento, slow

lettera, *f.* letter
letto, *m.* bed
levarsi, to get up, rise
lezione, *f.* lesson
liberare, to free, liberate
libro, *m.* book
lieto, happy, glad
lieve, light
limone, *m.* lemon
lingua, *f.* tongue, language
lodare, to praise
lontano, far, distant
luce, *f.* light
lucroso, gainful, lucrative
lume, *m.* light, lamp
lungo, long, along
lustrare, to shine
lutto, *m.* mourning

macchina, *f.* machine
madre, *f.* mother
maestro, *m.* teacher
magro, thin
mai, ever, never
male, *m.* evil, ache, pain
mandare, to send
mangiare, to eat
maniera, *f.* manner, way
mano, *f.* hand
mantenere, to hold, keep
marcia, *f.* march
mare, *m.* sea
marinaio, *m.* sailor
marito, *m.* husband
maschile, masculine
materia, *f.* matter, subject
mattina, *f.* morning
medico, *m.* doctor
meglio, better, best
membro, *m.* member

memoria, *f.* memory
meno, less, fewer, minus
mente, *f.* mind
mento, *m.* chin
mentre, while
mercato, *m.* market
mese, *m.* month
messaggio, *m.* message
mesto, sad, gloomy
metà, *f.* half
mettere, to put, set, place
mezzo, *m.* middle, means
migliore, better, best
minimo, least, smallest
minuto, *m.* minute
misero, wretched, poor
misura, *f.* measure, size
moda, *f.* style, fashion
modesto, modest, conservative
moglie, *f.* wife
mondo, *m.* world
moneta, *f.* coin
montagna, *f.* mountain
mordere, to bite
morire, to die
morte, *f.* death
mosca, *f.* fly
mostrare, to show, prove
muovere, to move
muro, *m.* wall
musica, *f.* music

narrare, to narrate
nascere, to be born
naso, *m.* nose
nave, *f.* ship
nazione, *f.* nation
neanche, not even
negare, to deny
negozio, *m.* store

nemico, *m.* enemy
neppure, not even, nor
nero, black
nervo, *m.* tendon, nerve
nessuno, no one, none
neve, *f.* snow
noia, *f.* annoyance, trouble
nominare, to name
non, not
norma, *f.* rule
notizia, *f.* news
notte, *f.* night
nulla, nothing
nuocere, to harm, injure
nuovo, new

obbedire, to obey
occasione, *f.* opportunity
occhio, *m.* eye
odiare, to hate
odorare, to smell
offrire, to offer
oggi, today
ogni, each, every
omaggio, *m.* praise
ombra, *f.* shade, shadow
onestà, *f.* honesty
onorare, to honor
opera, *f.* work, opera
opinione, *f.* opinion
ora, now
ora, *f.* hour
ordinare, to order, command
orecchio, *m.* ear
oro, *m.* gold
orologio, *m.* watch, clock
ospedale, *m.* hospital
osservare, to observe, note
oste, *m.* host, innkeeper

ostilità, *f.* hostility
ozio, *m.* leisure, idleness

pace, *f.* peace
padrone, *m.* master
pagare, to pay
pallido, pale
pane, *m.* bread
paragone, *m.* comparison
parlare, to talk, speak
parte, *f.* part, section
partire, to depart, leave
passare, to pass
passeggiare, to walk, stroll
pastore, *m.* shepherd
patria, *f.* fatherland
paura, *f.* fear
pausa, *f.* pause
pazienza, *f.* patience
peccato, *m.* sin
pelle, *f.* skin
pena, *f.* pain, grief
penna, *f.* pen
pensare, to think
per, for, through, by
pera, *f.* pear
perchè, why, because, so that
perciò, therefore
perdere, to lose
perdonare, to pardon, forgive
perfino, even
pericolo, *m.* danger
perire, to perish
permanente, permanent
permettere, to permit, allow
perpetuo, continuous, perpetual
piatto, *m.* plate, dish
piazza, *f.* square, plaza
piccolo, small, little
piede, *m.* foot

pieno, full
pio, pious
pioggia, *f.* rain, rainfall
piovere, to rain
pista, *f.* track
più, more
poco, little
poi, then, after, afterwards
polizia, *f.* police
pollo, *m.* fowl, chicken
polvere, *f.* dust
pomeriggio, *m.* afternoon
pompiere, *m.* fireman
ponte, *m.* bridge
popolo, *m.* people, citizenry
porta, *f.* door
portare, to bring, carry
posporre, to postpone
possibile, possible
posta, *f.* mail
potente, powerful
potere, to be able to, can
povero, poor
pranzare, to dine
preciso, precise, exact
predire, predict
preferire, to prefer
pregare, to pray, beg
prendere, to take, seize, catch
preparare, to prepare
presentare, to present
presso, near, by, close
presto, soon, early, at once
prezioso, precious
prezzo, *m.* price
primo, first
primavera, *f.* spring
principale, principal, main
principio, *m.* beginning
probabilità, *f.* probability

profondo, deep
profumare, to perfume
promettere, to promise
pronto, ready
proteggere, to protect
protestare, to protest
prudente, cautious, judicious
pubblicità, advertisement
pugno, *m.* fist
punire, to punish
punto, *m.* point, spot
purchè, provided
pure, also

quanto, how much
questione, *f.* dispute, question
questo, this
qui, here
quindi, therefore
quotidiano, daily

raccontare, to relate, tell
raffreddore, *m.* cold
ragazzo, *m.* boy
raggiungere, to reach
ragione, *f.* reason
rallentare, to slacken
rapido, rapid
rappresentare, to represent
raro, rare
re, *m.* king
recente, recent
regalare, to present, give gifts
regina, *f.* queen
regione, *f.* region
rendere, to produce, give
resistere (a), to resist
respirare, to breathe
restare, to remain
ricchezza, *f.* wealth

ricco, rich
ricevere, to receive
ricordare, to remember
ricuperare, to recover
ricusare, to refuse
ridere, to laugh
ridicolo, ridiculous
riempire, to fill, refill
rimanere, to remain, stay
ringraziare, to thank
rinunciare (a), to give up
riparare, to repair
ripetere, to repeat
riposarsi, to rest
risolvere, to solve
rispondere, to answer
riuscire, to succeed
rivelare, to reveal
rivista, *f.* magazine, periodical
robusto, robust, well built
romanzo, *m.* novel
rompere, to break
rosso, red
rumoroso, noisy
ruota, *f.* wheel

sabato, *m.* Saturday
sacco, *m.* sack, bag
sacrificio, *m.* sacrifice
saggio, wise
sala, *f.* room, hall
sale, *m.* salt
salire, to climb, come up
salutare, to greet
salvare, to save
sano, sound
santo, holy, saintly
sapere, to know
sarto, *m.* tailor
sbadataggine, *f.* carelessness

sbaglio, *m.* mistake, error
sbattere, to beat, dash
scala, *f.* ladder
scarno, thin, lean
scarpa, *f.* shoe
scatola, *f.* box
scegliere, to choose
scelta, *f.* choice
scemare, to decrease
scendere, to do down, come
  down
sciarpa, *f.* scarf
sciocco, silly, foolish
sciogliere, to untie
scodella, *f.* bowl
scolaro, *m.* pupil
scommettere, to bet, wager
scopo, *m.* purpose, goal
scorso, last, past
scortese, discourteous
scrittore, *m.* writer
scuola, *f.* school
scusare, to excuse, pardon
sdegno, *m.* disdain, scorn
sebbene, although, though
secco, dry, withered
secreto, *m.* secret
sedere, to sit
segnale, *m.* signal
sembrare, to seem, appear
seme, *m.* seed
semplice, simple, easy
sempre, always
senso, *m.* sense
sentimento, *m.* sentiment
sentire, to feel, hear
senza, without
sera, *f.* evening
serbare, to keep, save
serie, *f.* series

serio, serious, grave
serrare, to shut, close
servire, to serve
settentrionale, northern
settimana, *f.* week
severo, severe, grave
sfortuna, *f.* misfortune
sforzo, *m.* effort
sguardo, *m.* glance, look
siccome, since
sicuro, certain
sigaretta, *f.* cigarette
silenzio, *m.* silence
simpatico, attractive
sinistro, left
snello, slim
socievole, sociable
soddisfare, to satisfy
soffrire, to suffer
soggetto, *m.* topic, subject
sognare, to dream
sole, *m.* sun
solitario, solitary, lonely
solito, customary, usual
sollevare, to raise
solo, alone, only
somma, *f.* sum, total
sommo, very great
sonno, *m.* sleep
sopra, on, upon
sorella, *f.* sister
sorpassare, to surpass
sorridere, to smile
sospettare, to suspect
sostenere, to maintain
sottile, fine, thin
sottrarre, to subtract
spendere, to spend, expend
sperare, to hope
spesso, often

spettatore, *m.* spectator
spirito, *m.* wit
sponda, *f.* shore
sporco, soiled, dirty
sposare, to marry
sposa, *f.* wife, bride
sposo, *m.* spouse, husband
sprecare, to waste
stabilire, to establish
stancarsi, to become tired
stanotte, *f.* tonight
stare, to be
stento, *f.* toil
stesso, same, self
stima, *f.* regard, esteem
stipendio, *m.* salary, stipend
stivale, *m.* boot
storia, *f.* history, story
strada, *f.* street, road
straniero, *m.* stranger, foreigner
straordinario, extraordinary
strumento, *m.* instrument
studiare, to study
stupefatto, amazed, stupefied
stupidaggine, *f.* stupidity
stupito, astonished
stupore, *m.* amazement, wonder
subire, to undergo
subito, immediately
succedere, to happen
succoso, juicy, succulent
sud, *m.* south
suggerire, to suggest
suono, *m.* sound
superbo, proud, haughty
superiore, superior, higher

tacere, to be silent
tardi, late
tasca, *f.* pocket

tavola, *f.* table.
tazza, *f.* cup
tè, *m.* tea
telefonare (a), to telephone
televisione, *f.* television
temere, to fear, be afraid (of)
tempo, *m.* time, weather
tenere, to hold, possess
terra, *f.* land
terreno, *m.* ground, soil
tesoro, *m.* treasure
testa, *f.* head
tetto, *m.* roof
tipo, *m.* type, kind
toccare, to touch
togliere, to take away
torto, *m.* wrong
tosto, soon
tradurre, to translate
tranquillo, calm, quiet
traversare, to cross
tremare, to tremble, shake
treno, *m.* train
triste, sad
troppo, too much
trovare, to find
truffare, to cheat
tuono, *m.* thunder
tuttavia, nevertheless
tutto, all, everything

uccello, *m.* bird
uccidere, to kill
udire, to hear
ufficio, *m.* office
uguale, equal
mano, human

umido, humid, moist, damp
umile, humble, modest
umore, *m.* humor, disposition
unico, single, only
unire, to unite
uomo, *m.* man
uovo, *m.* egg
usare, to use
uso, *m.* use
utilità, *f.* usefulness

vacanze, *f.* vacation
vagone, *m.* car
valere, to be worth
varietà, *f.* variety
vasto, vast, large
vecchio, *m.* old man
vedere, to see
velocità, *f.* speed, velocity
venire, to come
vento, *m.* wind
veramente, truly, really
verde, green
verità, *f.* truth
vero, true, real
vestire, to dress
via, *f.* road
viaggiare, to travel
vicino, near, close
vietato, forbidden
vincere, to win
virtù, *f.* virtue
visitare, to visit
viso, *m.* face, visage
vita, *f.* life
vittima, *f.* victim
vivanda, *f.* food, dish
vivere, to live

voce, *f.* voice

voglia, *f.* desire

voi, you

volare, to fly

volgare, vulgar

vuotare, to empty

zaino, *m.* knapsack

zero, *m.* zero

zia, *f.* aunt

zio, *m.* uncle

zitto, silent

zucchero, *m.* sugar

INDEX